Merleau-Ponty between
Philosophy and Symbolism

SUNY series in Contemporary Continental Philosophy
Dennis J. Schmidt. editor

Merleau-Ponty between Philosophy and Symbolism

The Matrixed Ontology

Rajiv Kaushik

Published by State University of New York Press, Albany

© 2019 State University of New York

All rights reserved

No part of this book may be used or reproduced in any manner whatsoever without written permission. No part of this book may be stored in a retrieval system or transmitted in any form or by any means including electronic, electrostatic, magnetic tape, mechanical, photocopying, recording, or otherwise without the prior permission in writing of the publisher.

For information, contact State University of New York Press, Albany, NY
www.sunypress.edu

Library of Congress Cataloging-in-Publication Data

Names: Kaushik, Rajiv, author.
Title: Merleau-Ponty between philosophy and symbolism : the matrixed ontology
   / Rajiv Kaushik.
Description: Albany : State University of New York Press, [2019] | Series: SUNY series in contemporary continental philosophy | Includes bibliographical references and index.
Identifiers: LCCN 2018058274 | ISBN 9781438476759 (hardcover : alk. paper) |
   ISBN 9781438476773 (ebk.) | ISBN 9781438476766 (pbk. : alk. paper)
Subjects: LCSH: Merleau-Ponty, Maurice, 1908-1961. | Ontology. | Identity (Philosophical concept)
Classification: LCC B2430.M3764 K385 2019 | DDC 194--dc23 LC record available at https://lccn.loc.gov/2018058274

10 9 8 7 6 5 4 3 2 1

Contents

List of Abbreviations   vii
Acknowledgments   ix

Introduction   xi
   Matrix Events and Institution   xiii
   Sedimentation and Symbolism in Institution   xvii
   Symbolic Forms and Elemental Being   xx
   Outline of Chapters   xxiii

Chapter 1. Matrix Events: Methods and Antecedents   1
   The Homeric Diphthong   2
   The Platonic Dividing-Collecting   5
   The Merleau-Pontian *écart*   11
   Interrogative Method and *écart*   18
   Écart and Division in Heraclitus   20
   λόγος and ἁπτόμενον in Heraclitus   26
   Some Remaining Questions   27

Chapter 2. Space—Imagination   31
   Abstract Geometrical Essences, Morphological Ideals, and Phantasy in Husserl   33
   The Role of Imagination in the Substruction of Essences   41
   Sculptural Shapes and the Space of Imagination   45
   Beyond Sight and Image   50
   Some Remaining Questions   53

Chapter 3. Light—Dark/Awake—Asleep — 55
- The Light—Dark Opposition in Jean-Luc Nancy — 59
- Light—Dark and Elementality — 61
- Waking—Sleeping — 66
- Dark Sleep — 71
- Some Remaining Questions — 74

Chapter 4. Philosophy—Symbolism — 81
- Dreams and Passivity — 82
- The Positive Symbol — 85
- The Positive Symbol and Psyche — 91
- The Positive Symbol, Psyche, and λέγειν — 94
- The Positive Symbol in Philosophy: Analysis and the Analyzed — 97
- Some Remaining Questions — 100

Chapter 5. Philosophical Language—Literary Language — 107
- Ontology, Not Metaphorical Ontology — 108
- Finding a Hermeneutical Reverie with Proust — 112
- Some Remaining Questions — 121

Conclusion — 123
- Sedimentation, Elementality — 124
- The Different Politics of Metaphor and Symbolism — 126
- Politics, History, and Elements — 130

Notes — 133
Bibliography — 159
Index — 167

Abbreviations

Ép/IPP: *Éloge de la Philosophie et autres essais* (France: Gallimard, 1960), translated by John O'Neill as *In Praise of Philosophy and Other Essays* (Evanston, IL: Northwestern University Press, 1970).

Hes: "Préface," in A. Hesnard, *L'Œuvre de Freud*, 5–10 (France: Payot, 1960), translated by Alden L. Fisher as "Phenomenology and Psychoanalysis: Preface to *Hesnard's L'Oeuvre* de Freud," *Review of Existential Psychology and Psychiatry* 18 (1982): 67–72.

HT: *Humanisme et terreur, essai sur le problème communiste* (France: Gallimard, 1947), translated by John O'Neill as *Humanism and Terror: An Essay on the Communist Problem*, translated by John O'Neill (Boston: Beacon Press, 1969).

IP: *L'Institution, Passivité: Notes de Cours au Collège de France (1954–1955)* (France: Éditions Belin, 2003), translated by Leonard Lawlor and Heath Massey as *Institution and Passivity: Course Notes from the Collège de France (1954–1955)* (Evanston, IL: Northwestern University Press, 2010).

MPR: *The Merleau-Ponty Reader*, edited by Ted Toadvine and Leonard Lawlor (Evanston, IL: Northwestern University Press, 2007).

N: *La Nature, Notes, Cours du Collège de France* (France: Seuil, 1995), translated by Robert Vallier as *Nature: Course Notes from the Collège de France* (Evanston, IL: Northwestern University Press, 2003).

NC: *Notes de cours: 1958–1959 et 1960–1961* (France: Gallimard, 1996).

OE/EM: *L'Œil et l'esprit* (France: Gallimard, 1964), translated as "Eye and Mind" in *Primacy of Perception and Other Essays*, edited by James E. Edie (Evanston, IL: Northwestern University Press, 1964).

Par: *Parcours deux, 1951–1961* (France: Verdier, 2000).

PNP: *Philosophy and Non-Philosophy Since Merleau-Ponty*, edited by Hugh J. Silverman (United Kingdom: Routledge, 1988).

PP: *Phénoménologie de la perception* (France: Gallimard, 1945), translated by Colin Smith as *Phenomenology of Perception* (United Kingdom: Routledge, 1992).

PrP: *Le Primat de la perception et ses conséquences philosophiques* (France: Verdier, 1996) translated as *Primacy of Perception and Other Essays*, edited by James E. Edie (Evanston, IL: Northwestern University Press, 1964).

PW: *La Prose du monde* (France: Gallimard, 1969), translated by John O'Neill as *The Prose of the World* (Evanston, IL: Northwestern University Press, 1973).

RLL: *Recherches sur l'usage littéraire du langage: Cours au Collège de France Notes, 1953*, (Switzerland: MētisPresses, 2013).

S: *Signes* (France: Gallimard, 1960), translated by Richard C. Mcleary as *Signs* (Evanston, IL: Northwestern University Press, 1964).

SNS: *Sens et non-sens* (France: Gallimard, 1996), translated by Hubert L. Dreyfus and Patricia Allen Dreyfus as *Sense and Non-sense* (Evanston, IL: Northwestern University Press, 1964).

VI: *Le Visible et l'invisible, suivi de notes de travail* (France: Gallimard, 1964), translated by Alphonso Lingis as *The Visible and the Invisible* (Evanston, IL: Northwestern University Press, 1968).

Note: French pagination is cited first, then the English.

Acknowledgments

I would like to begin by thanking the International Merleau-Ponty Circle and its members. The Merleau-Ponty Circle is my intellectual home and much of my development is thanks to its investment in less-established scholars. I would specifically like to thank Duane Davis for inviting me to my first Merleau-Ponty Circle in Asheville in 2010. That was when I met several people, in addition to Duane, who continue to be significant to me personally and intellectually: Frank Chouraqui, Bernie Flynn and Judith Waltz, Véronique Fóti, Mauro Carbone, Stephen Watson, Galen Johnson, Gail Weiss, Glen Mazis, and Helen Fielding. These are all scholars whose work and thought are a constant source of inspiration and guidance. One need only read them to witness a generosity and good politics of thought: a kind of thinking that allows room for more and even different thinking.

I would again like to thank Duane Davis for reading chapters of this volume in different stages of their development and giving me some vitally important suggestions. I also want to thank Cheryl Emerson for inviting me to the University of Buffalo in April of 2017. Some of the ideas from the talk I gave there, along with certain arguments I began in recent articles in *Chiasmi International* ("Separations and Symbolics" and "Lighten Up"), have developed into the present book. Cheryl's comments on the talk were also invaluable. I finally offer my deep gratitude to my colleague, friend, and "constant ally," Drew Dalton, whose influence can certainly be found in these pages too, and whose friendship has kept me from dark and given me light these many years.

This book is dedicated to the members of my beloved family, who, like my own breath and lungs, constellate my inner and outer worlds: Natalie, Violeta, and Zubin.

Introduction

There is nothing about predictability that guards against unpredictability, nothing about it that guarantees the unpredictable will remain quiet. The predictable is not certain and does not exclude the unpredictable. Whereas the unpredictable intervenes in the predictable and interrupts the very scene in which its previous appearance would seem impossible. It ruptures. Referring to the notion formalized by set-theory ontology as the "void set," Alain Badiou calls this rupture an "event."[1] An event, he says, is a "pure inconsistent multiplicity."[2] It means nothing in itself, but counters in dramatic fashion the existent thing that otherwise presents itself as coherent and unified, what Badiou calls the "count-as-one."[3] If there is an event, in other words, the very conditions of existence, cohesion and unity, have been removed. Normality is perturbed, and a totally new space is opened up to rethink reality.

This is the context in which philosophies of the event are often positioned against phenomenology. The assumption is that phenomenology reorients incoherency to coherency, inconsistency to consistency, nonsense to sense, and therefore also closes itself to the truly abnormal aspect of events. According to Deleuze, though, Sartre comes closest to a philosophy of the event since he wants to think about "an impersonal transcendental field" that has "the form neither of a personal synthetic consciousness nor subjective identity."[4] This exception is telling: a philosophy of the event does not exclude the transcendental per se. It does not, for example, exclude the transcendental conceived in terms of nihilation. Only when it is conceived in terms of an intention, whether subjective or bodily, does the transcendental exclude the event. A more acceptable transcendental, one that accords with the event, would be afield from intentionality in general. It would be totally outside the apparent object, the subject conceived as the person to whom the object appears, and even the bodily situation that conjoins the two aspects of appearing. An event would break from all forms of intentionality so radically that it cannot be an origin, destination, or even a preexisting referent, and its eventfulness would instead be utterly spontaneous.

Whereas, as Deleuze points out, Sartre does not ultimately abandon the idea that the impersonal transcendental field is self-consciousness, in his *Institution and Passivity* lectures, Merleau-Ponty regularly speaks of the "matrix" and matrix events.[5] Matrix events do not emphasize self-consciousness at the cost of difference. They are, in fact, called matrices because they constellate difference as difference. It will prove noteworthy that, in the institution lectures, one of the initial mentions of a matrix has to do with the "symbolic matrix" Freud locates between human and animal.[6] A matrix event may be equated with differentiation in several ways: in addition to difference between human and animal, it can refer to the exterior and interior, public and personal, language and speech. A matrix event runs a circuit through these differences. But the loop of matrix events is never closed, and neither are the terms they snap up into them. This is crucial, for unless Merleau-Ponty thinks that, through the event, differences are reduced to an identity, he is not guilty of the typical criticism that befalls phenomenology—that it transforms nonsense into sense and makes what is incoherent coherent. It may be true that in phenomenology the transcendental field has the look of an ideal that excludes difference. This is undoubtedly so, for example, when Husserl calls transcendental consciousness an "absolute sense-bestowing consciousness" from which no other sense escapes. But, according to Merleau-Ponty, even this transcendental consciousness appears absolute by virtue of some alteration that has transpired, unprompted, within it. To the extent that there is some further condition to the transcendental field for him, he has a notion of its event that cannot be reduced to coherence and is not ideological.

Nonetheless, Merleau-Ponty at least initially says matrix events are temporal, and the key to understanding them is to trace out their character not reducible to the order of time's succession. For example, time conceived as a series of equally weighted and distinct instants will not explain the way an "event events" and always succeeds itself. If an event cannot be understood in causal terms, it is because it is instead promiscuous with times other than itself or even "distant from" and "non-coincidental with" itself. An event is not singular but plural. Its plurality, furthermore, prevents the event from being teleological. That there is a temporal character to the matrix event means neither that it is an origin from which other times succeed nor that it is a destination into which all times lead. The event is neither an origin nor a destination.

Matrix Events and Institution

As Merleau-Ponty would characteristically put it: events are always and only on an "adventure." These are monumental historical moments like the ones mentioned in the institution lectures—the Industrial Revolution, the invention of planemetric perspective, or Paul Klee's line. Engaging with the anthropological work of his good friend Claude Lévi-Strauss, Merleau-Ponty points out in those same lectures that monumental historical moments are not simply consequential instants. When Lévi-Strauss argues that all such moments are discrete chance happenings or aleatory, he prevents these moments from being interrelated.[7] Therefore, he also fails to show how history is *not* teleological. Yet, according to Merleau-Ponty, there are indeed monumental events that do interrelate moments and make history. These alter both our history and our understanding of ourselves within that history. If we conflate merely important historical instants with events that fundamentally reorganize a meaning-field, we will be unable to explicate the latter and how they reorganize this field. When we try to address these events, however, it is nonetheless difficult not to lapse into familiar terminology and presume that they are teleological from the past into the future. To explicate events, then, Merleau-Ponty instead turns to Husserl's notion of "institution." The exposition of institution shows how significant events work themselves in and through times other than when they occur. Indeed, institution reveals that matrix events are not merely previous occurrences or happenings but profound alterations with a meaning-field functioning in the present, of which we are ignorant and to which we remain blind.

In fact, Merleau-Ponty relates institution to the "crisis" which, for Husserl, results from the methodological inability to grasp truth claims in terms of their conditions of possibility. These conditions are ultimately not themselves truth claims for Husserl but involve a transcendental logic of their historical development. In his *"La philosophie aujourd'hui"* lecture, for example, Merleau-Ponty says that

> the transcendental is no longer immanent consciousness of constituting *Auffassungen* [opinions]. This would be what he calls in the *Vienna Conference "einseitige Rationalität"* [unilateral rationality]—there is, furthermore, for example, history which functions in us, not processes, chains of visible events, but intentional or "vertical" history with

> *Stiftungen* [institutions], forgetting which is tradition, reprisals [*reprises*], interiority in exteriority—*Ineinander* of the present in the past. As long as we have not recovered this transcendental, rationality is in crisis.⁸

Here institution (*Stiftung*) has the double sense of instituted and instituting. It is both that which *has been instituted* and that which *does the instituting or institutes*. It refers to the obvious norms of traditional values and practices that assemble a group of human lives in a particular way; and it refers to the more implicit means by which these traditional values and practices are gathered that do not raise to the level of norms. This reciprocity implies that the explication for any instituted norm is something not obvious to it. That every norm is in fact prepared by something not fixed, ongoing, and otherwise. There is no straightforward trajectory of human history here. The instituting is constitutive *within* the instituted and is repressed or "forgotten" therein. Its pastness is noticeable and visible while its insertion into and configurational character for the instituted is not. Because of this, the instituted is in fact doomed not to last and will always be supplanted with some alternate configuration. We might therefore say that institution describes every present epochal norm as both closed and open: though it seems determined, it is impossible for this norm to continue as is and always liable to continue in some other previously unpredictable way. Hence, Merleau-Ponty's opening sentences of "The Philosopher and His Shadow": "Establishing a tradition means forgetting its origins, the aging Husserl used to say. Precisely because we owe so much to tradition, we are in no position to see just what belongs to it."⁹

One could say that the whole direction of Husserl's phenomenology, from the static to the genetic, is to exhibit the otherwise secret configurational character of the instituting aspect of institution. That would give him, he thinks, a full picture of the historical development of truth claims and the transcendental structures that make them possible. It would be a relief to the crisis. But, in a Working Note to *The Visible and the Invisible*, Merleau-Ponty suggests that the phenomenology of institution could go even beyond the relief of this crisis:

> The *Einströmen*: a particular case of sedimentation, that is, a secondary passivity, that is, of latent intentionality—it is Péguy's *historical inscription*—It is the fundamental structure of *Zeitigung*: *Urstiftung* of a point of time—[Through?] this latent intentionality, intentionality ceases to be what it is in Kant: pure actuals, ceases to be a property of consciousness, of its "attitudes" and of its acts, to become intentional life—

It becomes the thread that binds, for example, my present to my past in its temporal place, such as it was (and not such as I reconquer it by an act of evocation) the possibility of this act rests on the primordial structure of retention as an interlocking of the pasts in one another plus a consciousness of this interlocking as a law (cf. the reflective iteration: the reflection reiterated ever anew would give only "always the same thing" *immer wieder*)—Husserl's error is to have described the interlocking starting point from a *Präsensfeld* considered as without thickness, as immanent consciousness: it is transcendent consciousness, it is being at a distance, it is the double ground of my life of consciousness, and it is what makes there be able to be *Stiftung* not only of an instant but of a whole system of temporal indexes—time (already as time of the body, taximeter time of the corporeal schema) is the model of these symbolic matrices, which are openness upon being.[10]

Whereas earlier transcendental philosophy, such as Kantian philosophy, assumes "pure actuals" behind reflexion that are then never themselves subject to reflexion, Husserl's phenomenology, through an act of suspension, ultimately aims at these and makes them phenomenally available for the first time. By undermining the pure actionality of consciousness, this phenomenology also reveals a movement of consciousness towards a meaning. That is, it reveals a primordial intentional consciousness, and shows nothing less than a co-substantiation of sense (this would be the noetic pole) and meaning (this would be the noematic pole).[11] What is more, phenomenology raises this correlation to the dignity of philosophical reflection and thematizes it as the proper transcendental structure underneath the pure actuals. Yet there is a problem here too: as long as Husserl thinks appearances always appear in the form of an intentional object, it follows that the transcendental structures of intentionality likewise appear in this form. This means that a transcendental ego never shows up in its purported role as the source of all intentions but only retrospectively and as an intentional object. The solution to this for Husserl is not to return to Kant's "pure actuals" but move away from them further still. Going from a static structure between sense and meaning to a genetic structure between them, what previously looked like co-substantiation is far more complex. There now, in the genetic structure of consciousness, appears to be a lapse between sense and meaning, so that every sense will have a meaning and meanings other to it. These other meanings do not exactly show but they are nonetheless at a crossroad with the meaning that does and has sense. This intersection is the model of institution: each intention between sense and meaning will have more and other meanings; these remain unsignified and yet configured within the intention so much as to make it available to reflection.

The phenomenology of institution passes through two dimensions, then: it disrupts Kantian "pure acts" to reveal their transcendental features; it then reveals these features in terms of the unreflexive meanings through which all conscious life streams. Merleau-Ponty says above, however, that even this second dimension does not reduce to an absolute source of all intentions but is in fact a peculiar case of sedimentation. Though at first it seems institution describes an original stream of consciousness, which is defined as the primordial structure of retentions into the past, the reduction applies to it; and so it is brought to reflection. There is, in other words, an unreferenced and unsignified institution that remains configured within and at the crossroads with the institution Husserl recognizes.[12] This matrix between institutions is itself impossible to reduce yet is what allows Husserl to signify institution as the lapse between sense and its alternate meanings.

Merleau-Ponty's analyses of institution are, as a result, wider in scope than Husserl's. Beyond human institutions, they also include evolutionary and natural institutions, such as puberty, menstruation, and animal morphology, etc. These biochemical transformations would fall under what Merleau-Ponty describes above as the "secondary passivity" and "latent intentionality" within Husserl's formulation of institution. Such passivity and intentionality come into view once phenomenology redoubles its efforts and recognizes the difficulty in which it is invariably involved: once it accepts that all reflexion, even reflexion on the primordial structure of institution, sediments whatever it reflects on, phenomenology can no longer demand a return to the things themselves or to the original stream of consciousness. But it has to be open to the organization and event of these themes. The event is, in this context, not spaced apart from or other to reflexion. It is not the simple negative of reflexion. That it is a matrix implies it is unavailable to reflexion from within that same reflexion. In fact, the very method of suspension in phenomenology, which is a deliberate act of disruption, is premised on what resists this act from inside it. One could say here that, if phenomenology relieves a crisis for Husserl, for Merleau-Ponty it discovers that crisis makes it possible. This is the double ground of the life of consciousness that for Merleau-Ponty is basic to institution and is the model of a symbolic matrix.

Sedimentation and Symbolism in Institution

It might seem that such a phenomenology would only form its own circumference and remain a "phenomenology of phenomenology." To the extent that Merleau-Ponty thinks reflexion sediments and ought to show itself as such, his phenomenology of phenomenology also reveals the phenomena as premised on a kind of resistance to sedimentation. It is no longer only concerned with the movement of consciousness towards its objects and these objects as meant for consciousness. It is no longer only concerned with reflexion and the reflected upon. These relations are instead revealed to be premised on something unsedimented and unthematic that constellates and delimits them. Such delimitation speaks to a primordial passivity that matrixes my capabilities for reflexion and those things I am capable of reflecting on. It is often said that, for Merleau-Ponty, all activity is passivity and all passivity is activity. A primordial passivity is, however, more than the crisscrossing of opposites. To the extent that it constellates both reflexion and the reflected upon, this passivity makes intentionality in all its forms possible and is in fact the formation of significance and thematization. It is for this reason a fundamental non-significance without which significance would be impossible. A primordial passivity is therefore not simply a passive-intentionality. In fact, equivalent to the event of institution, it is without origin and destination. When speaking about primordial passivity, it is thus important to keep in mind that it is not simply the reception of the exterior world into an interior consciousness. If anything, it is also the generativity by which an otherwise exterior world intercepts and intervenes into an otherwise interior consciousness. This is a passivity, as Merleau-Ponty says, "without passivism."[13]

The question such passivity forces is whether even the most radically reflexive philosophy can uncover the most radically un-reflexive moment before it. Can a reflexive philosophy really capture the very generation of reflexion *and* reveal this generation from its anonymous vantage point? It seems impossible to show a personal consciousness in the milieu of nonpersonal events. It seems impossible, furthermore, to show personal consciousness in the context of events that are public, like the historical matrix events Merleau-Ponty names in his lectures on institution and passivity. Merleau-Ponty is also often accused of being unable to think about symbolic structures, like the symbolic structure of language, which, in quite different terms, could explain the anonymous movement between personal and public. Without some sense of impersonal symbolic structures, for example, we can only assume that a personal narrative is just an uncritical perspective of someone plunged into the confusion of her present experience, or that history is a study independent of the immediate comprehension of events by those persons who undergo them. Of course, one lecture title in the institution course is, "Institution in Personal and Public History." He certainly wants institution to account for both the personal and the public, and, at least in some ways, turn them into one single problem. He certainly wants phenomenology to capture events that exceed phenomenological reflexion.

There is also no doubt that Merleau-Ponty is eminently a philosopher of the sensible and that, for him, the sensible is profoundly unreflexive. But he also says above that a phenomenology of institution eventuates in the discovery of "symbolic matrices." In the initial reference to the matrix in the institution lectures, Merleau-Ponty mentions a symbolic "displacement" that, according to Freud, exists between the human and animal, and this displacement, he says, is in fact the "*Stiftung* of a future."[14] It is through the symbolic, in other words, that institution is matrixed between consciousness and nature and between the personal and public, etc.[15] In fact, I think, it is by virtue of the symbolic matrix that consciousness and nature or the personal and public are not theoretical but "natural," that is, nonphilosophical, negations of each other.[16]

Such a symbolism is intimated in the lecture on "Artistic Creation as Institution." There, Merleau-Ponty mentions that developments such as the technique of planemetric perspective in painting are akin to philosophical ones,

> only if philosophies themselves are taken not as statements of ideas, but as inventions of symbolic forms. Shortcoming of Cassirer's philosophy consists in thinking that criticism is the endpoint, that philosophical sense has a directing value even though this sense itself is taken up into sedimentation. Consider criticism itself as a symbolic form and not a philosophy of symbolic forms.[17]

It is generally accepted that when the instituting becomes instituted without notice it works in some symbolic way. But, if institution is *equated* with symbolic matrices, this reading does not go far enough. The institution lectures themselves require some notion of symbolic form. Since Merleau-Ponty places institution at the core of philosophy and crisis, I would even go so far as to say that, for him, the symbolic form is configured in thought in general. His last sentence here, "consider criticism itself as a symbolic form and not a philosophy of symbolic forms," is sweeping and radical in its proposal to alter both the method and aim of philosophy. If philosophical criticism is itself a symbolic form, this would mean that the grounds for every truth claim in fact enfolds a symbolic component. The height of philosophical criticism would then, counterintuitively, eventuate in the symbolic. If so, philosophical criticism becomes absorbed by something very much counter to its usual goals, a form only ever discovered in mutation and that is never itself. The "secondary passivity" and "latent intentionality" that Merleau-Ponty earlier says is uncovered once phenomenology also recognizes itself as sedimentation is this very symbolic form. The form at once accommodates both reflexion and eventfulness. One could say that, like institution itself, the symbolic form is also both closed and open: closed, because on its basis consciousness grasps itself and what appears to it; but, open, because it is nonetheless genuinely impersonal or anonymous and not reducible to consciousness's grasp except in alteration. It is because of the symbolic form, in other words, that when consciousness grasps itself clearly, this is also a state of crisis.

Merleau-Ponty declares in "In Praise of Philosophy," his inaugural lecture delivered at the Collège de France in 1953, that, "it is useless to contest that philosophy limps," and that, "[t]he limping of philosophy is its virtue."[18] If "critique" belongs to the idea of knowledge and a theory of knowledge, the symbolic form of critique denies that these are on a straightforward march towards objective truth. In view of the symbolic form, in other words, Merleau-Ponty accepts that critique does not fulfill the aim of a theory of knowledge and even that there is no single project or trajectory of philosophy. In fact, he also says in the history portion of "In Praise of Philosophy,"

> [b]ut for the tacit symbolism of life [philosophy] substitutes, in principle, a conscious symbolism; for a latent meaning, one that is manifest. It is never content to accept its historical situation (as it is not content to accept its own past). It changes this situation by revealing it to itself and, therefore, by giving it the opportunity of entering into conversation with other times and other places where its truth appears.... Philosophical, aesthetic, and literary criticism, therefore have an intrinsic value, and history can never take their place. It is also true, however, that one can always recover from the book the fragments of history on which it has crystalized, and this is really necessary in order to know to what extent it has changed them in their truth. Philosophy turns towards the anonymous symbolic activity from which we emerge, and towards the personal discourse which develops in us, and which, indeed, we are.[19]

As soon as Merleau-Ponty proposes to show that philosophical critique is itself a symbolic form, that the symbolic form is the limit of critique itself, he also proposes a transformation of phenomenology. Though phenomenology may still be concerned with the possibility of knowledge, this same concern is now directed to symbolic forms instead of eidetic ones. But the term "directed" is already misleading. To interrogate the symbolic form of philosophical critique, phenomenology becomes the study of how thought raises what it examines to the level of signification and thereby modifies it. This is no longer a phenomenology concerned with the exhibition of some referent behind thought—it is not even concerned with what thought thinks. This is rather a phenomenology that reveals thought as a mutation of the symbolic form, which for its part remains unexhibitable and undisclosable. Even the earlier formulation of phenomenology, which called itself an "archeology of all thought," would be ignorant of this symbolic form. The "philosophy about the symbolism of philosophical critique" is in effect a transversal slice of philosophy where it meets its own internal and un-thought limit.

This transversal slice lacks a referent in any usual sense. It is not pointed to a precise object, principle, or foundation, and it is in fact not confined to direct signification. Yet Merleau-Ponty does quite explicitly say above that the symbolic matrix is also openness upon being. He also says elsewhere in *The Visible and the Invisible* that the symbolic is not just a model but the very event of phenomenality.[20] For Merleau-Ponty, in other words, being does not precede the symbolic matrix or is something to be uncovered by the symbolic form. Rather, being is symbolic and the symbolic is ontological. The symbolic does not, however, mediate or bring beings together with being but opens up and is the very difference between them. It is, in other words, on an adventure and is not a destination end or even a proper origin. It takes or is always on an excursion—between consciousness and unconsciousness, body and world, oneself and another, and the things of the world—while also being no place otherwise. For this reason, Merleau-Ponty can stress that the symbolic is anonymous—in between consciousness, humans, and things—and he may in fact associate it with themes more central to his thought such as flesh and *écart*.

Symbolic Forms and Elemental Being

The symbolic matrix thus proposes a variation in the relation between sense and meaning. While there may be a singular and specific relation between sense and its meaning, this relation is in fact owing to overdetermined meaning. Such overdetermination is not prohibitive. It may be clear that each sense corresponds directly to a meaning, but in fact this correspondence is due to some mutation and alteration that have transpired within the meaning. This implies that each sense is always open to other meanings and that these meanings in fact configure the otherwise obvious correspondence between sense and meaning. For example, in the theory of the sign: the relation between the signifier and the signified is obvious only because of the interventional character of meaning. Moreover, from the point of view of the relation itself, this interventional character is irreducible to either term and remains silent or mute, always unsignified. The issue is how meaning can mutate in such a way that it is at once both unsignified and integral to signification.

This question automatically demands a new thesis about sense and meaning, which differs from both intentional correlation and ontological difference. For example, if the unsignified configures and intervenes within the relation of signification, this relation cannot intend it. What is unsignified instead delimits both the apparent being and the consciousness to which it appears. It is therefore ontological to the extent that it slips within and pervades all the terms of the relation. In doing so, it makes consciousness and the world both interpenetrable and inter-penetrating. That is, it places each term within the other. When taken to its conclusion, this implies a further complication: the symbolic matrix that delimits each term of an intentional correlation also delimits what is in excess of the correlation. It stops being from sinking below its constellation within beings. This is in part the reason Merleau-Ponty uses the phrase "symbolic form" against Cassirer. The symbolic matrix is not what cannot appear, or on the other side of what appears, but is rather the limit of both what appears and what does not. It is, as such, always within visible things and the invisible spaces between them. It is where the contour and shape of one thing meet the contour and shape of another thing so that each may be what it is. In fact, it would be possible, only from inside this matrix, to grasp some difference between the meaning of being as opposed to beings. The symbolic matrix is, in short, an ontological tissue prior to formal ontology. It is inside ontology. It does not, and cannot, close difference but is from where it opens.

While I admit there is no thorough or consistent analysis of anything like an ontological symbolism in Merleau-Ponty, I find suggestions of it in his understanding and references to the elements. My interest in the elements here has to do with Merleau-Ponty's suggestion that, like the symbolic form itself, the elements also subsume direct intentions and reveal them in terms of inseparable but nonintended aspects. It is on the basis of these nonintentions that all intentions are in the world and remain concrete. Merleau-Ponty goes so far as to say, for example, that the intentions of perception are not first but rather the "*elements* (water, air), *rays of the world*, things which are dimensions, which are worlds; I slide over these 'elements,' and there I am in the *world*."[21] I would therefore like to depart from M.C. Dillon's claim that, for Merleau-Ponty, the elements are determinate and irreducible non-givens in the phenomena and are therefore dogmatic.[22] The elements are, to my mind, precisely the opposite: they are by no means determinate, by no means exterior to the explicit phenomenon, and do not oppose it. They are rather within the phenomenon even if they are not themselves phenomenal. They also therefore do not introduce a new reality. The only reason they cannot be located is because they are always differentiated and have no specific locale. If the elements thus refer to nonintentions that intervene within and make possible intentional relations, if they are unsignified within significations, they are also, I think, inextricable from the symbolic matrix—all the more so because they take particular shape and contour, persist in the middle of all phenomena and consciousnesses.

There is certainly a continuity between this work and my previous works, *Art and Institution: Aesthetics in the Late Works of Merleau-Ponty* and *Art, Language, and Figure in Merleau-Ponty: Excursions in Hyper-Dialectics*.[23] I believe, however, that this work is more foundational to the other two since it deals directly with divergence as the symbolic form. If *Art, Language, and Figure* found a place for the language-system in Merleau-Ponty's diacritical ontology, the present book is about the symbolic form that makes up this system and catches us all into it. Where Saussure argues that analysis of this system does not require discussion of its "ontogenesis," Merleau-Ponty thinks "ontogenesis" is the means by which language becomes a social phenomenon and therefore cannot be teased from the discussion.[24] This argument was intimated in *Art, Language, and Figure* although it received short shrift. There, I was more concerned with how artists such as Paul Klee and Cy Twombly are able to figure the play of language in the sensible world and therefore undermine the notion that they are distinct from each other.[25] The present volume is concerned instead with a symbolic matrix that would be the ontological limit of both language and world.

The ontological limit of what appears and does not appear constellates them both. To the extent that it delimits both terms from within them, this limit matrixes them and is their internal possibility. As such, it remains the limit of both beings and being—an ontological limit before formal ontology. This limit is also called the symbolic matrix. It remains between both language and world. It matrixes them and allows each to oppose the other. To borrow Merleau-Ponty's initial phrase to describe the symbolic matrix in the institution lectures, this is a symbolism that "displaces" language from the world and constellates them as two distinct regions of existence. Ultimately, I want to argue, Merleau-Ponty's phenomenology does not just retrace its steps back into some place where language and the world are not yet displaced from one another. The operation of the matrix, neither an origin nor a destination, in fact prevents a return to it. His phenomenology is thus eventful as much as it is recuperative, as much productive as it is unrepressive. The best it can do, in other words, is utilize a language that sets in relief some new displacement between language and the phenomena.

Outline of Chapters

The first chapter of this book, "Matrix Event: Methods and Antecedents" is a non-exhaustive history of diacritical methods in philosophy. The chapter identifies three major moments: the "diaeresis of the diphthong" in Homeric poetry, Plato's method of dividing/collecting as it is articulated in the later dialogues and especially *Sophist*, and Merleau-Ponty's *écart* of the flesh. Not only in this first chapter but throughout the book, it should be evident that Merleau-Ponty's place in the history of thought is unique. I continually place him alongside and against other thinkers—chief among them, Homer, Heraclitus, Plato, Husserl, Heidegger, Ricoeur, Derrida, and Nancy—each of whom engage in some transformation of the philosophical method or other.

In Merleau-Ponty's *écart*, divergence is primary and names the relation between the insensible and the sensible. This means that, for him, the insensible is not merely the "not-presently sensed" but only insensible because it *separates from* the sensible. The same holds true in reverse: the sensible is not simply what was previously insensible but sensible only because it is a *concretion from* the insensible. Thus, for Merleau-Ponty, *écart* describes an insensible *in the hazards of or in* the sensible, a genuine lacuna located between and in sensible things whereby these things become what they are. There is not a further phenomenological moment for Merleau-Ponty that would disclose *that from which* the terms sensible and insensible diverge. Their relation, he would say, is only ever diacritical. If there are identities, it is only because there are first differences. Indeed, Merleau-Ponty explicitly states that the flesh is diacritical and a system of oppositions.[26]

In the last section of this first chapter, I point to some crucial resonances between Merleau-Ponty and Heraclitus's first fragment. Already in the first fragment, Heraclitus stresses the unresolvable tension and strife between opposing terms and demands to think from within this tension on its own terms. In the comparison with Heraclitean opposites, Merleau-Ponty is at odds with Heidegger and his notion of an ontological difference that may ultimately undermine the first fragment. In effect, this contrast with Heidegger sets Merleau-Ponty in relief as a decidedly non-occidental thinker, which has consequences in his ontology for a role of the symbolic and its association with form and the formation of things.

The second chapter, "Space—Imagination," carries these reflections about opposition through to a discussion about space and imagination in Husserl and Merleau-Ponty. For Husserl, phantasy consciousness diverges essential forms from concrete shapes—it makes the difference between essences and particulars. This difference eventuates in the difference between geometrical forms and the shape of concrete bodies. Beyond this, for Merleau-Ponty, the imagination resides in the spaces where concrete bodies diverge from one another. It is this most resourceful "spacing" that Merleau-Ponty's ontology proposes. Consider, for example, this passage from *The Visible and the Invisible* in which he uses and takes aim at Husserl's analyses concerning inner-time consciousness once more:

> [A]ll this turns around the problem of an existence that is not a thought of existing—and which Husserl finds again in the heart of the psychological reflection as an absolute retentional flux (but in Husserl there is here the idea of a time of *Empfindung* which is not good: the present in the broad sense is [instead] a symbolic matrix and not only a present that breaks up toward the past—i.e., of a Self-presence that is not an absence from oneself, a contact with Self through the divergence (*écart*) with regard to Self.[27]

Again, inner-time consciousness for Husserl is "irrelational" to the temporal phenomena. It speaks to a succession only within the immanental horizon of consciousness. This inner-horizon also risks supposing a theory of consciousness that is self-relational, however. This is a critique I explore further in chapter 2. Breaking free of this theory of consciousness means finding in the succession of consciousness a thickness—a distance of consciousness from itself that is not merely towards its retentional past or even merely temporal. The thickness with which

Merleau-Ponty is concerned, where consciousness diverges from itself, is therefore not just a negative relation internal to consciousness but its spatial lapse. This does not just mean that interior consciousness has space, but also that interior consciousness is spatialized and held out into things. In that sense, the divergence of consciousness from itself also turns out to be one of and between things.

Where Husserl's phantasy consciousness remains at the level of an immanental horizon, the imagination for Merleau-Ponty is how consciousness comes to itself and grasps geometrical forms from concrete shapes but is also more profoundly within the spaces and separation between those concrete bodies and shapes. Merleau-Ponty again uses the phrase "symbolic matrix" here to refer to these spaces of separation. The symbolic matrix is, in other words, not simply the "not-presently visible" of the visible but also the insensible in the hazards of or in the sensible, making things sensible. These divergences of the sensible would be the most basic kind of symbolic form; they would be symbolic formation itself. The second chapter ends with two more discussions. It discusses the sculptural texture of things, the way sculpted shapes and contours play between light and dark. This play is not simply about sense-vision but the texture of a space in formation that Merleau-Ponty equates with symbolism. This is followed with a discussion of Merleau-Ponty's references to Schelling in the nature lectures. There, light is called a "quasi-concept" and "element" rather than a source of illumination.[28] This quasi-concept, Merleau-Ponty notes, is a "primordial symbolism of knowing" that constellates both what appears and what does not.[29] In other words, there is a symbolism that acts on what is lit up, keeping it from becoming an absolutely positive term, and what is dark, keeping it from becoming an absolute negation. One could say, then, that this primordial symbolism is not non-being itself but what in fact matrixes being and non-being.

The third chapter, "Light—Dark/Awake—Asleep," moves the play between light and dark in shapes into a discussion of the elements. This brings up the same contrast with Heidegger's reading of Heraclitus discussed the first chapter. In the same way that Heidegger reads Heraclitean opposites in terms of an ontological difference between particular beings that appear and the self-identical being that does not, he reads the opposition between light and dark in terms of particular phenomena and a fundamental recessed light source. This opposition is especially found in the seminars dealing with Heraclitus's fragments on waking, dreaming and sleeping. While waking and dreaming concern appearances for Heidegger, sleep concerns a covering over of appearances that is itself covered over—this is, in his view, why we cannot experience our own sleep. Whereas in waking and dreaming there is some structure of phenomenality and illumination between the human and sense or dream perception, sleep is an "open-standing" in a light event—the recession of the sun. For Heraclitus the first material principle is indeed the element of fire (e.g., the sun-fire that illuminates particulars). But, reading the concerning fragments, I see no need to turn this sun-fire into a unified source of illumination opposite to the particular things illuminated. Neither do I find that sense and dream perceptions are founded on a sleep, which does not appear because of its kinship with the unity of this recessed source. Heraclitus provides only the insight that sleep is a non-visible event and akin to the recession of the sun-fire. This darkness is itself the tension between waking and dreaming—it is in the middle of them—so that it can provide a movement between them. Merleau-Ponty also helps us think through how fire and the source of illumination may at the same time recess. Fire is of course also a touchstone for him in "Eye and Mind." An inspection of the passages where it is mentioned reveals that fire has no integrity of its own but is rather a non-luminescent "spark" that lights up the phenomena, both the things that we sense and our sensing of those things.[30] The elemental is in this way in the middle of these different points of view and is thus a sort of texture. It is in fact in all significations. Because this is so, however, the elemental is itself an unsignified event. As such, it is neither an origin nor a destination. Expanding from the previous chapter, I also propose to equate the elemental with a symbolic matrix that constellates the phenomenon.

In his passivity lectures, Merleau-Ponty also gives an analysis of sleep. There he shows that sleep is the deprivation of the phenomena that remains in the hazards of both waking and dreaming. Merleau-Ponty makes clear, for example, that sleep is not equivalent to dreams and the free ability of consciousness to present images and their non-being to itself. He also makes clear that sleep is not a simple passivity where the body is submitted to some external object or where it unifies with the external world and becomes a death. Thus, Merleau-Ponty calls sleep "being in the divergence."[31] It is not itself intentional except as the divergence between dreaming and sense intentions. It is, in other words, a limit that allows me to distinguish between my most interior life and the external world to which I am directed. Echoing the nature lectures, Merleau-Ponty in fact calls this limit a "primordial symbolism."[32] In this context, the primordial symbolism not only constellates and delimits the apparent and nonapparent but also the real and the fictive. It is, in other words, the limit between my waking and dreaming lives and is what allows me to take a stance on both aspects and know them as different. But, to equate sleep with a primordial symbolism, implies that even my own sleeping body is a limit of me and is not my limit. It is sleep, in other words, that prohibits and constricts me from gaining the properties of an absolute source of illumination, capable of illuminating my waking and dreaming lives, and indeed everything included in their difference, all at once. The phenomenology of sleep thus becomes a phenomenology of the non-signification, which makes all significations possible. As such, it becomes a phenomenology of the most profound, and concrete, symbolic matrix between me and the limit of all thought.

It is also important to note that the elements are likewise a limit to thought. In *The Visible and the Invisible*, for example, Merleau-Ponty says the being of flesh has no name in the history of philosophy except to designate it as an "element."[33] The element of light, for example, resists and is the ontological limit to thought; but the issue is whether even this element is concrete enough that it also intervenes into my individual life and allows me to tell the difference between my dreaming and waking lives. The fourth chapter is titled "Philosophy—Symbolism" and is initially concerned again with sleep and its connection to dreaming and sense perceptions. Merleau-Ponty describes the symbolic form of passivity as both a "censor" and "positive."[34] It is both positive and censorious, for example, when it delimits my dream perceptions from my sense perceptions. It is positive in the sense that it produces the distinction that I recognize. But it is also censorious because, from this very distinction, I cannot recognize the form that produces it. Inasmuch as the symbolic form produces and effaces itself in what I recognize, Merleau-Ponty also says it is "primordial": a nonpersonal and anonymous limit in personal thought. One could certainly say it is the delimitation of the personal from the public. But, to the extent that it does this, it also introduces the question of a limit to philosophy itself. To study this limit, phenomenology would become a sort of psychoanalysis of philosophy.

Note, then, that though the symbolic form is the censor of philosophy, it also produces philosophy—which is also to say that philosophy is at once both a repression and an expression of the form. A phenomenology of the symbolic form of philosophical critique cannot therefore treat this form as merely the repressed content of critique; it cannot trace this critique back to the original event of its expression. It is instead an analysis of a matrixed relation between repression and expression; and can no longer premise itself on the phenomenalizing and direct signification of the repressed symbolic form. In other words, an indirect ontology will also be the method of the symbolic form.

This is something Merleau-Ponty alludes to in *The Visible and the Invisible* and in the very recently published lecture notes on the literary usages of language. In one concerning passage from *The Visible and the Invisible*, for example, Merleau-Ponty speaks about the methodological adoption of an "eloquent language" in philosophy.[35] The point is to call into question a philosophical use of language that categorizes in language and yet takes itself to refer to real events. Precisely because it fails to interrogate its own language, this conceptual use of language is incapable of articulating the symbolism that evented it. Whereas, I think Merleau-Ponty ultimately demands that we notice the matrices between conceptual and literary language.

In chapter 1, I already note Merleau-Ponty's phrase in *The Visible and the Invisible*, "*Ursprungsklärung*" and his idea that we must start thinking "from behind [the] point" of philosophy.[36] Doing so entails thinking from behind an ontological difference and instead from within the "polymorphic matrix"[37] between being and beings. The point is neither to separate being from beings nor to meditate on their sameness. In fact, and even more radically, to think from behind the point of philosophy is to provide an ontology without origins. Here, difference and differentiation replace identity, and there is no room for some irreducible and self-related ground to beings. For this reason, Merleau-Ponty's ontology concerns the symbolic rather than ideal or fixed limit of beings. If this ontological matrix is a symbolic one, this does not mean it clarifies a symbol in-itself somehow distinct from its modes of symbolization. Finally, then, to show that philosophical critique is itself a symbolic form does not mean elucidating what philosophical critique is so much as showing its limits. This is, in a sense, a critique of critique. When Merleau-Ponty writes the literary language into conceptual language, I argue he allows for the recognition of such a radical critique. Here, one could say, Merleau-Pony wants his phenomenology to counterbalance the sedimenting effect of reflexion.

I develop this argument in the fifth and final chapter, "Philosophical Language -Literary Language." There is no question that Merleau-Ponty often employs a literary style in his philosophical writings. This is not so much an obfuscation of some otherwise lucid thought but an invitation for lucidity to operate a transversal slice of itself and catch a glimpse of its symbolic formation which still remains unsedimented. In this sense, I think, his phenomenology is eventful. It forces us to recognize the "ontogenetic" power of language itself.[38] If language is ontogenetic, it betrays neither a non-linguistic intentional object nor fundamental being but is the generation of meaning "as on the first day."[39] There is, in other words, no meaning before language, but language produces meaning and only then seems to refer it. This also means, as Merleau-Ponty says, the limit of language is "savage" and can never be signified because it intersects and is always inside language. The impossibility of reducing language, he thus also notes, *is* its reduction.[40]

In the end, the method most appropriate to this ontological symbolism involves an *exercise* of some medial language, between philosophy and literature, which reveals language in general in terms of the unsedimented meaning it produces. Such an exercise does not assume a philosophy of symbolic form – it does not concern an already theoretical and formalist symbolism. It is also not critical in the old sense of a systematic philosophy of reflection. But it is not uncritical. Still concerned with limits, it remains a phenomenology which shows the symbolic form of philosophical critique. Merleau-Ponty calls such an interrogation of the limits of philosophical critique a "hermeneutical reverie," and he finds this method in Proust.[41]

Chapter 1
Matrix Events
Methods and Antecedents

The phrase "matrix event" describes, for Merleau-Ponty, some event to which we are passively disposed all the more so whenever we try to actively reflect on it. It thus speaks to some event of which we are unconscious, so that we may not know from where or even that it has emerged. A matrix event is thus for Merleau-Ponty affective rather than dialectical. It describes the distances, oppositions, contradictions, and paradoxes internal to reflexive life. It is also therefore associated with Merleau-Ponty's other terms, "*écart*" and "diacritics," according to which differences are neither held decisively apart nor simplistically overlapped so as to lose their characteristics. The word "diacritics," for example, comes from the Greek word διαίρεσις, which means "taking apart," "division," or "distinction." It further derives from διαιρέω, "take apart," which is itself a compound of the verb αἱρέω "take" and the preposition διά "through" (in compounds, "apart").

In this chapter, I want to describe the matrix event inasmuch as it is associated with *écart* and diacritics. I also want to trace the points of continuity and discontinuity a philosophy that emphasizes *écart* and diacritics might have with the tradition of philosophy. If the main trajectory of western philosophy is dialectical and synthetic, Merleau-Ponty's seems at odds with and even to undermine this trajectory. This chapter is first about the origins of a diacritical philosophy but is in no way meant to be exhaustive. It begins with a brief explanation of διαίρεσις in the context of Homeric poetry and then proceeds to a discussion of "dividing-collecting" in Plato's *Sophist* and the later dialogues. If the import of *Sophist* is that it opens a dialectical situation of being—its fundamental relation to non-being, obscurity, and discourse—the method of dividing-collecting ultimately requires a dialectician who reflexively sees through multiplicity and into unity. It is argued that such reflexion assumes a second-order ontological structure wherein non-being has being. That is, for Plato, the dialectician betrays an ability to see into an ontological structure, which disambiguates the sensible world through a set of formal axioms, and he thinks that such disambiguation is real.

Merleau-Ponty's *écart* is a profound reversal of Plato's, and with it the aims of a diacritical philosophy are fundamentally altered. For Merleau-Ponty, the pursuit of diacritics does not resolve the dialectical situation of being but rather opens it. In that case, diacritics is understood as the production rather than solution of being and non-being. In fact, for Merleau-Ponty, any attempt at clarification and unification of an ontology is equally a production of obscurity. Thus, his *écart* also emphasizes a proximity between obscurity and discourse at the ontological level, but it problematizes any ontology suggesting we can supersede this discourse. We could say that, with Merleau-Ponty, the dialectical situation of being is posed in terms of discourse, a discourse that does not implicate a situation to be overcome. For him, a philosophy that closes the meaning of this discourse and gives it determination would be counterproductive to its stated aim. Following Merleau-Ponty, then, discourse itself ought to become both the object and the aim of investigation. Unlike for Plato, for Merleau-Ponty a diacritical method does not elucidate the obscurity of being but rather brings it to bear as the limit of ontology itself.

What appears to be a chronological analysis turns out to be explanatory. Since the Platonic diacritical method comes from a first engagement with the pre-Socratics, especially Parmenides and Heraclitus, towards the end of this chapter, I would like to turn to a connection between Merleau-Ponty and Heraclitus. This functions less to make the historical point of a re-emancipation of something original and more as an occasion to think of Merleau-Ponty's ontology within an alternate frame where discourse is not only associated with ontology but central to it. I suggest, then, that this ontology is matrixed and still operative within the traditional ontology.

The Homeric Diphthong

Compared to later Greek poetry, Homeric verse has a remarkable freedom to accommodate words to its meter. Many anomalies in language have historical explanations, and the first poets of the *Iliad* and *Odyssey* were also inheritors of a long and continuous tradition of epic composition going back to the Mycenaean Age. Certainly, over that time various changes occurred in Greek, and the epic language could not but be affected by them. The consequence is that some formulae that were originally metrical become un-metrical, or metrically imperfect. There are therefore verses in the text that become, in turn, metrically more satisfactory when they are translated back into an older form of the language. When this is done, previously unnoticed patterns of the language emerge. For example, sometimes it is simply a matter of resolving a vowel contraction, as in the line "*ἔνθα δ' ἀποβρίξαντες ἐμείναμεν ἠῶ δῖαν*" and a series of others where *ἠῶ* occupies the fifth foot.[1] This is an unusual placement for a word made of two long syllables but normal for a word scanning longer, as in the earlier form, *ἠόα*.

The most famous case of this phenomenon is the digamma. Greek once possessed a sound like the *w* in English, which occurred in many words. Some dialects still possessed it and wrote it with the letter *F*, called *wau*, which stood after *E* in the alphabet.[2] Later grammarians called it the digamma because its shape looked like a double gamma. The most obvious effect of the digamma is hiatus. The missing digamma may close a preceding short-vowel syllable and make it scan long (this is called "make position"), and it may even be treated like one of the consonants (λ, μ, ν, ρ, and ς) and be doubled, causing the effect of a preceding short vowel to scan long (*ἀποειπών* scanned u—). We find, then, that short syllables terminating in a consonant (for example *ος* and *ον*), are also often rendered long as if they were in position, just as they would be where they are not affected by the double gamma. In these cases, the position is produced by the final consonant of the word, and the initial consonant or digamma for the word coming after. It therefore seems that the digamma was, strictly speaking, a real consonant with the sound of the Latin *F* or *wh*, and regularly used when Homer's poems were recited, but lost much later when these same poems were written.

In Charles Anthon's 1866 metrical index to the first six books of Homer's *Iliad*, a special section is dedicated to the "shortening of long vowels and diphthongs at the end of a word"[3]: according to Anthon, every final syllable, which is long because of a vowel or diphthong can be made short if it stands in the "thesis" (the thesis being that part of the foot on which the stress of the voice does not fall), and if the next word begins with a vowel or diphthong. In Homer, this shortening is almost a constant rule. Anthon lists the following examples:

ἡμένη| ἐν βένθεσσιν ἁλὸς παρὰ πατρὶ γέροντι.
ἄμφω ὁμ|ῶς θυμῷ φιλέουσά τε κηδομένη τε.
αἰδεῖσθαί θ' ἱερῆα καὶ ἀγλαὰ| δέχθαι ἄ|ποινα.
κλῦθί μευ| ἀργυρότοξ', ὃς Χρύσην ἀμφιβέβηκας.[4]

The diphthongs that were pronounced in the common Attic dialect as one sound, are in the epic dialect often resolved by separating them into two sounds to make the poem's metrical requirements work. In his commentary on the forms of Ionic dialect in Homer, Carl Willhelm Lucas writes about this phenomenon in a section called "Of the Diaresis of Dipthongs," which is followed by a section, "Of the Change of the Rough into Smooth Breathing."[5]

If the diacritical method in philosophy has its informal roots in the epic poetry, these roots preserve the meter and recitations of the poems. If, as it is commonly noted, the Greek language operates by "sound symbolism," and the sonorous character of the language is not extrinsic to its sense and meaning, then analyses of phenomena like the diaeresis of dipthongs in the epic poetry are not simply historical analyses. It is possible to suggest, in other words, that Anthon's analyses of shortened vowels and diphthongs and Lucas's diaeresis of the diphthong may be read as more than just puzzles regarding the meter of Homeric poetry. They may also be seen to bridge the schism between sound and sense, and between the metrical and syntactical series. Lost pronunciations or changed meters in the later language may in fact eventuate in both a lost sense and an alteration in the syntactical rules of the language. It may in fact mark an alteration in both the practical and formal elements of the language. Reciprocally, the recitation in which a single vowel is split into two sounds would also be a new formal construction of sense and syntax.

To recuperate an intertwining between the practice of language and its formal construction means posing a set of questions like the ones Giorgio Agamben does in "The Dictation of Poetry" chapter of *The End of the Poem*:

> What does it mean for a living being to speak? Is language, as seems obvious, a creation and expression of the living human being. . . . Do life and speech constitute an articulated unity, or is there a disjunction between the two that neither individual existence nor the historical development of humanity can overcome?[6]

When it comes to answering these issues in the register of poetics, however, Agamben also notes that the solution is not immediately evident, and cannot possibly be immediately evident:

> When literary criticism and aesthetics finally came to formulate the problem of the relation between lived experience and poeticized experience with regard to the work of art, the terrain on which the problem

could have been correctly posed had already been covered over and forever altered.[7]

In other words, as soon as the distinction is made in poetics between speaking and the structure of the poem this very poetics proves unable to deal with their connection. Merleau-Ponty deals with these same issues in language in general and not just poetics. This becomes a more vivid issue in the fourth chapter especially.

The Platonic Dividing-Collecting

If diacritics has its roots in Homeric verse, it is Plato who formalizes it and turns it into a philosophical method.

In *Sophist*, Plato poses a very instructive question: "How many beings are there, and what are they?[8] This question is instructive only because it shows that being cannot be quantified, and there results a set of antinomies when we try to do so. When we say, "all of beings" or "the One is," for example, we are automatically also saying "two," since being is *also* all beings or One.[9] Thus, for Plato, being is neither "all of beings" nor "the One," and both definitions need to be excluded from its definition. In addition to the quantification problem, Plato says, this is also a language problem. When we say, "the One is," we are also giving the One a name, and doubling it again.[10]

In the first contradiction, Plato is in fact addressing a fundamental problem of the One that seemed intractable in *Parmenides*: while being adheres to a material model and has spatial and temporal determinations, "participation" of the One in spatial and temporal determinations would be a μεθεξις ουσιας μετα χρόνου του παρόντος (*methexis ousias meta chronou tou parontos*). This conundrum in *Parmenides* has also been noted by Kierkegaard in *The Concept of Anxiety*, where he says that Plato equates the now-moment, being, and the one:

> The one must nevertheless be, so it is said, and then "to be" is defined as follows: Participation in an essence or nature in the present time (*to de einai allo ti esti e methexis ousias meta chronou tou parontos*) ... the present (*to nun*) vacillates between meaning the present, the eternal, and the moment.[11]

Plato's failure to disassociate being from the One in *Parmenides* means that time is reduced abstractly to the present, and the concept of being means a truncated presence that excludes past and future. But, in *Sophist*, when the problem of being is posed in terms of quantification, it is immediately recognized that being *cannot* truncate the present and exclude past and future, while the One is also freed from its equation with the now-moment and being. The solution that Plato offers in *Sophist* to the problem in *Parmenides* is thus to tear the One away from being. The *Sophist* is radical to the extent that it gives up the ontological dogmatism of the One, and the impracticable problems that come with it, and it opens the question of being even at the expense of its degradation. This means that the temporal forms of "is, was, and will be" are no longer explained in terms of the singular, unchanging, and eternal moment like they are in *Parmenides*.[12]

In *Sophist*, in other words, the question of being is now evidenced in each being. The temporal form of each determinate thing that "is" is also what "was" and "will be." It existed in the past and will continue to exist in the future. A being that "is" in this sense is initially situated in non-being and the obscure. This non-being—how we are unaware of it even as a problem, and how this unawareness becomes obvious to us—is what fascinates Heidegger about Plato's *Sophist*, famously in the very opening of *Being and Time*.[13] He also spends a good portion of his lecture course on *Sophist* on the different articulations of the dialectic of being in the dialogue: the vexatious nature of being and non-being, the phenomenological sense of non-being, the positive sense of a non-being that discloses itself.[14] Thus, we can read phenomenology back into one of the *Sophist* course's opening remarks:

> This past, to which our lectures are seeking access, is nothing detached from us, lying far away. On the contrary, we are this past itself. And we are it not insofar as we are explicitly to cultivate the tradition and become friends of classical antiquity, but, instead, our philosophy and science live on these foundations, i.e., those of Greek philosophy, and do so to such an extent that we are no longer conscious of it: the foundations have become obvious. Precisely in what we no longer see, in what has become an everyday matter, something is at work that was once the object of the greatest spiritual exertions ever undertaken in Western history.[15]

Insofar as *Sophist* breaks open the dialectical situation of being, Heidegger also values it to *regain* that dialectic. Since the dialectic of being implies that being is initially non-being, its obscurity, Heidegger thinks, is always still at play, now only disclosing itself in its obscurity from us so that we are in fact unconscious of it even as a problem. The rectification of this obscurity is already at work in the condition of the dialectic itself, and it is key that, according to Heidegger, the initial dialectical situation of being could only ever be in its temporal form. Yet, to disambiguate being, Plato *does* want to put the temporality of each determinate thing to rest. This play between movement and rest is also exhibited when an idea becomes known: movement, because the idea has become known; and rest, because the idea is now what it is. There is no question that Plato wants the ideas to become known and known as what they are.

Let me now attend to the second contradiction of the One mentioned above: the One may not be named without doubling it. In this sense, the One is rather the limit of naming and language. Whereas, in its initial dialectical situation with non-being and obscurity, being for its part always remains within the limits of discourse and speech (λέγειν). To the extent that Plato wants to put being to rest, the question is how this rest may remain within the limit of discourse and speech as well. This difficulty appears in many dialogues, where the essence is what prevents discourse from being wholly free and coheres it. Plato draws support for this view from an opposition, typically posed in antiquity, between "by nature" and "by convention." If language is mere convention, then it bears the history of human acts and can be shaped by those acts. But Plato thinks that language is not so pliable. It is not merely shaped by our actions and is not just our conventions since it does not just bend to the human will to produce any sound whatsoever or to put unrelated words together in speech. In fact, Plato says, language is the initial "interlacing" of noun and verb that betrays a set of otherwise nonapparent set of grammatical, syntactical, or lexical laws. In the third Logical Study of his *Logical Investigations*, Husserl notes exactly this point of Plato's: the problem of essence is the problem of an absolute and right language.[16] The problem of an absolute and right language is in effect the refusal of a subjective language through and through.

This criticism of conventional language is also always apiece with Plato's criticism of pure becoming. When I say that "language is precisely how it appears," Plato thinks that I am in fact admitting "beings are becoming" and that "things are how they appear to me." If we think our conventions of language speak truths, in other words, then we ignore the both the epistemological and physical separation between being and appearing. In the *Cratylus*, for example, in the opening arguments against Protagoras's thesis "man as the measure of all things," Plato inserts his own thesis that being is the measure of language. Here, along with *Euthyphro* 11a, for example, being is suddenly given a substantive form to contravene Protagoras's subjectivism: "Do you believe that *ousia* is proper to each one?" Then, we would be "the measure of all things" only if language were nothing but convention.[17] Just a little later in the *Cratylus*, Plato tells us that we can "see" the significations and have our "eyes fixed on that which is the name in itself."[18] This name introduces us to a stop and prevent things from flowing.[19] Whereas, Heraclitus's flow, for example, prevents us from seeing how things can become known, and this is why Plato ridicules Heraclitus, calling him the philosopher of the "runny nose."[20]

Plato wants to get to the name in itself and sublimate the flow. He wants to navigate past the "verbal" copy to the "real" model—to get beyond the shadows, of which words are a species, and proceed to the reality of all words. It is not difficult thereafter for Plato to consider humans as proper legislators of language, who can attend to these models directly, and without words.[21] It is well known, for example, that for Plato geometrical essences are essences derived from out of the pluralism of multiple species (e.g., there is one and the same triangle across the different instances of triangles, one and the same circle across the different instances of round objects).[22] And if Aristotle is to be believed, all ideas would have eventually been numbers for Plato, which would turn philosophy into a meta-mathematics.

In his later dialogues, *Sophist, Politicus,* and *Philebus* especially, Plato calls the process of going to the "name in itself" διαίρεσις and συναγωγή, dividing and collecting (technically, "ordering-together"). If division is for Plato the initial possibility of deriving ideas, it is because he thinks thought demands recognition that one thing is not another. In the otherwise pluralized and confusing world, it is thought that separates and dissociates. Thus, division is a constructive moment. This also means that collecting is inherently linked with a disjointed vision of εἶδος, an εἶδος that is "each time" singular. This is to say that, in terms of the process of dividing-collecting, thinking for Plato is not synthetic but a question of grasping "each being" in terms of its nonconventional and collected nature.[23]

The *Sophist* therefore famously says that being is "mixed" with all εἶδος. Since he attributes being to *this* or *that*, for Plato thought is first and foremost situated on a level where there are multiple beings in the sense that there are distinct significations. This is because such thought is initially based on what is called the descending dialectic that has to do with discourse and language. If in *Parmenides* the participation of being in the sensible was thought on a material model, the notion of being "sharing in" and "resembling" the sensible fell short and was thought to be absurd. Whereas in *Sophist* Plato passes from the sensible to εἶδος through the method of dividing-collecting and is no longer asking the question of being on the basis of a material model. Understood in terms of dividing and collecting, the dialectical situation of being is instead grasped in terms of method and labor. Specifically, it is the work of reflexion itself. Socrates says, for example, that the dialectician is the one who sees past the multiplicity and into the unity.[24] If remaining at the level of discourse and distinct significations leads only to aporia, the method of diving-collecting these significations give rise to a second-order ontological question. We are ushered from the question of *beings* to the question of *being* as such, and now this question is answerable not in terms of discourse but an intuition of the unity εἶδος.

In other words, the *Sophist* ushers in a method that allows us to move from the divisions of the sensible to a reflexion on its unity—from the initial dialectical situation of being to the unity of being. Not only does this mean that, according to the *Sophist*, it is necessary to show the relation of *this* or *that* to being; we are also required to show the relation of *this* or *that* to their non-being.[25] After all, Plato still operates in a realist system of truth, and the reflexion of non-being does not result from a spontaneous transcendental "I think." The *Sophist* instead demands the impossible thesis that there *really* is non-being. Because it no longer works according to the material model of *Parmenides*, the dialogue implies that participation of the sensible in being instead requires yet another moment in which both being and non-being *are*. Paul Ricoeur forcefully notes this problem:

> The transcendental attribution of being to non-being and of non-being to being is the second-degree ontological structure that makes attribution possible at the first level of thinking (for example, when I say that the number three *is* odd). One could say the same thing in different terms: the problem of the *Sophist* and the *Parmenides* stems from a reflection on dialectic as a *method*, where attribution occurs simply by means of the copula; this reflection reduplicates dialectic, in a foundational dialectic, where being is attributed anew, no longer to essences but to otherness . . . in this way the reciprocity of being and non-being is uncovered.[26]

Thus, Ricouer also argues that *Sophist* is in the last analysis plagued with a "philosophical scandal":

> For Plato, it makes no sense to speak of a "philosophy of the concrete." By the same token, the participation of the sensible in the intelligible is a relation that is *practiced* daily in the act of speaking, of naming, of defining, but which cannot be thought through as a relation intelligible in itself; everything happens as if, from brute existence to "meaning," there were a *leap* worked by the *legein*, by Speaking, and as if, inversely, from saying to perceiving, there were an inverse leap, a *chairein ean*, a "saying farewell"—which is silence.[27]

This is a difficulty that, according to Ricoeur, Plato partially explains away in other dialogues, for example, with the introduction of the demiurge in *Timaeus*. But one could very well say too that, on the contrary, in *Sophist* Plato is everywhere concerned with language and rhetoric. That is obviously the very point of the dialogue. What Ricoeur notes here, though, is that there nonetheless remains a deep-seeded ambiguity in the relation between the discourse that is philosophy and the philosophy that looks for essential structures of that discourse. If the essences are tantamount to a collapse in the relation between philosophy and discourse, then we say farewell to the limits of λέγειν in which being initially appeared as a problem. This is what lets sensible determinations fall into utter silence and darkness since these are not the proper meaning of language nor of philosophy.

Ricouer therefore argues that, for all the laboring the *Sophist* does to get away from the question of the One, it also leads back to the One or the same source of illumination we find in the sun of the *Republic*. In the *Republic*, for example, Plato does not endorse the question of being beginning with the basic aporia of non-being. Rather, it is most famously the sun that makes the beings known and us knowledgeable of those beings. This sun is therefore a radical origin that philosophical discourse cannot in principle deny without leading to its own ruination.

If we follow the *Sophist*, we eventually must admit that, for one reason or another, the discourse of philosophy is such that it cannot ever explain itself. If its dialectic is insatiable, then being is in fact never clarified, rescued from its initially obscure situation, or apart from discourse. Alternatively, being is clarifiable and its dialectical situation comes to a rest. But in this case, it is limited by something outside of it that is not itself dialectical. One can say that Plato's critique of Heraclitus, and his insistence on a dialectic between becoming and being, leads back to Parmenides. In that case, as it is articulated in the *Sophist*, Plato's diacritical method on its own proves insufficient.

The Merleau-Pontian *écart*

While "diacritics" is not always seen as a focal point in Merleau-Ponty's late ontology, it is nonetheless closely aligned, if not outright equated, with the much more central theme of *écart*, which he describes as a "diacritical conception" of separation.[28] While the first reference to "diacritics" in *The Visible and the Invisible* comes much later in the text, "*écart*" appears very early in the book, in the first pages of the "Reflection and Interrogation" chapter.[29] As the translator's note mentions in the early reference to *écart*, it may be described variously as, "divergence," "spread," "deviation," "separation."[30] The word "diacritics" refers to these too, but, rooted in διαίρεσις, also makes clear that such terms do not assume something from which things diverge, spread, deviate, or separate. In this case, diacritics may be the more technical elucidation of *écart* since it emphasizes that divergent terms are ultimately not synthetic. It is additionally important to note that, when diacritics is mentioned, it is also associated with language or the behavior between signs in a language system in which no sign means anything positive except in relation to other signs that it is not. For example, when Merleau-Ponty describes *écart* as a diacritical conception, he says this is a critique of the positive signification or the theory of predication.[31] Just as we do not have one single word that says everything we could possibly say in a language, we also do not have one continuous sensible field or source of sensation that lets us see everything. Indeed, Merleau-Ponty connects the diacritical not with an origin but with "originating."[32]

At first, *écart* describes a reduction from "monocular vision"—the vision to which we reflectively refer when we think about perception—to the "thing perceived with both eyes"—the concrete, motile and binocular vision that is unreflectively and practically there in, but hidden to, monocular vision. Merleau-Ponty describes this monocularity in terms of "phantoms" and "pre-things," while the binocular he describes as perception of the "real" and "dense," actually sensible world. The former vision is phantasmatic and unreal inasmuch it does not account for the body's position-taking. It is nonetheless a coherent and singular point of view from which nothing differs, having only the envelope, general or universal contour of things. Merleau-Ponty associates the binocular, on the other hand, with a vision that, even for one person, has incommensurability and incoherency right within it. Such vision is at an intersection with the sensible, which for its part cannot be given over to just one perspective or seen from just one right or objective way. This vision is real and dense because it traverses into the polyspectivity of what it sees rather than just a set of universal and general outlines. In the discussion of geometrical and sculptural shapes next chapter, we see that, for Merleau-Ponty, binocular vision sees the real and dense character of things but is *already also* phantasmatic and unreal. An abstract geometry of things can only in this way be different or a divergence—not essentially severed as two independently meaningful terms—from binocular vision. Here, in this initial section on Merleau-Ponty, we are outlining the unique way he conceives of this difference and divergence more generally.

His association between vision and *écart* targets the idea that the former is the most veridical of senses since it beholds things from a distance and without investment. Unlike touch, for example, vision seems to be able to glance the whole of a landscape at once and may be associated with the intellect and the seeing of essences. The first appearance of *écart* in *The Visible and the Invisible* to describe the divergence of seeing universal contours from seeing the dense and sensible things is an initial strike against the idea that sight is the "higher sense." It undermines an entire philosophical trajectory based on this premise. This suggests that we can read *The Visible and the Invisible* as a classic phenomenological response to the Platonic method of dividing-collecting. Where for Plato division consists in the logical method of dividing species to get to a genus, which would consist in seeing a unified $εἶδος$ against the multiplicity of sensible content, Husserl's eidetic phenomenology grasps essences that are "inseparable" from contingent facts even if they are not categorically the same. According to this articulation of phenomenology, when we maintain with Plato the separation between essences and facts as a real one, this is already symptomatic of the natural attitude applied to both—making facts and essences two different, real things now impossible to relate. Husserl is very clear in the *Ideas I* that he is no Platonic realist.[33] The driving force behind his phenomenology is to offer a method according to which the realist picture of truth is obsolete. Husserl's eidetic phenomenology is radical to the extent that, by bracketing the natural attitude, it offers a new method that genuinely immanentizes essences within facts. A genetic phenomenology is even more radical to the extent that it explains the genesis of the correlation between essences and facts. I also note that, according to phenomenology, there cannot be any second-order ontology in which both being and non-being exists. Nor is there any transcendental reflexion from which non-being spontaneously arises. Husserl at least introduces the problem of figuring non-being into the correlation between essences and facts, making it a fact of appearing that essences have to accommodate rather than disambiguate.

Already in the opening passages of the "Reflection and Interrogation" chapter of *The Visible and the Invisible*, Merleau-Ponty says that the phantoms of monocular images "are only a certain divergence from the imminent true vision, absolutely bereft of its [prestiges?] and therefore drafts for or residues of the true vision."[34] Near to when he breaks off to some last thoughts and Working Notes, he returns to the *écart* and tells us that the "most difficult point," is to give a philosophy that outlines "the bond between flesh and idea, and the internal armature which [it] manifests and which it conceals."[35] The *écart* bookends Merleau-Ponty's final and supposedly radical text, but these two passages alone appear to say that *The Visible and the Invisible* will do nothing than what phenomenology in general purported to do: it will reveal that the vision of ideal things is itself divergent, not *really* different, from the vision that sees from within the density and poly-perspective character of things. This is a claim about the structure of knowledge itself. The actual and dense sensible field is brought to bear on the very notion of essences, and a phenomenology aimed at the *écart* between the sensible field and essences appears to be transcendental in nature even if, for Merleau-Ponty, the condition of possibility is ultimately found in the sensible world that is multiform.

But this is not the entire point of Merleau-Ponty's *écart*, and it is even quite misleading if not understood in its narrower context. Its later equation with diacritics in *The Visible and the Invisible* brings into sharper focus Merleau-Ponty's departure from both Plato and Husserl by emphasizing the non-synthetic nature of the sensible field. Note, for example, that Merleau-Ponty also says that the sensible field is *itself a* "diacritical, relative, oppositional system."[36] The sensible field, in other words, imposes a diacritical relation between facts and essences more fundamental than the phenomenological articulation of their inseparability. It is, as Merleau-Ponty says elsewhere, "the advent of difference" between facts and essences, or "a possibility for separation (two eyes, two ears: the possibility for *discrimination*, for the use of the diacritical)."[37] As such, the sensible field is neither itself essential nor factical. It accords neither with reflexion nor even with the reflected upon objects. Instead, it produces their difference. Indeed, that is the very point of mentioning *écart* in a chapter that is about reflexion. It should be made evident that Merleau-Ponty must also deny the originary and ontological character of the *categorial distinction* between essences and facts, which Husserl initially maintained to preserve the essential nature of the coherency of facts. Unsurprisingly, this makes *The Visible and the Invisible* more closely aligned with Husserl's genetic phenomenology. Yet Merleau-Ponty is concerned to penetrate further than even Husserl does in his later period. Merleau-Ponty's essential question may be phrased: how to grasp the event and occurring of a categorial distinction between facts and essences?

The "combining," "composing," and "putting together" of συντίθημι is second to "generation, "production," "creation," and "becoming" of γένεσις. True, when we fix our attention strictly to the event of a sensation, maintaining the deceptively simple method of attending always to the explanatory force of perceptual faith, we see that the sensible is a double-ness, both an active *sensing* and a passive *being-sensed*. As is well known, Merleau-Ponty does speak of a "reversibility" or of an "overlapping." Beyond these well-known references, he also speaks of "one sole Being,"[38] "unique Being,"[39] "the same Being,"[40] and so forth. But we will also miss a fundamental point of his if we just take reversibility and overlapping to simply mean a combining together of the activity and passivity of sensibility, in which case the double-ness would be superseded. If we take reversibility to be the erasure of difference, we will in fact miss the fact that the sensible is itself separating. We will be unable to see the importance of themes such as "fragmentation,"[41] "dehiscence,"[42] "explosion,"[43] or "promiscuity"[44] for Merleau-Ponty's ontology.

Consider the example of touching a table. When I touch the table, I am confronted with a series of appearances that are apprehended as belonging to the table. When my hand slides over it, I perceive its hardness, smoothness, and extension. It is also possible, however, to change my attention so that, instead of being preoccupied with the properties of the table, I bring to explicit awareness the touching hand and its pressure and movement, not apprehended as objective properties of the hand but localized in it and manifesting its function as a particular sort of experiencing organ. One and the same sensation can certainly be interpreted in two different ways, as both an appearance of the experienced object and as a localized sensing in the correlated experiencing bodily part. But, as Merleau-Ponty says, the touched object and the touching hand do not at all appear in the same manner. Whereas the properties of a table are constituted adumbrationally, this is not the case for the localized sensing. Now consider Merleau-Ponty's most famous example of the two hands overlapping, the right hand touching the left hand. The touching hand feels the surface of the touched hand, but when the left hand is touched it is not simply given as a mere object, since it feels the touch itself. Yet I never, in the same instant, experience my one hand as touching *and* as touched. Rather than saying here that one and the same sensation can be interpreted in two different ways, it is more appropriate to say that sensation itself contains two different dimensions *that do not strictly coincide with one another*. As Merleau-Ponty puts it, "[E]ither my right hand really passes over to the rank of the touched, but then its hold on the world is interrupted, or it retains its hold on the world, but then I do not really touch it."[45] In another stunning passage, he says:

> When I find again the actual world such as it is, under my hands, under my eyes, up against my body, I find much more than an object: a Being of which my vision is a part, a visibility older than my operations or my acts. But this does not mean that there was a fusion of coinciding of me with it: on the contrary, this occurs because a sort of dehiscence opens my body in two.[46]

The sensible, he says earlier in *The Visible and the Invisible*, is both an "absolute proximity," since there is a sensing that cannot be discounted as *my own*, as well as an "irremediable distance," since it is sensed and apart from me.[47]

In such passages, and in the many other places like them, Merleau-Ponty is pointing to sensation as *écart*, understood specifically as diacritical. He is stressing, in other words, that the sensible is itself differential. My body's activity and immanence are always short-circuited and there is an internal rupture where it lapses into passivity, out into something alternate to it. I see because I can be seen from a point of view not my own; I touch because I can be touched by the body of an another; I hear because I can be heard in the ears of someone else. In general, I sense and have a point of view because I am always opened up to another sensing and point of view that is not presently my own and that I cannot just take up. In these ways, my body is "opened up in two" and there is a sensible "older than my operations or my acts." Merleau-Ponty uses the term "dehiscence" here, which is, as is often noted, a botanical term referring to the splitting open of a flower's anther. It is also, however, a medical term that refers to the rupture of a previously sutured wound. It appears that this second meaning of dehiscence is equally relevant: when the body is opened up in two, there is exposed a gap between its passivity and activity. Precisely this gap, lapse or non-coincidence has not adequately been accounted for. It speaks neither to the apparition of a thing nor to a subject to whom appearances appear but to a more archaic sensibility. This sensibility is supposed to undermine Husserlian intentionality. It has no interior *telos* and lacks a specific route to a destination.

How are we to understand the sensible as an *advent of difference* if it is supposed to be nothing but the differences that rupture my body in two or that open up the distance between myself and another? As an advent or production of difference, is the sensible not initially non-differentiated? In that case, *écart* cannot be properly diacritical from the outset. If the advent of difference is not itself difference, then perhaps the sensible could be *made* obvious itself with a simple turn of our attention to it. It is nonetheless clear that, for Merleau-Ponty, the sensible not something just passively resting there, merely awaiting our regard to catch hold of it. There is not supposed to be a *sensation in itself*. The sensible is not itself a content so much as it needs a content and is for this reason always differentiated.

It is in this context that I mention the recurrent theme of depth in Merleau-Ponty's writings. One assumption about depth against which Merleau-Ponty often reacts is that it is not visible or sensible in any way, and that it is just an abstraction from the other dimensions. Typically, we say that depth is the "third" quantity of size. Merleau-Ponty likes to point out, however, that the original character of depth starts with and from our bodies. The body is, he says in "The Philosopher and His Shadow," "the absolute here to the there . . . *the source of distances to distance*."[48] As an "absolute here," the body is the originary site of depth. It is extra-ordinary in the sense that it is where I, and I alone, exist, because it is not at all "there" for me like everything else that surrounding and distanced from it. Yet the body—*my* body—of course *must be* there. It is an "absolute here" *to* "the there": to experience my own body as extraordinary from the rest of the world, my body must also belong to "the there" and inserted into that world. This is "the source of distances to distance." I am inserted into and am of the very distance that I see apart from me. My body is of the very same depth of the world that it holds out against it. But, in this distance and depth, there is no unbroken continuity. After all, I never do see my own insertion into the distance, and I never see the depth into which I am inserted. I never see "the there" of which I certainly am. What may be especially strange about "the there" is that, though I can cover each eye and notice that my vision is binocular, I never see this vision where it intersects with the real and dense sensible world and its poly-perspective character. Yet it is precisely this intersection that undoes the notion of a sensation in itself.

This is not only because the very notion of a sensation in itself is dispelled once we recognize that sensing is concrete and perspectival. It is furthermore because, insofar as sensing is concrete and perspectival, sensation is itself no longer unified. Glen Mazis explains, for example, that for Merleau-Ponty, depth is "the going together of incompossibles," "a sensed unity within disunity or within the tension of what can't go logically together."[49] Referring to an example in *Phenomenology of Perception* of seeing two roads converge in the distance even though reflectively we know they are parallel, Mazis again notes: "[T]he experience is the 'parallel in depth,' which means that the roads appear both parallel and converging into the horizon. These are incompossibles that give us depth."[50] The term "incompossibles" comes from the Liebnizian thesis of maximization, which is supposed to explain how possible worlds are made actual. There is an interpretive issue whether for Leibniz incompossibles exist all at once or whether the instantiation of one decisively prevents the instantiation of another. Gilles Deleuze, for instance, urges the former view, and points out that each instantiation is thereby split into an innumerable number of *determined* but not-actualized trajectories. With respect to the incompossibilities in depth, Merleau-Ponty takes the former view as well. In depth, the two disunities internal to the unity are both present trajectories. They are not determined in any way. Rather, they cut across the visual field, leading the field to any number of trajectories, and they can only do so because of the fundamental non-actuality of each.[51]

In anticipation of the discussion next chapter on the imaginary character of geometrical shapes and sculpture, I note here the similarities between the "parallel in depth" and the "fictive linkages" in Merleau-Ponty's well-known passages on Rodin's sculpted horses in motion in "Eye and Mind":

> [M]ovement is given, says Rodin, by an image in which the arms, the legs, the trunk, and the head are each taken at a different instant, an image which therefore portrays the body in an attitude which it never at any instant really held and which imposes fictive linkages between the parts, as if this mutual confrontation of incompossibles could, and could alone, cause transition and duration to arise in bronze and on the canvas. The only successful instantaneous glimpses of movement are those which approach this paradoxical arrangement.[52]

Both the "fictive linkages" and the "parallel in depth" betray the enjambment of distinct and exclusive moments that Mazis describes as piled into one another.[53] The connection here between "the fictive" and the "parallel in depth" highlights another way Merleau-Ponty distinguishes himself from both Plato and Husserl. For the former: there is no essential or real divergence between facts and essences; there is also no essential or real divergence merely between the facts. The divergences between contingent facts are not simply real ones that can be objectified. On the other hand, it will not follow from this that there is a real or even unbroken field between all things.

Interrogative Method and *écart*

Merleau-Ponty's interrogative method, beginning as it does with the explanatory force of perceptual faith, may appear simple but its repercussions are profound and far-reaching. It seeks to do away with any upper limit to philosophy that generates its categories and puts philosophy in the difficult position of being possible because of something absolute that it cannot bring into proper analysis. Instead, Merleau-Ponty's phenomenology tries to bring into focus a sensible field that is perpetually limiting, limiting one thing against another and making things discrete without itself exceeding limitation or being uniform and continuous. Such limitations are indeed the margins of sensible things—they are not themselves sensible things—but they are not thoroughly negative delimitations. Rather, they are aligned with the *écart* and its diacritical structure and are the accomplishment of Merleau-Ponty's "interrogative method" described from the outset of *The Visible and the Invisible*. This interrogation is ultimately supposed to be antagonistic to the traditional philosophical method of dialectic and the dialectic of being, exemplified, for Merleau-Ponty, by Sartre's analyses of being and nothingness.

So much has been written on how Merleau-Ponty's interrogation engages Sartrean dialectic, and I do not want to replicate those exegeses entirely. What I would instead like to point out here is the way Merleau-Ponty in *The Visible and the Invisible* invokes a decidedly Sartrean phrase, "negation of negation," to expose something anti-Sartrean and anti-dialectical.[54] While Merleau-Ponty's method of analysis often appears Hegelian inasmuch as it undermines a stance from within that stance, it nonetheless leads to a standpoint not readily reconciled with Hegel. Merleau-Ponty's phenomenology bears, I think, a strong kinship with deconstruction to the extent that they both reveal the internal counter-sense of any theoretical supposition. The "negation of negation," or what Sartre terms "nihilation," for example, is indeed opposed to Hegel's negation and aims to render a genuine transcendence over the world that is not mediated through being, like in Hegelian negation. However, as Merleau-Ponty points out, a proper and more radical "negation of negation" could not transcend the world just as much as it could not be mediated through it. A "negation of negation" instead stands in need of genuine explication to the extent that it implies a negation of both the notion that an appearance is an image of a thing and that the thing does not appear in principle. Regarding the latter notion, the "negation of negation" therefore undermines the objectivity of the object that affects us from outside. As Merleau-Ponty notes towards the end of *The Visible and the Invisible* in a small section titled "Presence," we should be critical of the notion of an object "spreads itself out before us by its own efficacy and does so precisely because it is gathered up in itself."[55] Regarding the former notion, the idea that appearances are images or representations, the very fact of appearing means that it is not wholly internal to me and something to which I alone have an absolute relation. Merleau-Ponty thus writes: "This *separation (écart)* which, in first approximation, forms meaning, is not an I affect *myself* with, a lack which I constitute as a lack by the upsurge of an end which I give myself—it is a *natural* negativity."[56]

If my own subjectivity is constituted by a natural negation, this means there is no I that affects me from outside of or prior to that affect. It may be only in retrospect of this affect that I find myself as myself or take myself to be distinct from this affect, but this is just to say that I am not the initial source of affect for my own identity. In fact, for Merleau-Ponty, the affect in which I discover my own subjectivity and to which I therefore consciously respond is not subject related at all. But, again, this does not mean that, rather than the self-identity of consciousness, affect turns out to be of a subject-less sensible world. The natural negation would have to apply equally to this world. Whatever the affect is to which I consciously respond, this is not the affect by which I am affected. There simply is for Merleau-Ponty no primary source here. If the question put to Merleau-Ponty is what is the event by which one is affected, the natural negation distinguishes him from both Husserl and Heidegger. From the former because appearances are not simply object-oriented intentions. From the latter because there is nothing that is original. It is in this context that Merleau-Ponty also calls for an *"Ursprungsklärung"* in the opening passages of his Working Notes to *The Visible and the Invisible* beyond both Husserl and Heidegger.[57] "We have to start anew," he writes, "from behind [the] point" of philosophy.[58]

If Merleau-Ponty's ontology ends with a primordial original clearing, it does not at last ask us to think through ontological difference. This is because it never supposes a meaningful initial separation between ground and things. The sense of negation Merleau-Ponty has in mind would undermine exactly this supposition. If the ground is a negation of negation of those things, it does not exceed particularization. It is not fulsome and distinct from beings. This also means, in turn, beings are not positive determinations of a being that does not itself appear. The most we can say about being, then, is that that it resists beings from within them and is in their midst. It twists, meanders, and zigzags all through the differences and refuses to be ossified as categorially opposed to distinct beings.

Merleau-Ponty uses the phrase "polymorphic matrix"[59] to express the idea that the negation between being and beings is not exactly located anywhere but is lateral to everything. This means the ontological register for beings is not some absolute plenum that erases difference and flattens beings out. I want to trace this diacritical ontology back to Heraclitus's notion of opposites to stress that it is not a new ontology so much as it is an unfamiliar one. What is particularly unfamiliar here, I think, is the notion of an ontological limit of things, which, rather than being distinct from things, is in the hazards of them. This is the Heraclitus who Plato buries. I also will not find this ontology in Heidegger's works and teachings on Heraclitus.

Écart and Division in Heraclitus

The kind of negativity Merleau-Ponty formulates in *The Visible and the Invisible* implies a topological or locational being. This brings us to one of the more striking Working Notes of the book, titled "The Invisible, the negative, vertical Being," where Merleau-Ponty describes being as a,

> negative that makes possible . . . the topological space and time in joints and members, in dis-junction and dis-membering . . . and the male-female relation (the two pieces of wood that children see fitting together of themselves, irresistibly, because each is the *possible of the other*)— and the "divergence," and the totality above the divergencies—and the thought-unthought relation (Heidegger) and the relation of *Kopulation* where two intentions have one sole *Erfüllung*.[60]

There is a well-known section of this Working Note, where Merleau-Ponty also indicates that "the invisible is not only non-visible," not just the *"possibly* visible" as in "different degrees of possibility: the past has been, the future will be able to be seen," since its "absence counts in the world . . . where the lacuna that marks its place is one of the points of passage of the 'world.'"[61] This footnote may seem very much at odds with the notion of reversibility so central to Merleau-Ponty's last philosophy of the flesh. Nonetheless, it is crucial because it prevents an analysis of reversibility that emphasizes a single totality above the various divergences, or a single fulfillment belonging to two otherwise distinct intentions, without any reference to the negative that intersperses itself between them. It keeps us from forgetting that each opposition expresses a non-presence that, for its part, cannot be different from the expression of either even if it does not properly combine them. In this way, the footnote echoes what was noticed in the problem of depth, that there is an internal contradiction that lets things appear in a coherent way and in relation to one another. These remarks, footnote included, are important because they implicate a diacritical nature in which the separation between opposites is not superseded by anything and that their negative relation is not outside of or apart from them. It is instructive to situate these comments alongside Heidegger's reading of the opposites in Heraclitus, and his reading of the origins of the problem of identity and difference in philosophy.

For Heidegger, the origins of the problem of identity and difference is not itself a problem—it is not the problem of a first and self-grounding being or a being in contradiction with beings—but an astonishment that beings *are in fact* and that they *all* come into existence. Heidegger describes this astonishment as a clearing (*Lichtung*) in which the rules of philosophy are not yet formalized and where contradiction, and in particular the contradiction that beings have being, stands first. In his Heraclitus seminars, Heidegger seeks to regain and inspire this wonder through Fragment B16, commenting that "because of its inner significance and ultimate implications, perhaps we ought to consider it *the first*."[62] The fragment reads: "τὸ μὴ δῦνόν ποτε πῶς ἄν τις λάθοι." The English translation of Heidegger's essay offers the Diels-Kranz German rendering of the Greek: "How can one hide himself before that which never sets?"[63] The occasion of the clearing connects to λάθοι and is rendered as "hide himself." This hiding is what drives the fragment for Heidegger because it points to the realm of ἀλήθεια in which we stand. To facilitate a rediscovery of "how this word speaks in Greek," Heidegger refers to Homer's *Odyssey*, VIII, 83ff., in which Odysseus remains concealed, ἐλάνθανε, with respect to the others while shedding tears. His point is that Λανθάνω does not so much mean "to hide oneself," as "to remain concealed." Thus, Heidegger says, λάθοι announces an original concealment or hiddenness, which ἀλήθεια is in fact meant to overcome.

In the fragment, for example, λάθοι is posed as a question to τὸ μὴ δῦνον, "that which never sets." Δῦνον is a participle of δύω, which means to "envelope," "submerge," and often describes the sun's setting into the sea; thus δῦνον also names going into concealment, and so "the two main—because substantial—words with which the fragment begins and ends, δῦνον and λάθοι, say the Same."[64] The two "main words" of the fragment amount to a notion of concealing, so this "same" seems to be the realm of concealing or that into which things are concealed. Yet the μή preceding δῦνον creates a distance from setting, and the question mark following λάθοι suggests that concealing is not at all definite. In fact, Heidegger says, "[T]he fragment does not operate in the realm of concealment, but in the utterly opposite sphere."[65] He does not mean here that the opposite of concealment is decisively distinct from concealment, but that concealment accepts revealing as its inescapable counterpart. Taking the word following δῦνον into consideration, Heidegger then points out that the fragment says "τὸ μὴ δῦνόν ποτε (the not setting *ever*)," and so may also be read as τὸ δῦνον, "the never setting."[66] It is not just ποτε or οὐκ but μήποτε that brackets δῦνον, and for Heidegger this suggests that the participle δῦνόν ought to be considered verbally: we should avoid representing concealment in terms of a thing—as presuming something *that* has now become concealed—and see it in terms of an "ever-rising."[67]

Heidegger's phrase for "the never setting" thus reads, "the still to be sure not to go under ever."[68] The phrase deserves attention because it offers some insight into Heidegger's notion of a clearing in which a concealment is simultaneously an un-setting and can never be totally and fully eclipsed. In other words, "that which never sets" is at the same time an "ever-rising." It is a setting and concealing that is at the same time an un-setting and revealing. Heidegger in fact takes this as the more accurate translation of Fragment B16. Notably, he calls this tension a "dispensing jointure." *Fügung* is Heidegger›s translation of Heraclitu's ἁρμονί, λήθη and ἀλήθεια, which constellates a series of words to describe that which simultaneously ever-rises and never-sets: *Fug, Fügung, Unfug*. These may be provisionally translated into English as "jointure," or "fit," and "disjointure," "being out of joint," or "not fitting."[69] The connection between ever-rising and never-setting, in other words, indicates to Heidegger an initial point of contact that dispels its parts from out of it. His earlier remark about an "ever-rising" notwithstanding, the characterization of being as a jointure that becomes disjointed implies that it has some initial moment where it is self-identical so that it can then show itself as self-differentiated. It is also crucial in this context that, echoing Merleau-Ponty's note above, Heidegger points to this basic accordance not as the invisible of the visible but as a non-appearing or non-showing (*unscheinbar*).[70] Where for Merleau-Ponty the invisible is not just privative, Heidegger abandons the perspective of visibilty-invisiblity altogether. One of the classical problems attributed to Heraclitus is the apparent logical fallacy of opposites, and Heidegger wants to explain the problem at the ontological level: being is the jointure that never *itself* shows but does so only in terms of its disjointure. It is a non-apparent continuity running under things that only ever shows in terms of discontinuity.

There is, however, no need to impute to Heraclitus any fallacy of opposites, and no reason to seek their jointure. For they may not themselves need reconciliation. Even if Heidegger claims to read Heraclitus in light of the wonderment that beings *are in fact* and yet *all* come into existence, he nevertheless fails to grasp that he need not reconcile facts and their becoming with being opposite to becoming. In their classic text, *Héraclite ou la séparation*, Jean Bollack and Heinz Wismann point out that Heraclitus certainly makes, "a contribution to a reflection that pursues unity, not separation." But, they say, he makes "radical separation as such the condition of identity."[71] This claim refers to the initial fragment in which Heraclitus speaks of division according to nature:

τοῦ δὲ λόγου τοῦδ ἐόντος ἀεὶ ἀξύνετοι γίνονται ἄνθρωποι καὶ πρόσθεν ἢ ἀκοῦσαι καὶ ἀκούσαντες τὸ πρῶτον· γινομένων γὰρ πάντων κατὰ τὸν λόγον τόνδε ἀπείροισιν ἐοίκασι πειρώμενοι καὶ ἐπέων καὶ ἔργων τοιούτων ὁκοίων ἐγὼ διηγεῦμαι κατὰ φύσιν διαιρέων ἕκαστον καὶ φράζων ὅκως ἔχει· τοὺς δὲ ἄλλους ἀνθρώπους λανθάνει ὁκόσα ἐγερθέντες ποιοῦσιν ὅκωσπερ ὁκόσα εὕδοντες ἐπιλανθάνονται

[Though this Word is true evermore, yet men are as unable to understand it when they hear it for the first time as before they have heard it at all. For, though all things come to pass in accordance with this Word, men seem as if they had no experience of them, when they make trial of words and deeds such as I set forth, dividing each thing according to its kind and showing how it is what it is. But other men know not what they are doing when awake, even as they forget what they do in sleep.][72]

I stress again that Heidegger proposes to make Fragment B16 the first fragment. Whereas Heraclitus's Fragment B88 is often cited to illustrate a division according to nature or the "coinstantiation of opposites":

ταὐτό τ' ἔνι ζῶν καὶ τεθνηκὸς καὶ [τὸ] ἐγρηγορὸς καὶ καθεῦδον καὶ νέον καὶ γηραιόν· τάδε γὰρ μεταπεσόντα ἐκεῖνά ἐστι κἀκεῖνα πάλιν μεταπεσόντα ταῦτα

[As the same thing in us are living and dead, waking and sleeping, young and old. For these things having changed around are those, and those in turn having changed around are these.]

Oppositive qualities are found in us "as the same thing." Their sameness is due to one thing changing around to another. We are asleep and we wake up; we are awake and we go to sleep. Both are of course found in us, but not at the same time or in the same respect. Oppositive qualities are thus the same only by some constituting system of connections: alive-dead, waking-sleeping, or young-old. Heraclitus is not conflating opposites or differences into a sameness or identity. He is giving a series of subtle analyses to point out the interconnectedness as well as movement between contrary states. In fact, if sleeping and waking were identical, there would be no change, and no temporality either, as required by the second sentence. Even if sleeping and waking were equal poles of equal opposites, still there would be no temporal change between them. Rather, change and temporality require the unequal weight of opposing forces. When sleep supersedes waking, this is not because of its confluence with or inner succession towards waking but because of its resistance to waking, when it is stronger against wakefulness. In general, we can say, the appearance of beings against being entails an unequal weight of the former against the latter. The beings are not simply balanced equally or the polar opposite of being nor vice versa; they are different from being because they resist against being and because being is the weaker, non-symmetrical opposite of beings.[73] The non-symmetry between being and beings reveals instead that each term opposes the other in terms of a divergence that accords with each. Each identity is what it is by a divergence according to or within it. This prioritizes divergence between opposites to allow for the temporal change and movement between them.

    This non-symmetry parts Heraclitus from Parmenides, and gives us no reason to think that each on his own would necessarily be lost to philosophy, as Plato claims. Merleau-Ponty's Working Note, especially with its references to "joints and members" and "dis-junction and dismembering," is certainly reminiscent of Heidegger's constellation of words to describe Heraclitus's Fragment B16. But he has in fact worked out a relation between being and beings more in keeping with Heraclitean division when he says, for example, that there is a negative that makes oppositions possible and that this negative is topological or locational. The point is that every sensible thing bears within it a non-sensible aspect, and this aspect mobilizes the thing and allows it to confront another thing. This confrontation is literal—it is the co-frontation between two sensible things that makes each sensible thing what it is by opposing another thing. There is no initial point of contact being has with respect to itself before it becomes dis-jointed.

Rather, the possibility of oppositions, and indeed their very existence, is due as much to their apartness and dis-jointedness, the non-appearing right within their opposition, making each thing what it is and how it is. No doubt, then, Merleau-Ponty in fact refers to the absence of being from beings in a quite distinct way than does Heidegger: being is absent from beings because it is non-diametrically opposed to what appears, so much so that it requires placement in the midst of beings and its absence counts in the world.

The placement of being within the beings implies a separation within each term of the opposition. It is true, however, that Merleau-Ponty ontologizes separation itself since he calls being *écart*. There is a structure to Merleau-Ponty's account of divergence here that I hope the reader will notice, since it recurs in his writing and pervades the arguments of this book (e.g., in the oppositions between space and imagination, light and dark, sleeping and waking/dreaming, and philosophy and non-philosophy). Where there is a separation in one identity of an opposition, there is also a separation in the other identity. If separation is within each identity, it does not follow that separation in fact unifies the identities, that separations in identities are the result of a sameness. By "sameness" I mean unification or synthesis. It only follows that separation between identities is their condition for existence. This separation in other words has no specific location. When Merleau-Ponty thinks divergence, for example, he ends up thinking about a lack of affective source within consciousness or of luminescent source to the world. He ends up pointing to the lapse or openness of each identity and the inability for this lapse to curl up into itself and become a hypostasis. In this sense, for Merleau-Ponty, divergence figures in all identities and distinct things—between objects, reflexivity and unreflexivity, between subject and object, between oneself and another. This follows from his phrase "natural negativity" and his critique of negation. Consider now Bollack and Wismann's account of Heraclitus's initial fragment with a view towards this negativity:

> The subject has only a dissociated, abstract, and punctiform existence, since it discovers the Other within itself.... Thus the separation that founds the intelligence of the saying forms the main content of all the fragments. In reality, the distinction that makes for the *self*, in reproducing the divergence between the saying and its object, enables one to find, by traversing the saying, the divergence that is within the thing, so as to divide it according to its nature.[74]

For Heraclitus, the height of philosophical insight does not require a meditation on the sameness between being and beings, and this is because we are not initially struck by the fact that beings require some fundamental being to which they are irreducible. It is not that we are stunned by the undifferentiated being behind the beings. Rather, for Heraclitus, the world of beings stuns us into silence because in it things are dividing according to their very nature; and it is this dividing by which things are what they are. Heraclitus does not say that this silence is totally deafening and covers over speech completely; rather, he says that dumbness makes speaking about each thing of the utmost difficulty. Any interpretation of the fragments ought to keep this feature in mind.

λόγος and ἁπτόμενον in Heraclitus

Heraclitus is undoubtedly a thinker whose thought is, as Véronique Fóti writes, "indissociable from the linguistic articulation of his discourse—a *logos* of incomparable refinement that does not situate itself on a meta-level but participates in what it speaks of."[75] But, because this is so, she also notes, the fragments offer entryways into the complexities and paradoxes of the senses—what makes them "provocative for thought and what prevents [them] from functioning unproblematically as a model for intellectual adequation."[76] To read λόγος consistently, in other words, we have to read it in terms of the division already announced in the initial fragment, indistinguishable from the distinctly human experience of being rooted within the material universe and its multivocal senses.[77] This is what Heidegger tries to do when he associates λόγος with λέγειν.[78]

Whereas, when William K.C. Guthrie associates λόγος in Heraclitus with the first material principle of fire, he argues that λόγος is responsible for the government of the world and therefore must be "rational."[79] In other words, for Guthrie, fire is equivalent to λόγος, and λόγος is equivalent to νόμος.[80] To see the kindship between fire and λόγος does not however require that we accept a reconciliation between opposites. Even if fire principally characterizes the material universe it does not have to be equivalent to νόμος or elide the double and even contradictory meanings announced in the first fragment. It is important to consider fragments such as B217 in this context:

κόσμον τόνδε, τὸν αὐτὸν ἁπάντων, οὔτε τις θεῶν οὔτε ἀνθρώπων ἐποίησεν, ἀλλ' ἦν ἀεὶ καὶ ἔστιν καὶ ἔσται πῦρ ἀείζωον, ἁπτόμενον μέτρα καὶ ἀποσβεννύμενον μέτρα

[This cosmos, the same one for all, was made neither by a god nor a man, but it always was and is and will be ever-living fire, kindling itself in measures and extinguishing itself in measures.]

This fragment may beget a problem in Heraclitus, noted by Heidegger, of a cosmos that is "same for all" and yet "self-grown" or "self-made"—always in the many even though it first emerges from itself and is not merely the many. But if we keep in mind that, for Heraclitus, the opposition between a cosmos that is self-grown or self-made is so only when it is non-symmetrically or weakly opposed to the many, then there is no problem of separation between the cosmos and its particulars. The fragment instead points to ἁπτόμενον or kindling as an unsetting or ever-present kind of illumination described as such only because it lacks an internal power of its own and cannot be disassociated from the very beings that are illuminated. If we are going to think about luminescence in terms of the first material principle, the question is how we ought to bring our thinking back into touch with its non-lucidity and latent or not necessarily resolvable meanings.

Some Remaining Questions

Merleau-Ponty's interrogative method and critique of negation is a critique of the dialectical situation of being and its relation with non-being. His ontology must unburden itself of a need for essences opposite or against the space and time of beings. It must likewise resist posing this space and time in terms of their primary difference between the beings that populate it. In *The Visible and the Invisible* Merleau-Ponty expresses a hope to replace the philosophy of "finalism" with a "cosmology of the visible" that "is no longer a question of origins, nor limits, nor of a series of events going to a first cause, but one sole explosion of Being which is forever." To do this, he says, requires a description of the "'rays of the world' beyond every serial-eternitarian or ideal alternative."[81] Previously in the text, Merleau-Ponty associates these rays with an "aesthetic world."[82] It is perhaps counterintuitive that an explosion of being—a fragmentation, shattering or breaking up of being—also includes a cosmology. If Merleau-Ponty's ontology is associated with Heraclitus, it is not because he is an occidental thinker. Instead, Merleau-Ponty begins with some of the same claims found in the initial fragment: if we start with the difference between being and beings, we already suppose that identity precedes difference. A proper ontology, which does not suppose this outright, first demands that thought takes place in the middle of things, remaining internal to them without the recuperation of an identity. Merleau-Ponty will equate divergence with the very symbolic form that is the limit of philosophy itself.

This divergence is also for Merleau-Ponty a matter of language structure taking place nowhere but between interlocutors and between the speaker and the object about which s/he speaks. When Merleau-Ponty reflects on the chiasm between speaking and hearing towards the end of *The Visible and the Invisible*, for instance, he is not led to a simple fleshly overlap or symmetry between the interlocutors. He points out that when I hear the voice of a speaker this is in fact the resonance of a sound within my own ear. If I hear from within my own hearing, the content of my hearing is from the mouth of an interlocutor to whom in a certain sense I am deaf. This internal discrepancy between hearing and deafness results in Merleau-Ponty's comment: "The others' words make me speak and think because they create within me an other than myself, a divergence (*écart*)."[83] A little earlier in the text, he makes a similar point:

> Speaking subject: it is the subject of a *praxis*. It does not hold before itself the words said and understood as objects of thought or ideates. It possesses them only by a *Vorhabe* which is of the same type as the *Vorhabe* of place by my body that betakes itself unto that place. That is: it is a certain lack of . . . such or such a signifier, which does not construct the *Bild* of what it lacks. There is therefore here a neo-teology, which no more permits being supported by a consciousness of, . . . nor by an ec-stasy, a constructive project, that does the perceptual teleology. The Saussurean analysis of the relations between signifiers and significations (as differences between significations) confirms and rediscovers the idea of perception as a *divergence* (*écart*) by relation to a level, that is, the idea of the primordial Being, of the convention of conventions, of the speech before speech.[84]

Merleau-Ponty is remarking here on a silence that operates between one's own speech and hearing as well as in relation to shared world with another. In both speaking and hearing there is a silence that for its part turns interlocution towards the sensible world and makes its activities transcend themselves in an unreflective and passive way. If Merleau-Ponty calls this transcendence "the awesome birth of vociferation," it is not only because both the spoken and the heard are sensible but because the reverse is also true: the sensible is an internal delimitation between both speaking and hearing and the interlocutors. The diacritics evidenced in vision therefore applies equally to interlocution, and in interlocution there is internal delimitation that also goes between speakers and the objects about which they speak. In effect, this delimitation is an endless circuit that prevents the sensible world from falling back into oblivion, or a totalizing and complete silence.

In general, any philosophical investigation of language, and any philosophy that recognizes its impossibility without the very language it investigates, has to retrieve the sensible world in which language is spoken. Merleau-Ponty may agree with both Heidegger's analysis of the more felicitous association between λόγος and λέγειν and his claim that language is more than a totality of words that holds humans under its own power. But ultimately Merleau-Ponty cannot say with Heidegger that, because it exceeds individual signs, language gathers otherwise disparate significations and is the revelation of a concealed jointure. I leave this last claim aside for the moment. It requires us to first deal with another claim, that Greek mathematicians use the word λέγειν to refer to the forms according to which separate significations are gathered. To the extent that these forms are the limits of language, the philosophy of them would likewise seek out the limits of language. The very power to gather significations in fact seems to account for both the physical and epistemological distinction between being and beings.[85] The issue for Merleau-Ponty is not entirely that the sensible intercepts the association between language and mathematics. It is more precisely that the sensible bounds and contours the form and shape of things; and this same sensible is where speaking and interlocution take place and is their symbolic matrix. If we can show that the sensible bounds and contours the form of things, that it is their internal delimitation, and that this delimitation does not supersede the concrete situation of language but is in fact also within it, then with Merleau-Ponty we have a symbolic matrix that is the limit of and within philosophy.

In the final pages of the completed portion of *The Visible and the Invisible*, Merleau-Ponty writes: "We shall have to follow more closely this transition from the mute world to the speaking world."[86] Leonard Lawlor remarks about this passage, and in the context of diacritics:

> Who knows what would have happened if Merleau-Ponty had had the time to follow this transition more closely? Perhaps, if he had had the time, he would have felt compelled to change the title of this book one more time; perhaps he would have felt compelled to change it from *The Visible and the Invisible* to something like *Ousia and Grammé*.[87]

Chapter 2
Space—Imagination

Despite its influence on Heidegger and the question concerning the meaning of being, Plato's *Sophist* implies a higher transcendental and ontological level, in which being is attributed to non-being and non-being to being. This attribution makes possible a philosophy in which we may say the number one or geometrical space *is*. That is, it makes possible both the ability to see a set of axioms that disambiguate the sensible world and the notion that this disambiguation is itself a real one. This chapter explores the way phenomenology does not require the secondary ontological level in which being and non-being are attributed to one another and instead reveals the debt geometrical forms have to the very sensible world they purport to elucidate.

The problem this chapter deals with is also one that Husserl points out in *The Crisis of the European Sciences*, especially in his historico-phenomenological analysis of the mathematization of the world, starting with Euclid and Galileo, and in the "The Origin of Geometry." It is also helpful to note a small section that outlines the difference between the "dimension of depth" and "the plane" that appears in *The Crisis*, just before Husserl's introduction of the great theme of the life world. In the section on depth and plane, he writes:

> This schema for a possible clarification of the problem of objective science reminds us of Helmholtz' well-known image of the plane-beings, who have no idea of the dimension of depth, in which their plane-world is a mere projection. Everything of which men—the scientists and all the others—can become conscious in their natural world-life (experiencing, knowing, practically planning, acting) as a field of external objects—as ends, objects—and, on the other hand, also, in self-reflection, as the

"plane," which is, though unnoticed, nevertheless only a plane with an infinitely richer dimension of depth. But this [image] practical in the usual sense or a theoretical life, [i.e,] scientific experiencing, thinking, planning, acting, or scientific experiential data, ideas, goals of thinking, premises, true results.[1]

Husserl thinks of depth against the flatness or horizontality of a "plane-world." On this plane-world, only the surfaces of things show. Here, everything, including the margins or edges of what appears, can be connected by a straight line. The plane-world thus reduces everything to their measurability. In this way, things are themselves abstract, thought to be what they are only in terms of their predictable or deducible abstraction, and related to one another abstractly. If Husserl analogizes our sciences with the plane-world, it is because for him the sciences are concerned with the surficial phenomena to the exclusion of a depth that is never itself so straightforward. If we abide solely by the sciences, then, we remain "plane-beings" concerned only with superficial phenomena. The dimension of depth is, on the other hand, a sort of demand to think past the surface of things, the object-field in general, and down into their resources, which Husserl describes here as "infinitely richer." A few pages later in *The Crisis*, he equates depth with a life-world that is "intuitable in principle," and opposed to the "objective-true" world, which is "in principle nonintuitable" and only a "'logical' substruction" of the former.[2] What was merely a schema in the depth and plane section is stated outright: the richer dimension of depth, in which we practically live, in fact grounds our sciences. Although its praxis remains unnoticed by our sciences, nevertheless it is constantly operant within them such that they are always being "substructed" by this dimension. This means that the superficial attitude of the sciences is actually the work of depth, which functions by hiding in the superficial. Husserl, like Wittgenstein, thinks that depth is at the surface.

Husserl's notion of depth also anticipates Merleau-Ponty's interest in it, especially with Merleau-Ponty's desire to reveal it as the "first dimension." Once we notice this depth, we may well be on the way towards preventing the scandal in which thought is unable to explicate itself and remains ignorant of what is basic to it. Nonetheless, as I want to highlight in this chapter, Husserl still leaves depth unexplained in some important ways, and never entirely interrogates the *substruction* of it by the sciences. For instance, he conceives of abstract geometrical essences constitutively. They are cut off from both phantasy and from the sensible. This in turn implies that the sensible is a "plenum," a general thing incapable of operating on its own. What makes a robust account of geometry's substruction of the sensible impossible is these two effectively autonomous poles. If we take up what Merleau-Ponty calls the "interrogative method," however, the exegesis of substruction should instead show the geometrical essences and the sensible world in one another. This would mean finding the sensible as more determinated than a plenum and located at the intersection of every possible reflexion.

To this end, we should also recall from last chapter Merleau-Ponty's early description of the plane-world as a monocular one that is phantasmatic as opposed to the sensible and deep world that is "actual" and "dense." If Merleau-Ponty is going to accomplish the project that Husserl initiates, he will have to deny Husserl's claims that geometrical essences are constitutively distinct from phantasy and that this phantasy is distinct from the sensible. To keep up the exegesis of how the geometrical sciences substruct the sensible world, in other words, Merleau-Ponty needs to retrieve the space of imagination. That is, he needs a notion of the imagination in which: the sensible world and the phantasma are not negatives of one another; and, as genuinely intuitable, in fact impossible for geometrical essences to foreclose.

Abstract Geometrical Essences, Morphological Ideals, and Phantasy in Husserl

For all of Husserl's analytic rigor, he nonetheless gives phantasy a central role in his phenomenology. Indeed, he thinks phantasy is what makes his rigorous science possible. The role of phantasy, for Husserl, is threefold: it frees us from naturalistic theses of all kinds; it makes explicit the phenomena as they are lived-through; and it allows consciousness to wrest from itself the cognitive acts essential for the phenomena to be however they are lived-through. Thus, Husserl conceives phantasy as an "inner" or "imaginative pictorial consciousness" that is in relation to both sensorial content and its form.

In other words, for Husserl it is necessary to gain an ontological standpoint on sensorial content; and this requires his phenomenology to get rid of an image-theory of consciousness and hence representation itself. But this should not, in turn, mean confusing phantasy with sensation. In *Ideas I*, for instance, Husserl makes every effort to distinguish between the presence (*Gegenwärtigen*) of concrete bodily movements or sensations and the presentification (*Vergegenwärtigung*) of phantasms.[3] This distinction involves four different kinds of conscious modifications, which I highlight here:

1. Consciousness is modified by an immediate and actual sensory impression, which means that whatever impression consciousness was just having is now altered.
2. Consciousness must also, in turn, modify this immediate and actual sensorial impression to guarantee its association with the previous, just passed impression.
3. The passivity of consciousness's association between the past and present sensorial impressions needs to be superseded by an equally continuous memory so that, in addition to living through them, consciousness can also recall the past impression and associate it actively and reflexively with the present one.
4. There must be a modification that makes this active memory possible, and this is the role of a phantasy-consciousness no longer associated with the former two modifications.[4]

While actual sensory impressions alter and change, we can understand them to belong to one and the same thing because consciousness of our present is itself a continuous temporal transformation of its past. That is, consciousness of the present both undergoes the succession appearing before it and grasps itself as having experiences in succession. Meanwhile, the phantasmata for Husserl are evidence of an inner-consciousness that is already passively self-aware and capable of grasping itself. They are, in other words, evidence of a pre-reflexivity that is the innermost structure of the acts of consciousness according to which it grasps itself as having experiences in succession. Thus, Eugen Fink can write that in Husserl phantasy supplies a "universal modification of our whole life experience."[5] He means that, for Husserl, the phantasmata reveal consciousness as a pre-phenomenal being across all the more basic diversities and modifications of both the intentional acts and objects. They are apiece with the most basic immanental feature of consciousness where it is irrelated to other regions, "absolutized," and operates as a "sense bestowing consciousness that for its part exists absolutely and not by way of another sense-bestowal."[6]

Husserl thus rejects space as an essential dimension of our inner experience, and certainly as a dimension of phantasy-consciousness. He thinks we are unable to describe living and experiencing in spatial terms, since it is from the intentional activity of conscious that the dynamic field of spatial objects acquires its meaning. Husserl chooses time, temporality, and time-consciousness as the main criteria to distinguish perception from phantasy and its presentations. This means that he also must allow for the following distinctions between: a spatial object; the mode in which this object appears; and a pure consciousness related to the appearance of a spatial object.[7] To this end, Husserl famously speaks of a "transcendence in the immanence of a pure ego."[8] Even though he insists that this not be taken as the real exclusion of objective and transcendent spatial things, still one can conclude that, whereas time is essential to consciousness, space is not. We can thus point out two apparent theoretical suppositions that follow: The first is that space is an objective dimension that does not itself interfere with the interior and subjective sphere of consciousness; it is considered an exteriority that subjectivity should suspend to proceed to its own lower-most and immanental limits. The second supposition follows from the first and is that Husserl seems to support a strong theory of conscious life where it is a continuous presence to itself that can always be discovered and maintained despite all the changes and modifications happening to it.

When Husserl gives phantasy its authoritative role in phenomenology, he does so with the understanding that it bears an inner-temporality that excludes spatiality from it. Indeed, in his 1907 *Thing and Space* lectures, Husserl pays almost no attention to phantasy, since he considers it a mode of appearing opposite to the concrete perceptions that are the focus of his notes.[9] At one point in the lectures, though, he elaborates what he calls the "obscurities" of these perceptions, mentioning that they have differing modalities—proper or improper, empty or full, determined or undetermined—and says that phantasy could be considered akin to the improper data in perception.[10] That is, phantasy could be considered *like* the hidden and non-presented phases of an object. This is a simple comparison that should not be overlooked: according to Husserl, a spatial object presented in perception is not very different from an object presented in phantasy since each has a presently appearing face and hidden faces, and thus each is discovered in its unity only through a progression. In neither do we see the front side at the same as the backside, and so each is marked fundamentally by limitation and the inability to bring into expression a total object seen from all perspectives at once. Thus, Husserl says in *Thing and Space* that phantasy is as unilateral as perception.[11]

This point allows Husserl to succeed in making intelligible a parallelism between the immediate intuitions of what is present to the body through perception and the non-intuition of what is not presented to the body in phantasma. Because they are both equally unilateral, and so limited in what they present to consciousness, they each expose a need to go past their limitation; but how they each do this is fundamentally different. In what is bodily present in perception, limitation is exceeded by a motility or just the possibility of movement, which mediates the non-present and makes it appear or always an "actual potential" appearance (Husserl calls this "potentiability"). In phantasy, on the other hand, there is no such need for mediation. This is because what is presentiated therein is "inactual." I do not actually experience all the immanent experiences, but only presentiate them to myself, perform them only inactually. To overcome the unilaterality of phantasies, then, I have only to imagine them from another side. This is true more generally and speaks to a more potent power of phantasy. I can always phantasize myself into an experience: I can feel "as if" I were experiencing, seeing, hearing, speaking, doubting, questioning, willing, desiring, and so on. The whole affair, be it a coherent phantasy-world or an incoherent sequence of individual phantasy situations, is given as unreality in the modification of this "as if," which prevents a believing or positing consciousness from taking hold. Whereas perception always has the *Urdoxa*, for Husserl, phantasy does not. Whereas perception is positional, phantasy is neutral.

But, notably in section 70 of *Ideas I*, Husserl refers to "pure phantasy" as a "positing presentation," and no longer thinks of it as merely distinct from the primordial belief of concrete perceptions just because it is neutral.[12] Here, Husserl wants to make clear that phantasies are still unreal and lacking the certainty of its existence. The "as if" remains, but because of this I *posit* the unreality of a phantasy-object. Although this positing does not require a mediation of the body, Husserl's aim is to remove the parallel between phantasy and perception and to rather claim that phantasy transcends perception. The former is what makes perceptions possible and therefore also what one can discover and disclose from out of perceptions. Because of phantasy, I perceive both the front side of an object while apprehending its backside, which is precisely the possibility of experiencing spatial objects. This means that, in addition to perceptions, there must also be non-perceived or empty intentional components that take care of the obscurities of perceptions. Phantasy is thus also a "positing presentation" in the sense that, when I posit the non-perceived aspect of an object, I am in a certain position; the positing is, in other words, bodily and positionally related to the perceived side. The empty intentional components of perception are as transitory as my bodily ability to move around an object. When I move around an object, then different plenary aspects are being connected to an equally repositioned intentional component. Whenever something is clearly presented to me, it is so because of an *intentional act* that has succeeded to reach down into its content, which is always in some way to be found in the perceptual field and so really is of a hyletic (material) manifold. Where the concrete perceptual data is distended off into a horizon I likewise find a subjective life that is not merely actively object oriented. With this, Husserl may yet avoid the two theoretical presuppositions noted above that assume the exteriority of a phantasy against perception.

The truly difficult point here is not really that this non-objectifying subjective life has transcended itself and gone into that objectivity. Rather, Husserl discovers a moment of experience that does not expel from it an obscurity of the hyletic manifold itself, which is thus no longer incompatible with the intentional acts of subjective life. Where in his initial considerations these acts were simply the form of their material content, they are now dissolved into something more primitive and non-active. They participate in a hyletic stratum that is itself not yet objectified. With this insight, a host of new concepts comes to figure prominently in Husserl's writings. Some of these are: genetic constitution, passive synthesis, pre-predicative intentionality, horizon intentionality, operative intentionality, bodily intentionality, and anonymous intentionalities. In these, Husserl always suggests some aspect of the life of consciousness that is no longer simply directed to objects or to objective space but opened up into a horizon, and the novel, unexpected, and surprising aspect of horizonality itself. That is, he suggests a life of consciousness, underneath the plane and its predictable state of affairs, connected to depth.

Such intentionalities are still not cause for Husserl to give up his claim that consciousness lives across the more basic modifications of the manifold and therefore lacks space. Even in the *Crisis*, for example, he in fact forecloses on this claim on the basis that the lower intentionalities belong to a "universal unthematic horizon." This unthematic horizon is for Husserl a series of "inactive [*inaktuelle*] validities,"[13] and "[i]mplied in the particular perception of the thing is a whole 'horizon' of nonactive and yet cofunctioning manners of appearance and syntheses of validity."[14] When this horizon is displayed we see that, "the objects and the world would not be there for us and that [they] exist for us only with the meaning and the mode of being that they receive in constantly arising or having arisen out of those subjective *accomplishments*."[15] These subjective accomplishments are the "necessary subsoil of obscure but occasionally available reactivatable validities, all of which together, including the present acts, make up a single indivisible, interrelated complex of life."[16] In other words, subjective accomplishments are precisely the accomplishments by which the modifications of manifold "are not dead sediments."[17] If consciousness lives across the more basic modifications of the manifold because of the phantasmata, then these same phantasmata make the manifold a series of living sediments, of bodily extension and perspective. This is why Husserl will maintain a distinction between sensible and morphological essences. The sensible field, he thinks, has no shape, figure, or form. It is pure content, uniform, general, and a plenum—whereas phantasy forms this field. It makes it into what Husserl calls "pregeometrical forms" and "morphological essences."

The distinction between the sensible world and morphological essences in fact also explains the distinction between morphological and geometrical essences, which are released from both the sensible world and phantasy. Husserl is very careful to free geometry from both the order of the sensible and of phantasy, for example, in the *Crisis*:

> No matter how arbitrarily we may transform these bodies in phantasy, the free and in a certain sense "ideal" possibilities we thus obtain are anything but geometrical-ideal possibilities: they are not the geometrically "pure" shapes which can be inscribed in ideal spaces—"pure" bodies, "pure" straight lines, "pure" planes, other "pure" figures, and the movements and deformations which occur in "pure" figures. Thus geometrical space does not signify anything like imaginary space.[18]

Husserl's own example of a circle is informative. A circle is an abstract geometrical shape. Below it, as it were, there are types of roundness. These types are not simply reducible to the multiple and different shapes we find in concrete perception. It is through phantasy that the multiple and different shapes are given their type. Whereas these types have to do for Husserl with pregeometrical or morphological essences, he thinks the circle is released from these essences through a method of variation: "[P]roceeding from the factual, an essential form becomes recognizable through a method of variation."[19] Whereas typification has to do with practical elements of "perfecting 'again and again,'" the method of variation instead tends towards "limit-shapes" that are "pure" and "invariant."[20] This method, Husserl thinks, substructs geometrical shape from its types, while this phantasy distinguishes types in the plenum.[21] For geometry, however, it is only a facto-historical point that its essences are produced from these morphological types. The field of geometry in fact requires that these types be nullified, and geometry circumscribes its own ground. It demands, that is, an internal sense of its own. From this internal sense, geometry stops precisely at what has conditioned and is its own kind of static analysis. Abstract geometry thus has general essences that are abstract, while the source of these essences in their pregeometrical and morphological forms is left in the dark. The methodological consequence of this is that geometry does not proceed descriptively but deductively: from its axioms, it derives its content; it defines things only analytically; and the countless spatial shapes that may be sketched are in fact never *themselves* seized upon by this analysis.

This is what allows Husserl to diagnose the abstract study of geometrical space as being in a state of crisis, confused as the truth of the very field it conceals. Meanwhile, phantasy gives rise to its own kind of space and to a science of that space. This leads Derrida in his analyses of Husserl's *The Origin of Geometry* to claim that such a science would be concerned with the unforeseeable proliferation of morphological types.[22] It is crucial that Derrida also calls the unforeseeable proliferation of morphological types "inorganic."[23] Through typification, in other words, pregeometry betrays a set of morphological forms that are surprising and eventful, but still these essences are not found in the sensible field and are therefore ideal.

If the question is to what extent the science of geometry is subtended by the science of phantasy,[24] this is a question that remains unanswerable so long as one assumes a strong theory of consciousness and the supposition of an objective space unable to intervene into the interior of consciousness life. Since Husserl thinks the sensible world is distinct from the phantastical space that typifies the world, he is also able to claim that geometrical space signifies something other than phantasy space. Whereas, if phenomenology undoes this notion of phantasy altogether and shows that it does not have the autonomous power Husserl initially claims it does, then the morphological forms of this phantasy are no longer inorganic. The manifold previously thought to be shapeless, figureless, or formless without phantasy is in fact never shapeless, figureless, or formless—it is in fact never properly speaking a plenum—and therefore never itself without phantasy. Moreover, because the sensible is itself already shaped, figured, and formed, geometrical essences cannot be the invariant limit-shapes Husserl claims they are.

The entire substruction of abstract geometrical essences puts phantasy at the core of its investigation and departs from the notion that consciousness is immediate to itself and absolute. I leave Husserl behind here and look to John Sallis's profound and far-reaching analyses of imagination in *The Logic of Imagination*, where he argues:

> [I]magination opens a space across which it can draw together different moments in their difference.... In this connection, the opening of a space must be construed in an originary way. It is not that a certain space is already somehow there, though closed off, sealed in an enclosure, so that imagination would then dissolve the closure, opening up and freeing the space, letting it perhaps expand into—or at least relate to—a broader space. Rather it is only in and through imagination's coming to hover that there is a space, that space is there.[25]

And:

> In other words, in its hovering, imagination opens the very space in which the hovering takes place. To this extent—though only to this extent—imagination is nothing other than spacing itself. As also—within a certain limit—it is nothing other than the drawing that takes place across the space opened up.[26]

It is not simply that the objectivity of space is opened up by the imagination. It is also not simply that space impinges itself on the interiority of the imagination. The point for Sallis is to resist any theory of consciousness or any idea of objective space to see instead that consciousness is spatialized and that space is non-objective and itself imaginary. Thus, the imagination hovers or floats because it is expanded out into and amongst the different things, and the very separation or spacing of one thing from another is the imagination.

Even though Husserl's analyses of intentionality aims to undermine the naturalistic relation between consciousness and its world, the notion of a phantasy-consciousness that prohibits space from entering into it amounts to a natural relation. Sallis also deals with this point by reinvigorating the question of relation between imagination and space as a question of separation:

> The hovering of imagination can be thematized as separation, that is, as a spacing in which two moments are kept separate, each in its difference from the other. Yet to keep the moments separate, is at the same time to hold them together. For separation is also relatedness; that is, one moment can be kept separate from the other only insofar as, in connection with the one moment, account is taken of the other—hence insofar as relatedness is maintained. In different terms, two moments can be kept apart only insofar as each is positioned with respect to that (other moment) from which it is to be kept apart; otherwise it would not be separated from other but simply independent of it.[27]

For Husserl, the plenum is uniform. It lacks perspective and depth, and only acquires its morphology through the inner-sphere of phantasms. Whereas, in his chapter on motor-movement and space in *Phenomenology of Perception*, Merleau-Ponty argues that homogeneous space depends on the concrete and orientated space.[28] The body, he further says, is the basis for the symbolic function of intentional consciousness to project and throw itself into the orientated space.[29] Merleau-Ponty thus invites the notion of a function that works from within a nonuniform world and a series of motor-intentions. This of course requires him to give up on the premise of a neutral position in contradiction to classical psychology. Since the symbolic function of motor-intentions is always orientated in such and such a way, it is never in a neutral position. It can never be so, furthermore, because the orientated space in which it operates is never itself neutral. This is ultimately how for Merleau-Ponty the space of the imagination turns on the notion that the sensible must itself separate or differentiate.

The Role of Imagination in the Substruction of Essences

In "Phenomenology and the Sciences of Man," Merleau-Ponty outlines the points of contact and differences between psychology and what Husserl calls "eidetic psychology."[30] Whereas psychology is the investigation of facts and the relations between them, an eidetic study concerns their meaning. If the focus of an eidetic study is not facts or their relations, it is instead the essence of perception, image, and consciousness. The eidetic psychology is in effect a phenomenology that gathers lived facts together and subsumes them under one essential sense to find the same conduct in all of them. In this way, Merleau-Ponty points out, phenomenology is to psychological facts as geometry is to physical facts: the former clarifies the internal meaning of the latter. Moreover, while phenomenology is necessary to the clarification of psychological facts, it remains a distinct study from psychology. The purpose of phenomenology is to contact the psyche through phenomenological reflection in order to understand the results of the empirical investigations of psychology. With respect to images, then, phenomenology asks the more fundamental question: what does an act of imagining mean in a subjective life?

We should resist the temptation to think of a phenomenology of the imagination only as a unification of empirical psychological investigations and instead as directed to the life of a psyche for which such unification would have meaning. According to Merleau-Ponty, Sartre fails to do this. He is thus unable to grasp how the imaginary life predominates and is meaningful for a given subject or even how an image enters into relation with the thought that uses it. Whereas, for Merleau-Ponty, the eidetic psychology is,

> an analysis which would show us that, in principle, the image is not something observable, though it pretends to be—that it is, in short, essentially deceptive. We all believe that images are observable like the things we sense. But when we try to observe them, we find that this is impossible and that, as Alain says, we cannot count the columns of the Pantheon in our images of it. The image is, therefore, a claim to the presence of the imagined object, which is unfounded. It is an absence of the object which tries to pass as its presence. It calls up an object, as one speaks of calling up a spirit. The thinking self is referring to such and such a real object existing in the world, with the presence of making it appear here and now just where I am.[31]

This is again a description of the kind of relation intentional consciousness is supposed to highlight, and it is misleadingly simple. Merleau-Ponty anticipates here the "natural negation" or "negation of negation" mentioned last chapter: there is no original affective source within consciousness that stands outside or apart from whatever appears to that consciousness. When a thing appears to me, the appearance is not just negative of that thing. When I grasp the appearance as an appearance *of the thing*, I am already recognizing both something that is not merely thingly and something not only internal to me. The very notion of appearances in phenomenology, on Merleau-Ponty's account, in fact prohibits me from understanding the interior of consciousness to be radically self-reflexive. This is even so for images and phantasy. The latter is not simply the presence of an absent object or derived from the ability to nihilate presence. The image is an apparent object derived from the ability to locate oneself as oneself and where one is in fact. It preserves the "as if" of phantasy objects, for instance, as when I daydream that a tiger is there in front of me. But Merleau-Ponty, unlike Husserl, in fact denies the neutrality of this modification. The image is born of the same "distance of distances" Merleau-Ponty ascribes to the "absolute here to the there." He no longer maintains disinvestment of an image-consciousness, and he no longer maintains the inertia of a plenum. At its depths, the imagination is spatialized, and the spaces between things that allow them to be distinct from one another is imagination.

The previously central role of phantasy in intentional consciousness and the discovery of our own constitutive power is hereby revealed in terms of its ontological import for Merleau-Ponty. Its negation, both between subject and object and between the objects of the world, orients us towards a new kind of relation between the "regional ontology" of Husserl's eidetic psychology and a "general ontology." Merleau-Ponty touches on this point in his institution lectures:

> Direction of the analyses of sleep, dreams, the unconscious, the past: not to seek inductive and dispersed solutions to these problems one by one ... but to reveal ... *the dimension* in which the solution can appear and the opening to the truth to be established. For example, sleep (or dreams or the past, or the unconscious): what is its *theater*, which modalization of being does it realize? To learn through these modalizations the notion of being at which we need to arrive. To loosen up the sedimentation that links us to *natural being* or *psychical being*, or encloses us in the dichotomy of humans and things. Far from this being either reduction of philosophy to psychology or sociology, or superimposition of philosophical being on the ontology of these disciplines, [it is] an occasion to make philosophical being surge up as integral being at the intersection of these regions. (The "regions" in Sartre are simple specifications of a being that is defined from the outset as being in-itself [with its correlative, the For-Itself.] Cf. when he says that language poses *only* regional problems and conceives metaphysical problems as *beyond* these regional problems. For a truly phenomenological philosophy, the relationship of regional ontologies to philosophy is not the subsumption of the specific under the general, but the relationship of concentric circles.[32]

I leave aside how Merleau-Ponty positions language here, both in contrast with Sartre and in terms of its general ontological implications. In all, I think Merleau-Ponty is assuming his comments in "Phenomenology and the Sciences of Man" and elsewhere. Husserl's eidetic method begins by questioning the psychological notion of intentionality, which accepts an immanency of actions proceeding from and remaining within the subject. The aim of Husserl's method is to free itself in a radical way from such immanency as well as its naturalistic implications, and to instead rediscover a meaning regional to the intentional correlation between an appearing object and its constitutive acts. That would be the eidetic grade of intentionality. But as soon as this eidetic project begins, Merleau-Ponty is pointing out here, as above, it is also forced to proceed downward, to a more general ontology concerned with what makes each general region possible in the first place. There are two further claims Merleau-Ponty brings to our attention in his comments here. The first claim is that, though each constituted field of study gives the impression of a static analysis, a general ontology would intersect with each self-constitution and undermine its self-authority. This general ontology crisscrosses each otherwise independent field of investigation, and is equally within geometry, psychology, and philosophy, etc. The second claim Merleau-Ponty makes is one about substruction: if a general ontology does not juxtapose any regional ontology but intersects with them all, this does not implicate a being to which we can go directly; there is no more appropriate region or universal study that circumnavigates all regions. In this sense, a substruction of any regional ontology must work in concentric circles, and every region—geometry, psychology, philosophy, etc.—operates by virtue of a transversal being which is impossible to appropriate. Thus, the question basic to an eidetic psychology, "What does an act of imagining mean in a subjective life?" is instead phrased here in terms of a general ontology: "For example, sleep (or dreams or the past, or the unconscious): what is its *theater*, which modalization of being does it realize?"

The latter question assumes that a general ontology is a diacritical one, where being is always defined by its lack of immediacy or lack of self-relatedness. The point of this ontology is to find the being that surges up and is integrally there at the intersection of all regions, a being that is not just regionally immanent to any particular constituted field or itself a circumscribed region, but rather always indirectly or laterally announced as the excess to all immanent fields. In this ontology, being is diacritical in the sense we explored more deeply last chapter along with Heraclitus and against Plato and Heidegger: there is neither a radical upper nor fundamental lower limit of beings but an ontology from within the middle of things.

The latter question above assumes, too, that precisely this ontological space is the space of the imagination. This expands our findings in the previous section in some important ways. When we are concerned with a general ontology in Merleau-Ponty's sense, one which does not just counterpoise regional ontologies or things but works itself into them and delimits them from within, then we cannot have a being that is categorially distinct from those ontologies or things, as another positive or equally real term. The imagination is at this point revealed to be crucial to Merleau-Ponty's ontology, but it must be one that follows the radical interrogation of its role within intentional consciousness. It is ontologically non-positive. It floats within the spaces that separate things from one another. These spaces are not themselves objective or intentional but always taking specific routes through discrete things with neither a starting point nor end. This texture would explain the genuine ontological import of the imagination for every regional ontology. For example, rather than by the internal structures of an abstract geometry, the shape, contour, figure, or form is due to a profound imaginational texture that belongs to both consciousness and things. From this perspective, there are no essential forms of the sensible but only certain and possible ways to give form to it. It is in this context that I want to turn now to sculpture and to sculptural shapes.

Sculptural Shapes and the Space of Imagination

Husserl notes in *The Crisis of the European Sciences* a plane-depth schema, depth being the hidden unpredictability behind the plane phenomena. He also says, however, that this depth is a plenum and is therefore non-differentiated. It is only the activity of phantasy consciousness, for Husserl, that typifies the plenum into shapes. But, if he is right, then the sensible never itself arises or events itself amidst the plane, and we have to proceed to it directly, if we can at all. To proceed straight to depths of the sensible would effectively be to negate the plane. Conversely, if we remain at the level of the plane this would amount to a total eclipse of depth. In the "Interrogative Method and *écart*" section last chapter, I note that Merleau-Ponty undermines the idea of discrete beings identical to themselves and separate from being. He invites a phenomenology that disrupts both polarities, and thus a phenomenology that disrupts formal ontology. In this disruption, the planar phenomena—their surfaces, contours and outlines, etc.—are grasped in terms of a depth that is neither the proper negation nor potential of surfaces but always occurring even if it is non-obvious.

It is not that Merleau-Ponty's depth contains a reservoir that in principle does not appear, or that is the single horizontal point of all the surficial outlines. If there is no single point in depth, then it should also be possible to demonstrate the multiformity of depth from the surface. This in large part is why Merleau-Ponty turns to art and in "Eye and Mind" borrows from Erwin Panofsky to say that perspective is itself a symbolic form.[33] It is also, I think, why Merleau-Ponty often refers to the sculptural aspects of painting, for example, in his descriptions of the color plane in Cézanne and Matisse or the way pigment on a Klee canvas is like a patina or mold. The history of painting is however closely tied to abstract geometry. Renaissance authors, such as Alberti and Vasari, often repeat one of the oldest origin stories of painting that relate it to the sun, describing painting as the trace or outline of a shadow. The idea is that painting is fundamentally about outline instead of modeling, schematic simplicity instead of tonal or chromatic complexity, and surface reality instead of representational illusion. That is, outline, schematic simplicity and surface reality are foundational to painting, whereas the application of color and tone just give the image an appearance of a less stable and contingent material reality. What becomes essential to painting, then, is the pure contour, and this contour does not have to do with the body of a sensed object but with the basic structure of an abstracted geometrical ideal of that sensed object.

This distinction between abstract geometrical contour and depth is exactly what Merleau-Ponty seeks to undermine all throughout his writings, and is anyways, he says in "Eye and Mind," premised on an act of bad faith.[34] This bad faith is evidenced, for example, when Merleau-Ponty compares the play of light and dark in Rembrandt's *The Nightwatch* with the blank spots of so-called modern painting:

> We see that the hand pointing to us in *The Nightwatch* is truly there only when we see that its shadow on the captain's body presents it simultaneously in profile. The spatiality of the captain lies at the meeting place of two lines of sight which are incompossible and yet together. Everyone with eyes has at some time or other witnessed this play of shadows, or something like it, and has been made by it to see a space and the things included therein. But it works in us without us; it hides itself in making the object visible. To see the object, it is necessary not to see the play of shadows and light around it. The visible in the profane sense forgets its premises; it rests upon a total visibility which is to be re-created and which liberates the phantoms captive in it. The moderns, as we know, have liberated many others; they have added many a blank note [*note sourde*] to the official gamut of our means of seeing.[35]

Merleau-Ponty points out that, in the Rembrandt painting, depth and shadow are not simply the result of two lines of sight that cannot go together but are what make the two lines of sight go together, how we see their togetherness. We do not see the dark or shadow as we do the scenic objects so much as the shadow-play lets those objects come into the light. This is a reversal of what Alberti and Vasari claim about the origins of painting; it is not that painting is the line around a shadow of the sun but that, in painting, the shadow and darkness of a scene are how there is a scene. In this sense, depth is how there is light; and the surface of things that play in that light could not be without this depth. Conversely, abstraction is not free in the sense that it has nothing to do with figures and forms. It is free in the sense that it has been liberated from the substructed geometrical ideals so that we may now see two incompossible sight lines without the need for their coherence and togetherness. Especially in "Eye and Mind," Merleau-Ponty is interested in Henri Matisse and Paul Klee because of their explorations of the "systems of equivalencies," and their deliberate attempts to undermine the categories stressed by Alberti and Vasari.[36] This means that, for such painters, outline, schematic simplicity and surface reality are returned to modeling, tonal or chromatic complexity, and the application of pigment onto a surface.

The distinctions Renaissance theorists made were, however, never really systematized in sculpture, so it is not surprising that when Merleau-Ponty writes about painting there are a lot of resonances with the medium. Consider Henry Moore's *Double Standing Figure (1952)*, a bronze presented at the famous "Geometry of Fear" exhibition in the 1952 Biennale in Venice. This sculpture is a doubling of the original *Standing Figure (1950)*, and thus it references its own figure. For Moore, this self-referencing aims to increase the cohesion and stability he thought was lacking in the original, when it was placed in the landscape of his sheep farm in Dumfriesshire, Scotland. What is interesting to me here is that achieving a stable meaning by duplicating the original figure implies counter-posing the proper limit or contour of the first figure with another, incommensurate figure, and yet *Double Standing Figure (1952)* is not two separate sculptures. It is one sculpture that reveals a space in which there are different possible positions at once, and where this difference is the creation of two discrete objects or bulks. There may be two internal axes in one assemblage, or two bulks that are sectioned off from one another, but this confrontation (co-fronting) brings the two bodies face-to-face. Where they come face-to-face—where they enter into a relationship with one another is at their outer limits, surfaces, or contours. It is also in this confrontation that they also become the specific bulks that they are. That is, the sculpture creates two bulks by showing how and in what manner each is exposed at its limits in order to be what they are. This is what Henry Moore called "simplicity in carving," which, "interpreted as a lack of surface trimmings, reveals the contrast in section, axis, direction, and bulk between different shapes and so intensifies the three-dimensional power in a work."[37]

In a text published as "Remarks on Art-Sculpture-Space," delivered at the opening of the Bernhard Heiliger sculpture exposition on October 3, 1964 at the Erker Galerie in St. Gallen, Switzerland, Heidegger writes: "Now one is quick to point out that today plastic art, and here above all sculpture, proceeds once again to find its proper place.... This lies in the fact that it has an exceptional relation to space, that it can be understood in a certain regard as a confrontation with space."[38] Again, at the 1969 exhibit of the Spanish Basque sculptor Eduardo Chillida, in a text called "Art and Space," he notes that sculpture invites "the question of what space as space is." It "is indeed a matter of questioning about what is proper to space," and an answer to this "must show itself from space itself."[39] Heidegger says that what is most proper to space is its intervallic character, and to think space would mean to think from some standpoint within the separation between objects. This is what, according to him, the sculpture allows us to do by design. It confronts its space and lets the opening of space show itself.

Heidegger's view on sculpture is however complicated by his talk of its "bodying" (*Leiben*) to express the fact that it is not simply about material bodies on display but their embodiment of the space. He writes:

> [S]pace is space insofar as it spaces (clears out), freely gives the free area for regions and places and paths. But space also spaces only as space insofar as the human arranges space, concedes this free giving, and lets himself in it, establishing himself and the things in it, and in this way protects space as space.

Therefore, he continues, "in order to think space as space, space needs the human being."[40] To think the proper of space, and to think from within space itself, one really has to think about the way humans inhabit it, because it is only from within this inhabitancy that space is arranged and existent. Without any arrangement space is not anything for Heidegger. There is nothing homogenous or cavernous about it. In fact, sculpture seems to turn the problem of relation between ideal and morphological essences into one of bodying, in which the human body arranges specific figures or forms to create the specific space. Here sculpture touches on a complex of relations between human and things, and between humans themselves, in which the body is a node. For Heidegger, in other words, thinking the proper of space ultimately means thinking about an embodiment that holds things apart, separates them, and lives or even exists in the space of that separation. For Merleau-Ponty, however, there is no initial standpoint from between separate things, and the proper of space is already an abstract space.

Thinking about the space of sculptural bodies in terms of their own volume allows us to draw a comparison to another motif in Merleau-Ponty's oeuvre, that of silence. When I say that sounds have volume, I refer to its amplitude. The amplitude is the degree of loudness a sound has, but even silence is amplitudinal. What keeps sound from being an indecipherable chaos of sensations is the amplitude of silence that figures between each separated sound or precedes and follows from a succession of sounds. It is even possible that silence is implicitly *within* the succession of sounds, what lets the succession be heard as a genuine succession. In these cases, silence is not an absolute zero-degree that stands outside of sound but rather what gives each sound or each succession of sounds the specific expressive character that it has—forceful, overwhelming, soft, lilting, etc. When I say that a mass has volume, I mean this magnitudinally, suggesting that different masses take up different amounts of space. Instead of some static and preexisting empty cavity that gets filled up, then, space is differentiated. It is portioned off or expanded, occupied or contained. There is no homogenous space but rather space participates in and between voluminosities and is what gives these voluminosities their character. Sculptural bodies demonstrate this. They reveal their space according to their metallic or stony quality, their roughness or smoothness, or their edginess or curvature. But though the sculpture has particular features and figures, it reveals these features and figures according to the space in which it has them. That is, it forms an environment that has no independence or homogeneity of its own.

There is yet another feature of the voluminous qualities of metal or stone, rough or smooth, edgy or curved; and that is the various ways these characteristics let light play. The apparently surficial features of the sculpted figure—its material, its specific availability to touch, its lines or run of surfaces—all expose the figure to the light in specific ways, and even let that specific luminescence to itself come to the fore. Yet, in addition to letting the very light by which things are seen to evidence itself, the sculpture also disallows us from thinking of this light as a primary source. As much as the sculptural figure is exposed to light according to the specific characteristics of its matter, touchability, or lines, these characteristics also let the figure recede into certain aphotic depths and prevent us from seeing its surficial characteristics all at once. Like the silence that itself has amplitude in sound, a figure's recession into depth is the place that holds it apart from another figure and prevents it from collapsing into one singular sensible plenum. What Derrida describes as the "inorganic unforeseeable proliferation of morphological types" is revealed here as an *organic* unforeseeable proliferation of morphologies. These morphologies are no longer types but genuinely surprising and unpredictable.

This aligns very nicely with Henry Moore's surrealism, for example, and the way he understands metamorphosis against pure abstraction.

For Moore, there is no difference between pure abstraction and abstract geometrical shapes, which he thinks are sculpturally uninteresting.[41] Whereas metamorphosis encourages a movement and alteration of every shape along many possible and extraordinary avenues. Through a simple switch in a viewer's position, coaxed along by the run of a surface, aspects of depth may at any time come into the light, becoming more than a shadow but exceeding every expectation. Yet there is no one stance we may take that gets rid of all the depths of any figure, and any depth can be genuinely eventful. That is, every figure is always capable of being otherwise than it now appears.

One of the things Merleau-Ponty claims sculpture evidences for us is a non-anthropological psychoanalysis.[42] This psychoanalysis would recognize that sensible things are superficially distant from human interiority, and at their depths are in fact proximate. A deep proximity such as this involves neither the reduction of an otherwise distant and inhuman world to the human nor the opposite. It is instead the mark of a syncope that runs all the way through the human body, between things, and turns them all out against one another. Another way to say this, it seems to me, is that there is an anonymity within me that also belongs to things. The inability to mark out the specific place of anonymity is precisely because anonymity implies a failure to overlap with itself. This failure is in everything, and thus it is on an adventure. It twists, meanders, and zigzags through the intervals between the contours and surfaces of all bodies.

Beyond Sight and Image

Husserl intimates that the changes of a body's position could also be changes in phantasy. So long as he thinks that phantasy bears an inner-temporal structure, however, he is also incapable of articulating how this may be so. To show that phantasy is always spatially oriented, one also has to show that its interior is not neutral. This would mean that phantasy is not the spontaneous act of consciousness it initially seems to be. Yet another reversal is required: the notion that space is interior to consciousness and not only sensible. To show that phantasy is invested and oriented in space, in other words, this implies an anonymous limit that constellates both phantasy and space. Merleau-Ponty understands this as an imagination and a depth, or more precisely as the depth of imagination.

This depth of imagination is at stake, for example, when Merleau-Ponty writes about the cave paintings of Lascaux in "Eye and Mind." These paintings have movement because they genuinely use the undulations and moorings of the cave wall.⁴³ They do this so "adroitly" that it is problematic to describe them as a "second thing" like a copy.⁴⁴ If the images on the cave are not a second thing, it is also because the cave is not a "first thing" like an origin. All at once, in other words, there is *an image on the cave wall*. This sudden configuration already disrupts some basic notions: the image may be a non-being, but it is not nowhere. The cave is a being, but it does not remain as it is concealed behind the image. Furthermore, between these, the imagination takes place at some depth where non-being and being are not neutral to one another. That is, it does not reproduce the non-being or image to itself and leave the being or origin untouched. The imagination instead holds out both aspects and takes place from a position where neither is immediately what it is nor opposite to the other.

Despite being a depth, then, this imagination is in fact at the instant of vision. If, as Merleau-Ponty writes, I see "according to, or with"⁴⁵ the cave paintings, it is because my vision neither starts with the image nor ends the wall. It neither starts with the copy nor ends with the origin. It neither starts with non-being nor ends with being. It is lost and wandering, Merleau-Ponty writes, because it always affirms the difference between these and rents them apart. This is in part why he says one always sees "further than one sees."⁴⁶ He means that vision is difference itself. For the eye to see, it needs the facial side of the eyelid that it does not see. It needs the obscure or the dark. To the extent that this is so, vision is no longer sense-vision. Merleau-Ponty remarks, for example, that vision always has a "blind spot" or *"punctum caecum."*⁴⁷

Even at the instant of vision, then, there is some blind spot that constellates both my sight and what I see. It is important to note that this blind spot is not neutral. Although it takes place between my vision and what I see and is an anonymous limit, it does not reconcile them but constellates them as incompossible. The blind spot is therefore not even the reconciliation between what is present and what is absent, or what is being and what is non-being. It is at least evident from "Eye and Mind" that, for Merleau-Ponty, the instant of vision where I at once see non-being and being configures this difference without a proper solution—without an origin or destination. Some of his commentaries in the nature lectures helps clarify this. Merleau-Ponty writes there that "[t]he reality of the organism supposes a non-Parmenidean Being," and this reality is of "a form that escapes from the dilemma of being and non-being."⁴⁸ He makes a similar remark in the Schelling portion of the nature course: "Because I myself, as a human being, know that at the moment when my consciousness poses a question, I am aware that Nature already gives me a response."⁴⁹

To question nature, or to posit nature as a question, consciousness must assume it in advance. To assume it in advance, nature does not present so much as it has already issued itself in terms of the positing acts of my consciousness. The explicit relation between consciousness and nature thus assumes something has already taken place. This is why Merleau-Ponty says that the subjective and objective status of consciousness and nature is one of "[m]orphogensis."[50] This is sometimes described as Schelling's dialectic of procreation, and apparently Merleau-Ponty recognizes this dialectic when he says: "We are the parents of a nature of which we are also the children."[51] If consciousness is the child of nature, it takes nature's place by substituting it with an image and non-being. In the same moment, nature is the also child of consciousness in the sense that, having been reproduced in terms of non-being, it maintains its integrity apart as being. If nature is the parent of consciousness, though, it is because its reproduction in terms of non-being is impossible without the integrity of its being. Finally, if consciousness is the parent of nature, this integrity cannot make sense and is impossible unless it has been reproduced in terms of non-being. The key is to hierarchize neither the non-being of consciousness nor the being of nature. They configure an impossible situation in which each is both the older and younger generation to the other. Merleau-Ponty's most famous reference to Schelling from *Signs* moves in this direction: phenomenology must "understand its relationship to non-phenomenology. What resists phenomenology within us—natural being—the barbarous source Schelling spoke of."[52] That is, the end of phenomenology is to find out that it is first premised on a non-phenomenological source or natural being. It is to furthermore see that, even if it makes phenomenology possible, this non-phenomenological source cannot be phenomenalized. This is to say that phenomenology discovers itself as premised on an impossible ontology.

There is, in other words, no sublation or synthetic moment between nature and consciousness, only a constant mirroring between the two. This is a problem, Merleau-Ponty notes, of which the systematic philosophy of reflection after Kant is ignorant but Schelling attempts to grasp. It is the problem of the very emergence of the visible plane and thus of light and illumination. Schelling, as Merleau-Ponty notes, understands this light only as a "quasi-concept"[53] that refracts nature and consciousness. Accordingly,

> light may be considered as matter, but light is also something other: it is subtle, it penetrates everywhere, explores the field promoted by our gaze and prepares it to be read. Light is a sort of concept that walks

among appearances; it does not have a subjective existence, save when it becomes for us. Light does not know the world, but I see the world thanks to light. We cannot consider its penetrating power as being nothing. There are three kinds of beings illustrated by the table, the light, and the I. To refuse this third meaning of Being is to make every carnal relation with Nature disappear.[54]

The issue is not whether light illuminates the beings to which we otherwise remain blind. It is not that light illuminates everything at once. It is that light remains within the very beings to which we are always also blind and even that light is itself dark.[55] It is in this sense that light is not a source from which we "know the world" but penetrates everywhere and explores the phenomenal field. This light is also why Merleau-Ponty ultimately rejects the representational model between consciousness and nature.[56] The reality of the organism, he writes, "is formed directly without the theme having to become an image."[57]

While "the barbarous source" is usually equated with flesh and wild being, light for Schelling, as Merleau-Ponty also notes, is associated with an "*Urwissen*" and is the "symbol of primordial knowing."[58] This *Urwissen* cannot only have the properties of self-reflexion, or else, on its basis, the table would not appear to the subject. It also cannot only have the properties of objectivity, or else the appearing of a table would not implicate any subjective state of knowing it. It is instead a symbolic form—neither properly subjective nor objective—on the basis of which both me and the table appear. It is also therefore a symbolism irreducible to the image as the copy of an origin. It furthermore prevents the origin from supplanting the copy as though it were its truth.[59] This is a symbolism that pulses at the heart of both non-being and being, explains them in such a way that each cannot escape the other, even while it is reduced to neither. This is a symbolism at the core of the reality of an organism and its place in nature. It is therefore not distinct from the barbarous source.

Some Remaining Questions

One result from these last remarks is that Merleau-Ponty maintains a "negation of negation." But now I think we are able to see more clearly that this "negation of negation" implies a restriction of non-being that means it is not simply supplanted by being. The "negation of negation" is, in other words, not an affirmation of being so much as it is a positive sense of its negation. When Merleau-Ponty says vision contains a blind spot, for example, he suggests a negation that is in fact in the midst of both my vision and the things that I see and is not another side to them. This blind spot is therefore not simply an anonymous-intention and does not accord with the model of objectivity or foundation. It is right there, in the middle of vision and delimiting it, so that there is vision. The blind spot is in this sense a positive negation that genuinely undermines the notion of a light source illuminating everything from out of itself. It is evidence of a non-being that is constricted so as to become a concrete and internal limit to beings instead of their condition of possibility. It is not a matter of "going back up the 'conditions of possibility,'" Merleau-Ponty says, "[a]nd this is why it is a question of an ascent on the spot (*ascension sur place*)."[60]

If this positive negation is not a condition of possibility, it is because it is not predictable or deducible from what I see. One other thing it introduces, then, is the notion of a primordial symbolism. Merleau-Ponty again mentions a primordial symbolism in the passivity lectures, this time in relation to sleep. There, he indicates that, whether I am awake or dreaming, what appears always possesses a relation to the non-visibility and darkness of sleep, and this darkness is equal to the tissue between consciousness and nature. This symbolism will also be called "positive" but only inasmuch as it opens the difference between the being of waking and non-being of dreaming, not because it is above both.

In the next chapter, I want to further explore the element of light in Merleau-Ponty, the way it penetrates everywhere and explores the phenomenal field and yet is not an origin of our vision and the things that we see. I also want to explore the nature of this element in Merleau-Ponty in relation to his discussions of sleep in the passivity lectures. But, intervening in these two discussions, is Heidegger's and Fink's seminars on the sun and fire-light in Heraclitus and their importance to his fragments on waking and sleeping. I take the same issue with these seminars as I did last chapter so that Merleau-Ponty's passivity lectures may be set in relief as both about Freud and an elemental ontology. It is in this connection that I hope to gain the full picture of an ontological event that is at once both symbolic and concrete.

Chapter 3
Light—Dark/Awake—Asleep

There are a couple of ways light is thematized over the course of the history of philosophy. One way is according to the geometrical model. In this view, the essence of illumination is a perfect line or angle that exists whether perceived by the human or not. These lines are the subject of both a catoptrics (the science of reflection) and a dioptrics (the science of refraction). This is the sense of light characterized as *lumen*. An alternative version of light, *lux*, emphasizes the actual apprehension of light by vision. According to this version, color, shadow, and movement may be equally important, if not more important, than form and outline.[1] As Martin Jay points out in *Downcast Eyes*, his monumental work on vision and philosophy, this dual concept of light nicely complements the dual concept of vision that we also witness over the course of the history of philosophy.[2] There is speculation with the intellect and observation with the two eyes of the body, idealism and empiricism, etc.[3] The former is initially, and most famously, emphasized by Plato, who has a "light metaphysics," as Hans Blumenberg calls it, which conceives of a clear and distinct perception of essences, removed from sense-vision.[4] Whereas observation could be understood as the unmediated assimilation of stimuli from the outside, either the collapse of perception into pure sensation or as a more complicated interaction of sensations and judgment.[5]

If the tension between speculation and observation, already existent in antiquity, involves two types of light, this is because there is already a complicated relationship between what we see and the objects that we think about. The Greeks did think the eye both transmitted and received light (this is called the "theory of extramission" or the "fiery vision" thesis), and that there is a participatory dimension in the visual process.

Even Plato held the view that the eye and the sun are "like" substances. In holding this view, he kept up a basic assumption in Greek thought, that what was over the horizon was the sum of all possible knowledge. On this assumption, vision happens in the firmament where there is neither any object nor subject but rather a vision of the totality of things to be seen.[6] This highlights the potential that sight may become absolute and that pure knowledge is the eventuality of a sort of self-reflective sight from which nothing escapes.[7] I note here that the Latin *speculation*—along with *contemplatio*, the translation of *theoria*—contains the same root as speculum and specular, and designates both sides of the mirror at once, and the end of light's refractive character.

Undoubtedly, Merleau-Ponty is the eminent philosopher of vision in the twentieth century, so it is unsurprising that references to light are everywhere in his writing. In fact, as has already been recognized, some of his most central themes, chief among them invisibility and depth, are also about light. Both the invisible and depth, for example, undermine the notion of geometrical outlines, the idea of a single and unitary light source, and a singular point of view from which the subject looks. The historical notion of light with which Merleau-Ponty most closely aligns might be *lux*, although he does not once mention the term. When speaking about light (for example, in the lamp and bust passage from *Phenomenology of Perception*, mentioned below), he certainly does emphasize its play between what is apparent and non-apparent, that what appears does so by virtue of what does not. It is in this context that, as I point out last chapter, Merleau-Ponty speaks of a blind spot in the visible that is not so much a condition or foundation but an "ascent on the spot." The invisible is, in other words, not simply the other side of the visible, capable of being made otherwise.

Merleau-Ponty's version of light, also noted last chapter, does not assume a hierarchical dialectic between being and non-being and are thus not reconcilable through some higher synthesis. For this reason, Merleau-Ponty speaks of light in the same way Schelling does. In this chapter, though, I want to draw a comparison between Merleau-Ponty and Jean-Luc Nancy. Nancy does of course explicitly mention *lux* in several places. For him, *lux* pertains not simply to observation but with the fact of their observability, that things make themselves observable and this fact about them is not itself observable. In this way *lux* pertains for Nancy to what he calls the "*phaos* of phenomenality," to what shows itself as properly separated and apart from us so that it strikes us as irreducible to the ground of which we are a part. This is meant as an anti-phenomenological claim. Nancy's analyses of *lux* are especially antagonistic to Hegel and Heidegger, but the theme of light is so closely tied with philosophy itself that any philosophy giving a central role to the irreducible fact of light—something about light which is invisible or dark—may just upend the whole tradition and point to something extrinsic to it.[8]

Neither Merleau-Ponty nor Nancy is happy with a notion of light that conceives of it as observable. That would be to conceive of illumination as having a source that can itself be illuminated, and therefore to in fact miss the possibility of examining how observation is possible in the first place. This kind of criticism takes both thinkers back to the shadows of light. While an underlying compulsion to reorient light and illumination towards the dark is evident in both thinkers, there are still contrasts between them that are instructive.

Merleau-Ponty would seem to want to think about the relation between light and dark in terms of a positive negation: what appears is never merely visible but arises and made possible through what is never itself visible. Merleau-Ponty refers to the visible as a *filigrane* to say that it shows through what resists showing.[9] By its very nature, though, this *filigrane* effaces itself within the appearing. If such effacement is the inherent and informative milieu of what appears, phenomenology cannot concern itself only with what appears obvious and must also plunge into what resists the sensible. If the model of visible shapes, for example, depends on the margins and spaces between them that are in fact invisible, phenomenology needs to concern itself with these margins and spaces. This is why for Merleau-Ponty perception and its directionality are not initial and why he ultimately stresses the need to replace them with elementality. Recall here Merleau-Ponty's Working Note quoted in the introduction: "Perception is not in the first place the perception of things but of *elements* (water, air), *rays of the world*, things which are dimensions, which are worlds; I slide over these 'elements,' and there I am in the *world*."[10] The point is in part to undermine directedness that is always towards some content and to install in its place a basic situation that is itself without content though it requires it. The elements are in this sense transitive. There is no color in itself, for example, but only specific colors. Similarly, there is no light in itself and only specific things that are illuminated. But if Merleau-Ponty wants to shift from intentionality to elements, one wonders if he does not end up making these elements a non-transitive form and therefore does not undo the model of directedness and objectification.[11] If he is interested in the separation of light from dark, for example, does he really speak only of specific things that are illuminated? Does not separation become the general term for the appearance of some specific thing from out of something nonspecific? These are questions that one can ask from the particular perspective of Jean-Luc Nancy's account of the separation between light and dark. For Nancy, there is likewise a blind spot internal to what appears, but this spot is irreducible to the visible and evades thought altogether.

I have already attempted to get beyond this criticism on Merleau-Ponty's terms. Regarding the model of essences, the sensible field that functions as their background is not for Merleau-Ponty a straightforward background or plenum, as it may be for Husserl. The phenomenology of geometrical essences, for example, does not result in the discovery of the margins or spaces of those shapes that can be apprehended or thematized, but rather those margins or spaces make apprehension and thematization possible. Yet they do not follow the paradigm of objectification, and there is no need to assume that they must be turned into a focus to which we can attend. For example, if the margins or spaces between things is to be characterized in terms of a background, when this background is apprehended it is not now an object since there are yet other margins or spaces elsewhere. Now I insist on my claim from last chapter moving beyond Husserl's initial supposition that phantasy only plays an ideating role: the most trenchant of paradoxes operating between things is not only that the margins and spaces of perception are non-apparent, and this non-appearance is the possibility of the thing; it is also that these spaces are the spaces of imagination. Moreover, I show last chapter, these spaces are basic to, not an exception in, Merleau-Ponty's general ontology.

I want to show now that this general ontology amounts to Merleau-Ponty's cosmology and the elemental.[12] The elemental, I think, explains how the space of imagination is not the intention of some non-being but an anonymity that takes a route through both reflexion and the reflected upon while being irreducible to either and avoids becoming a fixed target. It explains what constricts both the positivity of sense-perception and the negativity of dream-perception. This is the importance of the theme of sleep, which also marks the difference between sense- and dream-perceptions. Some of Heraclitus's fragments mention sleep in this very context. Heidegger points to these in his seminar with Fink, for example. But, given the criticisms of their general treatment of Heraclitus outlined in the first chapter, I think there is ample reason to be critical of their reading of the dreamless sleep in Heraclitus. It can be read instead in terms of the elemental according to Merleau-Ponty. I want to keep this elementality in mind when I turn to Merleau-Ponty's treatment of waking, dreaming, and sleeping in Freud for the purposes of ultimately discovering a symbolism that is as ontological as the elements.

The Light—Dark Opposition in Jean-Luc Nancy

In a short essay about one of Guerrero's photography exhibits called "Lux Lumen Splendor," Jean-Luc Nancy notes the historical versions of light, *lux* and *lumen*, and indicates that their antagonism may not be strictly oppositional: "At the very edges of bodies," he writes, "*lux* is folded, modulated, and diffused in *lumen*. The limbs that supply the title for this series, Lux Lumen Splendor, are a name for edges or frames, for what wraps around them, their hem, their nimbus."[13] Nancy is making the simple point that bodies have explicit sides, and the understanding of light as *lumen* may well be derived from these sides. For example, the idea that light is linear and geometrical is perhaps true with respect to a figure's explicit sides; and light may bear the characteristics of *lumen* when we have a straightforward view on them. But the same figure is also folded, modulated—it also diffuses *lumen*—and, on the peripheries of my straightforward view, there are no geometrical and linear light rays. Instead, light bounces from surface-to-surface, works around the edges or frames, and is a halo radiating outwardly from some interior non-radiance. Nancy thus intimates what we have already noticed in relation to sculptural bodies. If, on its explicit side, a thing has a definite look, it does not on its margins; yet it is only at these margins where the thing becomes what it is and separated from other things. For Nancy, then, *lux* is the more archaic version of light.

Nancy also says, however, that *lux* is decidedly anti-phenomenological. Since it is not per se associated with how a thing shows itself as a proper thing, Nancy conceives *lux* outside the bounds of the structures of intentionality, distinct from the appearing of something to a consciousness. It does not so much disclose itself to a subject as it registers itself impossible to appropriate by phenomenal consciousness. Here, *lux* is intimately associated with works of art, which likewise work outside of the domain of disclosure. Nancy writes in *The Muses* that,

> [t]he things of art are not a matter for a phenomenology... because they are in advance of the phenomenon itself. They are of the patency of the world. Or else, that's what the phenomenon is, but not in the sense of what appears in the light: rather than the *phanein*, it is the *phaos* itself, light, and not the light that appears (*lumen*) by clinging to surfaces, but the light that flashes (*lux*) and that causes to appear, itself nonapparent as such. *Lux* without fiat, having neither creator, subject, nor source, being the source but in itself refracted, in itself radiant, exploding, broken.[14]

Since it resists phenomenality, in other words, *lux* originates from nowhere and appears to no one. It betrays nothing of intentionality, having neither a single point of origin nor a single spectator. From this articulation of *lux*, we gather two further points. The first is that such light is not per se a source by which things become apparent, but it belongs to some fact that makes itself apparent. It is aligned with "the groundless basis for all sense: Not what it is but that it is."[15] This is what Nancy also calls the "presentation of presentation," which is "not a representation: it does not relate presentation to a subject for which or in which it would take place. The presentation of presentation relates to itself."[16] The second point we gather from Nancy's articulation of *lux* is thus that, having no singular source or viewer, it betrays a *world* apart from viewership, a world identical to itself or self-intimate.

There is one short text, "Euryopa: le regard au loin,"[17] which I want to highlight for the striking way Nancy associates the impossibility of disclosure with light. There, Nancy engages specifically with Husserl, who more or less stands in for the western need to search out grounds. In particular, though, Nancy focusses on the implicit philosophical suppositions of Husserl's "earth-ground" and shows that it, like the notion of ground in general, underpins the history of Europe's relation to the rest of the globe. In keeping with a major trajectory in his oeuvre, in "Euryopa" Nancy also offers a counter-reading of the idea Europe, one that would be free of its apparent narcissism. He first notes that the word itself, "Euryopa," is an epithet of Zeus that means either "wide-eyed" or "far-sounding" and might also be translated to mean a "far-sounding and looking-far into the distance."[18] In this sense, at the very root of the concept Europe is a colonization of its opposite side, which we might still notice in the idea of, say, global trade. Nancy points out that European vision is also *formally* a looking into the distance, a "particular way of looking whose singular sighting is the universal as such."[19] This would mean that, inherent to the idea of Europe, is a conceptualization of its own regard as having a special form such that it can see that which has made it. In this way, it understands itself as returning to itself and, at this very point, as forming its own foundation. It brings differences into itself and contains a point of view that forecloses multiplicity.

Yet, in his etymology of "Europe," Nancy also appeals to the Semitic, pre-Greek, word "*ereb*," which means "obscurity." In addition to or instead of "looking into the distance," Europe also more originally means, "looking into the obscurity," and even "into its own obscurity." The European way of looking has a "blindspot," Nancy continues, recoiled into its heart where it is affected in advance of itself. Here, he says, there is a "nocturnal vision" before the seeing of anything in particular, where the visibility of vision is in fact most distant from itself. At the very point at which vision is identical with itself, then, it also turns out to suffer from a kind of "alienation."[20] The usage of "alienation" needs to be highlighted since it is very much dialectical, and here it also suggests that the ideals of a European vision must be undermined. At the very least, this European vision needs in fact to see "that it does not see."[21] This is one of Nancy's overarching concerns, to free up a notion of world not at all informed by the universal and its totalizing or occidental effects. The point, for him, is to indicate the particularities of a world without recourse to a horizon that grounds it—to let the world remain in the darkness of particularities and not subject it to an absolute light source that claims to illuminate everything.

Whereas, according to Hegel in his lectures on aesthetics, art presents the idea in terms of the sensible—a unity in terms of a multiplicity—for Nancy, art presents nothing more than the multiplicity of the sensible. Moreover, for Nancy, Hegel's conception of art is untenable. When Hegel famously says that art overcomes itself and requires philosophy, that philosophy is the end of art, this perpetual overcoming should not lead to *another* ground that sublates multiplicity but rather prevent precisely this sublation from ever taking hold. To say that art overcomes itself, or is a constant self-overcoming, means that it always undermines itself in such a way as to allow only multiplicity, rather than unity, to lay itself bare. Overcoming itself, art leaves room only for matter. It leaves us, Nancy says, with the "induration of the arts in an irreducible material difference."[22] Elsewhere, in *The Sense of the World*, he speaks of this material difference as a "dis-location without appropriation of the place by another," and as "sites and places, distances [*écarts*]: a possible world that is already a world."[23] We may note here the kinship between *lux* and *écarts*, which is conceived by Nancy as an untraversable distance that asserts itself as such. When it does, it presents the fact of a world that cannot be undermined by appeal to some knowable ground other to it.

Light—Dark and Elementality

One might think Nancy's overall project is very much akin to Merleau-Ponty's. After all, Nancy's meditations on *lux* also lead to a blind spot in vision and to an *écart*. Consider, however, Nancy's further articulation of *écart* in *The Ground of the Image*:

> Continuity takes place only within the indistinct, homogeneous space of things and of the operations that bind them together. The distinct, on the contrary, is always heterogeneous, that is, the unbound—the

unbindable. What it transports to us, then is its very unbinding, which no proximity can pacify and which thus remains at a distance: just as the distance of the touch, that is, barely touching the skin, à fleur de peau. It approaches across a distance, but what it brings into such close proximity is distance.[24]

Nancy does not fully relinquish the heterogeneous space between distance and proximity here. He makes distance and proximity unbridgeable in such a way that what is proximate to us is our distance from things. That is, he radicalizes the heterogeneous space between distance and proximity so that the distant things are left completely on the other side of our proximity, and they are able only to present itself through extraordinary means. While Merleau-Ponty also recognizes the proximity of distance, he does so in such a way that neither their heterogeneity nor their homogeneity is at stake. It is not only that the sense of the world's distance is proximate to us. It is also that, at our core, we are also distant from ourselves, of apiece with the world's distance, and that we feel this distance most intimately. This is what Merleau-Ponty suggests, for example, when he repeats that anonymity resists us *from within us*. This is to say, *écart* is the divergence between my conscious and unconscious, things, and oneself and another.

Where for Nancy the blind spot is, like separation itself, an untraversable separation made intimate, for Merleau-Ponty it is an anonymity that situates itself between separate terms. His account of light likewise speaks to this blind spot. In the "The Thing and the Natural World" chapter of *Phenomenology of Perception*, and in a passage ostensibly about color, Merleau-Ponty refers to what in *Der Aufbau der Farbwelt*, Katz calls "*Lichtführung*." This is the "essential character of lighting":

> If we move a lamp round a bust at a constant distance from it, even when the lamp itself is invisible we see the rotation of the source of light in the complex of changing light and colour which is all that is given. There is, then, a "logic of lighting" or again a "synthesis of lighting," a compossibility of the parts of the visual field, which may well be specified in disjunctive propositions.[25]

This "logic of lighting" is mentioned later in the text too:

> The visual thing appears when my gaze, following the indications offered by the spectacle, and drawing together the light and shade spread over it, ultimately settles on the lighted surface as upon that which the

light reveals. My gaze "knows" the significance of a certain patch of light in a certain context; it understands the logic of lighting.[26]

In these passages, Merleau-Ponty is making a simple observation like Nancy's at the start: the surface of an object is always lit up against other darkened surfaces where light is diffuse. The logic and context of luminosity is also its invisibility. Part of what Merleau-Ponty contests about Descartes's analyses of light, for example, is that Descartes leaves aside this logic and context to clarify it. Because of this, he cannot give account for the light by which we see. On the other hand, when we return to its logic and context, we discover very quickly that no lighted surface is fixed as such. It contains dark spots that must also be able to shift to the light so that I can apprehend each surface as belonging to one and the same mass as before. It is the play between the two poles, in other words, that is illuminative; and this means that illumination, which is of course the touchstone of phenomenality, is not original. What seems compossible in the light is in fact incompossible and disjunctive. A full account of how we see things in the light, then, demands an account of how we see from within and according to an invisible that is not the other side of the visible but its internal disjunct.

Yet we may also be tempted to say that, even in Merleau-Ponty's bust example, the lamp rotates like the sun around the bust and is still a single source of light. In this case his descriptions of light do not get outside a "light metaphysics." When Merleau-Ponty speaks of a "new light" in "Philosophy and Non-Philosophy Since Hegel," he calls this light a "pharisaism."[27] This, I think, is a more drastic affirmation of the logic of lighting: light is impossible the moment it is affirmed. It cannot be traced back to its source because it does not have a source. When we posit its source we in fact deny the very light according to which we see things. Moreover, Merleau-Ponty further intimates with the term "pharisaism," the very contrast between a metaphysics of light and the experience of it already misses the logic of light. In the discussion period after delivering "The Primacy of Perception and Its Philosophical Consequences" to the *Sociéte française de philosophie*, Mme. Prenant asks a question that prods Merleau-Ponty in this same direction: does not Merleau-Ponty place "a higher value on the sun of the astronomer or on the sun of the peasant?"[28] His answer is significant:

> Recall the famous phrase from Hegel: "The earth is not the physical center of the world, but it is the metaphysical center." The originality of man in the world is manifested by the fact that he has acquired the more

exact knowledge of the world of science. It is strictly necessary that we teach everybody about the world and the sun of the astronomer. There is no question of discrediting science. It is only when one has conceived the world of the natural sciences in all their rigorous that one can see appear, by contrast man in his freedom. What is more, having passed a certain point in its development, science itself ceases to hypostatize itself; it leads us back to the structures of the perceived world and somehow receivers them. For example, the convergence between the phenomenological notion of space and the notion of space in the theory of relativity has been pointed out. Philosophy has nothing to fear from a mature science, nor has science anything to fear from philosophy.[29]

And:

This does not mean, however, that what is at the bottom is to be suppressed. It seems to me, for instance, that if we make it our goal to reach the concrete, then in certain respects we must put art above science because it achieves an expression of the concrete man which science does not attempt. But the hierarchies of which you are speaking suppose a point of view; from one point of view you get one hierarchy and from another point of view you get another hierarchy. Our research must be concentric rather than hierarchized.[30]

Merleau-Ponty also makes the point about concentric ontologies in the lectures on institution, as we see last chapter. The issue for him is to see a general ontology lateral to any regional one so that the former does not become hypostatically abstract and prevent us from tending to the concrete. In the logic of light, it is important to Merleau-Ponty that what issues illumination is also within the illuminated. This means that, for him, illumination contains no original source or point of view that can itself be illuminated. It means, in other words, that illumination is in effect also dark—that it is in fact darkness that makes illumination possible. There can therefore be no general ontology of light that does not have to do with its regional context and its inability to be seen. This same argument, pursued in the nature course notes in reference to Schelling, leads Merleau-Ponty to say that the highest ontology of light would acknowledge its lowest fact, that it penetrates everywhere, explores the phenomenal plane, and yet can never be a single source from which we know about visible things. In "Philosophy and Non-Philosophy Since Hegel," Merleau-Ponty therefore describes light a "polysemic" (he in fact uses the word "*Vieldeutigkeit*").[31] Rather than a source, light is an endless refraction and flash-like. This refraction never shows. Its primary character is diversion. Yet both the phenomenon as well as its disclosure are because of the very texture of this always diverted light.

It is commonly noted that Merleau-Ponty's later ontology often revolves arounds the elements, especially the element of fire in "Eye and Mind." In that essay, he writes, for example:

> There is a human body when, between the seeing and the seen, between touching and the touched, between one eye and the other, between hand and hand, a blending of some sort takes place—the spark is lit between sensing and sensible, lighting the fire that will not stop burning until some accident of the body will undo what no accident would have sufficed to do.[32]

And later in the essay we read that

> the painter touches the two extremities. In the immemorial depth of the visible, something moved, caught fire, and engulfed his body; everything he paints is in answer to this incitement.[33]

It is certainly important that Merleau-Ponty's uses the element of fire to describe how seeing and the thing seen are illuminated. Fire is by no means a fixed light source. When it flickers, for example, it illuminates aspects of a thing in an undefined and unsteady way, while also similarly darkening other aspects of that thing. Like the lamp rotated around the bust, the flicker of fire always shifts the way light and shade spread over a thing. A fire can of course also grow or shrink, spread or die out, either on its own or by exposure to other elements. Moreover, and I think this point requires stressing, in these passages the seeing and the seen thing do not point back to a fire per se. They point back to the *spark*, *incitement*, or *kindling* of fire, which are not equivocated here with the fire-element itself. There is no fire-element equal to a sameness between seeing and seen or between activity and passivity. It is the spark that kindles this difference. To account for fire, in other words, we go back to a clash or friction that happens between two otherwise resistant surfaces. I also note that, elsewhere in "Eye and Mind," Merleau-Ponty uses the word "deflagration" to describe being—a term indicating that, for him, being is in fact away or down from what is burning.[34]

Notwithstanding Aristotle's description of the "first philosophers" as those for whom matter is the primary source of things,[35] I read such passages and terms in Merleau-Ponty as radicalizations of Heraclitean opposites and of Heraclitus's first principle of fire. In Fragment B217, recall, Heraclitus describes the cosmos as a self-made-thing that "kindles itself" and "extinguishes itself" in measures. The word Heraclitus uses in this fragment for "kindling" is ἁπτόμενον. Heidegger likens ἁπτόμενον to the "sun-fire [that] surrounds everything πολλά."[36] He thinks of the πολλά aspect of light as surrounding everything and being everywhere. This is why, for him, the unsetting sun is also concealed: we do not see the light that surrounds everything and is everywhere. Merleau-Ponty, however, avoids having to say that, when it reveals and extinguishes itself, light operates inexplicably and distinct from us because it assumes an everywhere point of view that accounts for everything. His emphasis on the spark or incitement of fire is, in other words, an emphasis on a locality of light that situates itself concretely and secretly between our vision and what we see. Thus, for Merleau-Ponty, the earth and not the sun is the place to begin a metaphysics of light.

Waking—Sleeping

In chapter 1, I note that Heidegger resolves opposites in Heraclitus in terms of a singular ground of appearing that does not itself appear. I argue that this contradicts Heraclitus's claim in the first fragment that things are "divided according to their nature." It is separation, in other words, that makes identities for Heraclitus. When Heidegger deals with the opposites of light and dark in Heraclitus, however, he resolves them in terms of a singular light source—the sun—that is the non-appearing ground of appearing. In the seminar discussions with Fink, which deal with the opposition between waking and dreaming, such opposition is resolved by a sleep that at least bears a kinship to the sun to the extent that it likewise does not itself appear.

Consider this conversation between Fink and Heidegger from the seminar titled "The Dreamless Sleep: Sleep and Dream—Ambiguity of a ἅπτεσθαι (Correlated Fragments: 26, 99, 55)":

> FINK: In dreaming, we must distinguish the one who dreams and the dreamed I. When we speak of a light in the dream, this light is not for the dreamer, but rather for the dreamed I of the dream world....
> A phenomenological analysis of the dream indicates that not the sleeping, but the dreamed I kindles a light. Although the sleeper does not see, still, as a dreamer, he has a dreamed I that has encounters.
> HEIDEGGER: Thus one cannot identify sleeping and dreaming.

FINK: Sleeping is a vivid form of human absorption.... The I of the dream world, and not the sleeping I, kindles a light. If one wishes to interpret fire-kindling as a dreamy fire making, then on the one hand the phenomenological distinction between the sleeping and the dreamed I will be overlooked and, on the other hand, the human situation, aimed at in the fragment, of standing between light and night gets lost....

HEIDEGGER: We must notice that the thesis "no sleep without dream" is an ontic discovery that suppresses the existential distinction of the sleeping and dreamed I and only claims that all sleeping is also dreaming.[37]

Fink makes the distinction here between the dreamed subject and the dreaming subject. The latter dreams the former and is able to kindle a light. It is indeed significant that dreams are described here as kindling or ἁπτόμενον and likened to a candle light. The root of both ἁπτεοθαὶ and ἁπτόμενον is "apt," which means "to aim towards." This is why both dreams and dreamed subject are intended by a dreaming subject for Fink and Heidegger. Both the dream-object and the dreamed subject are apt to the dreaming subject who lights them up. To the extent that the dreaming subject is therefore a "fire-kindler," this subject aims towards its dream content. Though the subject kindles a light, however, "[H]e is not able, like Helios, to kindle a world-fire that never goes out, that drives out the night."[38] If dream content is intentional, this intentionality is driven out by the sun. If dream content is intentional, sleep is decidedly not: no sleep without dream is merely an ontical claim that ignores the ontological import of sleep. The question is whether sleep is the same as the sun and "still not to go under ever." The question is whether in sleep we fall into the light source itself.

This issue highlights that the concerning terms are not waking-sleeping but waking-dreaming on the one side and sleeping on the other. Fragment B26 reveals this most profound entanglement:

ἄνθρωπος ἐν εὐφρόνῃ φάος ἅπτεται ἑαυτῷ [ἀποθανὼν] ἀποσβεσθεὶς ὄψεις, ζῶν δὲ ἅπτεται τεθνεῶτος εὕδων, [ἀποσβεσθεὶς ὄψεις], ἐγρηγορὼς ἅπτεται εὕδοντος

[Man in the night grasps a light, having died for himself, his sight extinguished. Living, then, he touches the dead one while asleep, his eyes extinguished; waking, he touches the sleeper.]

It may be that, when it is dark, the sense of touch dominates the sense of vision. But it is not clear from the fragment what "touches" means. If the dominance of touch is the collapse of the distance between us and things, then the ambiguity of ἅπτεσθαι will be effectively undermined. In the seminar titled "The 'Logical in Hegel.—'Consciousness' and 'Dasein.'—Locality of Human Beings between Light and Night. (Correlated Fragments: 26, 10)," Fink indeed moves in this direction: "To touch on here does not mean to touch, but aims at a relationship of adjoining. And it is also important to notice here that it is not a question of simple bordering, but of a relationship of adjoining."[39] Whereas Heidegger warns that Fink goes "much to fast into the speculative dimension" and says that the fragment is instead "a question of an open-standing touching on. That goes with the fact that the kindles light also grants an open-standing quality to the little orbit of the room that is illuminated by the candle." The discussion between Fink and Heidegger continues:

> HEIDEGGER: The dark is in a certain sense also the openness, if a light is kindled in it. This darkness openness is only possible in the clearing in the sense of the *Da*.
> FINK: I would suppose that we may think the concealment of the dark not only out of the relationship of clearing of the *Da*. There is the danger that one understands the dark only as boundary of what stands open, as the exterior walling of the open. I would like above all to indicate that a human relates himself at the same time to the open and to the concealing darkness.
> HEIDEGGER: what you say may be true, but it is not directly mentioned in the fragment. I will not contest the dimension you have in view.[40]

One of Heidegger's points here is that in sleep the dominance of touch over vision requires a darkness so utterly concealed as to be impossible to notice in any way. So utterly concealed is it, in fact, that even its own concealment is impossible to notice. The sleeper is in other words incapable of witnessing herself fall asleep. Thus, for Heidegger, sleep is in fact the result of a recession of an original light source: in the dark we are open-standing because we are in fact indistinct from the same sun-fire that surrounds everything but is impossible to witness as such.[41] But at the same time this also entails a distinction. When the sleeper sleeps she at the same time creates through her dreams an orbit of light in the otherwise vast darkness. The reason Heidegger thinks Fink's claim about absorption moves too much in the "speculative dimension" is, in other words, because sleep is at once the dominance of touch over vision and the success of vision to see, through dreams, in the dark.

The ambiguity between sleep and dreams is thought in terms of precisely this duplicity. This duplicity turns on the fact that there is an intentional structure in dreams, which is one of vision rather than touch. Fink:

> [B]rightness that a human brings forth, in the light shine kindled by him, there emerges a relationship of grasping human to grasped state of affairs in his surroundings that has the character of distantiality. Seeing is a distantial being with things.[42]

Instead of denying this claim, Heidegger pivots to a consideration of the extent to which the different senses are related. Especially with respect to touch and sight, this discussion ultimately concerns the extent to which distance and proximity are related, and whether touch is in fact a "small distance" that maintains rather than undermines the intentional relations of dreams.[43] Without saying it directly, though, Heidegger points out that Fink's position depends on the secondary meaning of ἁπτόμενον, which means both "to hold" and "to be held":

> Here there is an immediate proximity between feeling and the felt. This proximity is not transmitted through the medium of distance in which the seer and what is seen, or the hearer and what is heard, are set apart from one another. In seeing, the grasping in light is separated from what is grasped. In the unity of light that surrounds the one who grasps and the grasped the manifold of πολλά shows up. A distantial distance holds sway between the one who grasps by seeing and what is grasped. . . . Contrary to that would be an understanding grounded in a being-in-the-proximity in the sense of immediate touching on. Touching on is an understanding that does not come out of the survey, out of the expanse, or out of the region toward what is grasped.
>
> HEIDEGGER: what about when I now give you my hand?
> FINK: That is an immediate touching of hands. In Περὶ Ψυχῆς [On the Soul], Aristotle calls flesh the medium of the sense of touch. But a phenomenological objection must be made here, because flesh is not the medium in the proper sense for touching and what is touched. Seeing is referred to a visible thing, to a visible object, which, however, meets us out of a region. Encounter out of the open ambit,

which is cleared by the brightness, is distinctive of the special kind of grasping that consists in the distance between the one who grasps and what is grasped.[44]

Finally, we must admit, then, that the proximity sleep to touch and to the darkness of night is not an ontical matter:

> HEIDEGGER: Body is not meant ontically here . . .
> FINK: . . . and also not in the Husserlian sense, . . .
> HEIDEGGER: . . . but rather as Nietzsche thought the body, even though it is obscure what he actually meant by it.
> FINK: In the section "Of the Despisers of the Body," Zarathurstra says, "Body am I entirely, and nothing else"; Through the body and the senses a human is nigh to the earth.
> HEIDEGGER: But what is ontic proximity?
> FINK: Human lack of ontological affinity with other entities belongs together with the ontological understanding of his manner of being. But if a human exists between light and night, he relates himself to night differently than to light and the open, which has the distinguishing joining together structure. He relates himself to night or to the nightly ground in so far as he belongs bodily to the earth and to the flowing of life. The dark understanding rests as it were on the other principle of understanding according to which like is cognized through like.
> HEIDEGGER: Can one isolate the dark understanding, which the bodily belonging to earth determines, from being placed in the clearing? Fink: True, the dark understanding can be addressed from the clearing, but it doesn't let itself be brought further to language in the manner of the articulated joining.
> HEIDEGGER: When you say ontic proximity, then no small distance is meant in what you call proximity, but a kind of opening.
> FINK: . . . but a twilight, dark, reduced openness that has no history of concepts behind it, to which we may have to come sometime.[45]

Whether touch and sight are different or the same may be an ontological rather than ontical issue. The earth and body may only be *cognized* as like one another, but they actually belong to one and the same matter. This sameness is not itself cognizable. If sight is distantial, for example, the ontological kindship between eye and world is not. Here we have an absolute limit that does not seem to admit of difference. Ultimately, I think, both Heidegger and Fink are forced to say that Heraclitus holds a version of the "fiery eye" theory of vision: since our vision is like the sun-fire, when sun recedes and we fall asleep so too does the distance between our seeing and what we see, and there is darkness; when sun-fire rises and we wake, a space is suddenly injected between our seeing and what we see, and there is light. If Heraclitus holds this theory of vision, what extinguishes the light and what lets it shine is impossible to know or fundamentally inexplicable. Of course, and again, just before his consideration of Fragment B16 in which the source of light both goes into hiding and never sets, Heidegger considers wonder in terms of a clearing (*Lichtung*) in which we are stunned by the conflicted nature of the emergence of beings—an emergence that is inexplicable in terms of further beings being or a self-grounding being.[46] Yet, I argue, his description of sleep as an absorption into sunlight, equivalent to darkness, effectively undermines the clearing and its basic lack of resolution. Whether or not touch collapses the haptic relation between what holds and what is held, the "open-standing" replaces irresolvable conflict with an inexplicable fiat.

It is unclear, though, that Heraclitus holds the fiery vision thesis since he never explicitly claims it. Furthermore, Heraclitus would only have to hold this thesis if he also thought in general that opposites require unification. Since he does not have to posit the necessity of unity, there is also no need to say that sleep unifies waking and dreaming, or that sleep is where we are adjoined to a light source that recesses and self-encloses. It follows, then, that we are welcome to reject the claim that dreams form a small boundary of light, like a candle, against the expansive darkness where the source of illumination is everywhere and accounts for everything. We are likewise welcome to reject the claim that dreams betray an intention whereas the ontological importance of sleep is its lack of intention. These two claims of course depend on one another. If we get rid of the notion that some original light source stands open, then the intentional acts of waking and dreaming cannot happen against the background of this source and indeed these acts are not merely ontical opposed to the ontological ground of their source. In other words, when we interpret ἁπτόμενον in such a way as to preclude the original difference between these two moments of light, then the standpoint of the human alters in a fundamental way. That is, the light of her dreams contains the same invisible aspect of light that illuminates the manifold of the world.

Dark Sleep

I note above that Heraclitus's opposition is not per se between waking and dreaming but between waking-dreaming and sleep. According to Fink, at least, this is because sleep for Heraclitus marks the collapse of waking and dreaming where there is no longer any proper difference between the touching and the touched. It is however surprising that, for Merleau-Ponty, sleep likewise does not collapse the difference between the touching and the touched. In the passivity lectures, for example, he in fact says that sleep is a "being *in the divergence*"[47] and that, rather than a synonym for being, sleep is rather its "internal possibility."[48] If sleep is being in the divergence, it is the very site from which being can be seen distinctly from particular beings. This site is not itself seen. It is however not merely ontological but the concrete limit of ontology—an ontology before ontology. Merleau-Ponty also speaks in a similar vein in *The Visible and the Invisible* where the "internal possibility" of being is called an "endo-ontology." This ontology, pursued from inside it, reveals dimensions of beings and being or one's being and being in general.[49] It seems sleep is inside ontology, itself endo-ontological.

Such primordial ontology is already anticipated in *Phenomenology of Perception* when Merleau-Ponty writes one of his more elegant passages about falling asleep:

> The relations of sentient to sensible are comparable with those of the sleeper to his slumber: sleep comes when a certain voluntary attitude suddenly receives from outside the confirmation for which it was waiting. I am breathing deeply and slowly in order to summon sleep, and suddenly it is as if my mouth were connected to some great lung outside of myself which alternately calls forth and forces back my breath. A certain rhythm of respiration, which a moment ago I voluntarily maintained, now becomes my very being, and sleep, until now aimed at a significance, suddenly becomes a situation.[50]

When sleep comes, I go from being directed to some significance to a situation. There is a clear absence of an external cause for this alteration. That is, sleep is directed by or to nothing other than itself and this is why it never signifies. Merleau-Ponty suggests, like Heidegger, that one's own sleep does not appear to the sleeper. But now his explanation for this lack of directedness and signification is quite different. If for Heidegger the non-apparitional character of sleep is due to the crossing out of difference, for Merleau-Ponty one's own sleep is not phenomenally available because it betrays the lapse at the core of our bodily existence. My own lungs and breath, the palpitations of my heart, are most intimate to me even as they as distant from my volition as are external things. They are outside aspects to my own interiority.

Two things stand out from this. The first is that sleep produces itself. In the passivity lectures, Merleau-Ponty in fact goes so far as to say sleep is "conduct"[51] or even an "act."[52] He points, for example, to Henri Piéron's discovery that sleep is less the straightforward result of intoxication but of the production of a chemical called "somnolence," which defends against the bodily reactions of intoxication. Merleau-Ponty notes in this context that the conduct of sleep is in fact defensive, and even that "[t]here is an intention of sleep."[53] Yet, he also says, "When I lie down I do something, I not only await sleep, I *lend myself to sleep*—indulgence. But I do not cause sleep; the will to sleep prevents sleep. The sleep of consciousness is not consciousness of sleep; sleep is the opposite of consciousness."[54] That is, if we deny that consciousness is opposite to its exterior, that it may be overwhelmed from its exterior, we can also deny that this exterior has no interior life of its own and that its passivity is the result of some other activity. When Merleau-Ponty says that "sleep is the opposite of consciousness," in other words, he supposes it a conduct that is non-conscious which overwhelms conscious life from inside of this very life.

The second, not unrelated, feature that stands out from the *Phenomenology of Perception* passage is that sleep does not itself signify because it is difference. Merleau-Ponty arrives at this same point later in the lectures in a description of coming to consciousness from having been asleep:

> But even in a normal position, if sleep is really heavy, I "lost all sense of place"—in light sleep, therefore, the body holds onto the place—And holding onto the place is also to hold onto personal identity. No longer knowing where I am, I no longer know who I am, I am in nothingness, irremediably . . . the body that we find upon reawakening is not a clearly articulated whole. It is a tiredness which merely has one form, at least as long as it is numb and immobile. As soon as it is ready to move, there is a place, in the form of its attitude, something which announces a time, a place (the body: general capacity to inhabit diverse situations), a house, an openness to total situations, to types of situations (for example, situations comparable for it, and equivalent for it by means of the multiple of space-time).[55]

The body is the capacity to inhabit diverse situations or to live in multiple spaces and times. This capacity is its potential. But there is an instant in coming to consciousness before this capacity and potential when there is in fact no I, body, or even precise world. "A man who sleeps," Merleau-Ponty writes, "is nowhere, in no span of time," but is instead "possible everywhere and at all times."[56] In other words, the sleeper is not simply a body. She does not inhabit a definite site but has the capacity to be "everywhere and all times"—to inhabit diverse situations, multiple spaces and many times at once. That is, there is no region or depth forbidden as a matter of principle to the sleeper. Where in *Phenomenology of Perception* the one who sleeps moves from significance to a situation, in the passivity lectures the situation of the sleeper is that she is in the midst of an event. Merleau-Ponty in the lectures:

> To avert misunderstanding: there is no determinism here, submission to a foreign power; the event often only occurs after decision (to sleep, to seduce). But the event is not caused by it, only permitted by it, such that it is not what was decided that occurs. This is also applicable to the production of a work of art, perhaps to any action or undertaking as it is truly lived or done.[57]

If the event is plural rather than singular, insofar as sleep is an event it is likewise plural. This entails that sleep is the opposite of consciousness because it requires an event and a dimension that articulates itself in fields otherwise to itself: in sense and dream perceptions. These perceptions would only be superficially intentional. They would also bear the traces of the primordial passivity that is sleep—neither the simple reception of the outside world to the inside nor the obliteration of that world. They would bear the traces of the being in divergence. I am separated from myself in sleep. But there is no original source for this separation. It is the same separation phenomenality and illumination has from itself. This is the dark in which my sleep is. There is no direct phenomenology of sleep, then, but this does not mean there is no phenomenology of sleep.

Some Remaining Questions

There is no way for me to see myself go to or out of sleep. These events, according to Heidegger and Fink, depend on a light event that is always hidden from us. They thus think that sleep happens by virtue of a sun event that cannot itself be seen. Nancy, on the other hand, argues that sleep is in fact opposite to the ontological. In keeping with his treatment of the blind spot, for example, he claims there cannot be a phenomenology of sleep because sleep is the complete absence of experience. Instead of falling into a ground of appearing, the fact that sleep does not appear entails an instant in which consciousness ensconces itself within itself and, for the time being, suspends the difference between itself and what it reflects on. This "tomb of sleep," as Nancy calls it, is an absolute proper: it has solitary existence and cannot relate to anything, including itself.[58] But sleep sometimes betrays even this absolute. I may wake up right before my alarm if I have to get up early. If I have to get up for something important, I may even wake several times throughout the night to see if my alarm is working. I wake to the cry of my child yet sleep through all kinds of other noise. I know when I have been asleep. Sleep does not preclude waking and sense-perceptions any more than it does dreaming and dream-perceptions. The ontological character of sleep for Merleau-Ponty is precisely this interventional character. Whatever of sleep resists appearing also intercepts and continues to intercept the intentional structure of consciousness and experience. Merleau-Ponty does not disassociate the blind spot and the absence of experience from experience. He writes for example:

> What do we mean when we say "it is the body which sleeps"? We mean, just as when we say "it is the body which perceives," sleep is not an act of *Sinngebung*. . . . However, dreams are not sleep; they are a compromise between sleep and waking. Dreams [are] evidently reckless *Sinngebung*, fulfillment of the *Sinngebung*. But this, then, is not sleep (and consequently it is no longer truly the dream as cut from the cloth of sleep). The symbolism is going to appear as sliding of sense upon materials. To understand it well, it is necessary to take stock of an alteration of sense itself, which consists in 1) [the]lowering of the barrier of the official personality, predominance of immediate desire through distancing of the world; 2) however, [the] control of this desire which, if it were overtly manifested, would provoke anxiety and reawakening. Thus semi-repression—semi-barrier. The disguise of symbolism, for Freud himself, is not uniquely due to repression. The renunciation of direct, adequate expression, *Erfüllung*, is a consequence of the fact that one sleeps, i.e., that one distances the discriminating apparatus and that one goes toward undifferentiation, aphasia, apraxia (cf. Freud showing that one does not truly speak in dreams, that there is no expression of logical relations in dreams). But this does not mean limitless freedom of an arbitrary *Sinngebung*.[59]

For Merleau-Ponty, too, sleep occurs when the distinction between consciousness and what appears to it is suspended. It is not equivalent to the intentions between the dreaming subject on the one hand and the dream-objects or dream-subjects on the other. Sleep is what in fact slips between the terms of such intentions and disrupts both their sense and meaning.⁶⁰ This amounts to an important claim about sense and meaning: the sense of the phenomenon and its meaning are not one and the same but also not dislocated from one another. In every intentional relation between sense and meaning, then, there is yet other possible meanings that are not per se intended even as they are not dissociable from the first relation. This non-intention is therefore not simply the repressed meaning of what appears in my dreams but a kind of repression, Merleau-Ponty calls it a "semi-repression" here, that in fact expresses itself in terms of dreams and their meanings. This semi-repression, sleep itself, is thus not the limitless freedom to produce meaning out of nothing. It is better understood as a complete lack of reference. It is because of sleep, for example, that I wake up from a dream still terrified or I am perturbed by a nightmare all day—confusing what appears and the place from which it appears. Behind this lack of reference, for Merleau-Ponty, the dreamless sleep is not only temporal but also spatial. Here we can connect the deprivation of phenomenality that is sleep to the non-directional event and thus to the elements. One could say that in Merleau-Ponty's account of the dreamless sleep there is no essential point of contact: sleep happens in a darkness, which is in the middle of the phenomenal world.

Merleau-Ponty notes that what constellates sense and dream perceptions is a kind of symbolism. This implies a distinction between symbolism and non-being. The former would conscribe non-being so that it does not amount to a radical negation as in Sartre. It also implies that sense-perceptions are more than perceptions of things. In all, such symbolism implies a primordial passivity between consciousness and its world that generates an intervention between our otherwise interior life and our otherwise exterior life. Merleau-Ponty says he is looking for the "[e]xact relation between the 'imaginary' and the 'real.'"⁶¹ He thinks that the primordial passivity would offer this. He thus also thinks that "the touchstone of a theory of passivity," is a "notion of oneiric symbolism."⁶² One is now reminded of Merleau-Ponty's suggestion, in his lecture on nature in Schelling, of a primordial symbolism that conscribes both non-being and being, makes them appear distinct, and yet for its part exceeds neither.

It is perhaps hardly surprising that Merleau-Ponty's discussions of Freud in the passivity lectures should remind us of Schelling. Schelling writes in *The Ages of the World* about "[t]hat primordial deed which makes a man genuinely himself precedes all individual actions; but immediately after it is put into exuberant freedom, this deed sinks into the night of unconsciousness."⁶³ Freud, for his part, quotes Schelling in his paper on the uncanny: "Uncanny is what one calls everything that should have stayed secret, hidden latent but has come to light."[64] Moreover, psychoanalysis likewise discerns a structure of symbolism in the manner Schelling outlines between what is and what is not. For example, the son wants to be the father of the father (Freud), or the infant is the mother of the mother (Klein); these conflicts animate the real relationships between son and father or infant and mother even though they are impossible situations to achieve. But when Merleau-Ponty approves of the "structure of oneiric thought" in Freud, there is this more obvious connection:

> Freud did not seek to reduce symbolism to repression (as he never reduced the constitutional to the acquired; on the contrary, without constitutional constraints, he said, traumatisms would not be neuroses)—He wanted us not to limit research through considerations of structure (as Sartre and Politzer do). But he does not deny the existence of an oneiric structure which is responsible for part of the way dreams look; he began the examination of it. He began with the exploration of "unconventional thought"—*The Interpretation of Dreams*. It is here that we seek the picture of primordial symbolism.[65]

Freud does point out that Schelling is a philosopher rather than a psychoanalyst and interested less in the etiology of mental illnesses than in "an ontology capable of representing the independence of individual."[66] In the final sentence above, Merleau-Ponty also seems to want to discover a symbolism integral to the etiology of the individual: through something like an interpretation of dreams, "we seek the picture of primordial symbolism." Merleau-Ponty also thinks, however, that Freud's "unconventional thought" suggests a more exact relation between the fictive and the real irreducible to that relation. This symbolism may efface itself in the conventions of thought, in other words, but it also constricts and interdicts that thought. Thus, following Freud, Merleau-Ponty thinks the symbolic form has to do with the specific site in which the life of consciousness unfolds. But he also thinks that precisely this site evades the conventions of thought and is its ontological limit.

One way to understand the primordial symbol is to try to place it in the context of sleep, which also constellates the limit between consciousness and world. Merleau-Ponty's engagement with Sartre's reading of the hypnagogic image is helpful here. The hypnagogic image is an image appearing in the liminal state between consciousness and world: "Let us allow, in addition," Sartre writes, "the subject a certain sleepiness, a state of suggestibility: the hypnagogic image will be born."[67] In the hypnagogic image of a cat, for example,

> [o]ne does not posit the image as object but one posits it as a representation. One sees, if not a cat, at least a representation of a cat; or, again, to be more exact, *one is in the act of seeing a nonexistent cat* . . . because consciousness feels itself imperfectly chained that it posits its object as nonexistent. It pretends to be seeing a cat; but, as if it feels itself, in spite of everything at the origin of this vision, it does not posit its correlate as existence. Whence this paradox: I really see something, but what I see is *nothing*.[68]

For the hypnagogic image to be possible, according to Sartre, consciousness self-suspends and transcends the world. It is for this reason "entopic."[69] It arises as an image from out of consciousness, and consciousness grasps this feature of both itself and the image with which it is now fascinated. As Merleau-Ponty puts it, in the hypnagogic image, "I stop opposing myself and verifying the form-matter relationship," and I am "not confused with these illusions, nor are they confused with their object."[70] If the hypnagogic image requires that consciousness no longer maintain the form-matter relation, it also requires that consciousness self-suspend its relation to the illusions that appear to it and thus also the relation between those illusions and their objects. This is the "sleepiness" Sartre notes. But, as Merleau-Ponty says, sleep is in fact "an abandonment of this possibility" and may also be examined from beyond the limited perspective of its passage to and from dreams.[71] It is in fact a profound confusion that one does not anticipate in an analysis of the hypnagogic image alone: I am confused with the illusions that appear to me, and these illusions are confused with their object. At this moment, according to Merleau-Ponty, there is an "abundance of the imaginary" in which the sleeping consciousness loses the "notion of the full to such an extent that it does not apperceive itself from its nothingness, and that, in the absence of a ground of being, it considers nothingness valuable." Here, Merleau-Ponty says, the "barrier" between the seeing and the seen is removed, and this removal implicates a "fate" in which "every intention to see is at once sight."[72] But whereas this fate would seem to make sleep "ultra-objectivist and ultra-subjectivist," it is in fact an ambiguity complete enough as to require a recasting of "perceptual and imaging consciousness" altogether. Indeed, the preceding lecture on the nature of perceptual and imaging consciousness introduces the notion of a primordial symbol.[73]

Because, in the lectures, sleep produces sense and dream perceptions, it is clear that sleep is not what is real behind our dreams. As the limit between consciousness and world, it is instead their symbolic form. The phenomenology of sleep becomes for Merleau-Ponty the phenomenology of a symbolic limit to thought.

I want to outline in the next chapter how exactly the symbolic form is a positive negation. This positive negation would at once *produce* both our conscious and non-conscious life and yet at the same time *erase* itself in what it produces. It is in this sense both a limit situation and a limit of thought itself. Any phenomenology of the symbolic form would, at this point, become concerned not only with a form that produces both conscious and non-conscious life but also the limit of philosophy itself.

Chapter 4
Philosophy—Symbolism

Heidegger and Fink pose the "ambiguity of ἅπτεσθαὶ" in Heraclitus's fragments as an opposition between waking-dreaming and sleeping. While both waking and dreaming imply intentionality, sleep is non-intentional. While both waking and dreaming imply direction to some phenomenon or other, sleep implies a loss of such direction and an open-standing in the source of all phenomena. Not only is sleep the loss of vision, in this case, it is an inability to see one's loss of vision. One does not see one's own sleep. Merleau-Ponty agrees that sleep is the deprivation of phenomena, though he does not think that it implies the erasure of difference. In fact, he says,

> sleep [is] an activity of distancing the world.... But is to sleep simply to work in the imaginary? Are dreams even sleep? [For] Freud dreams are the protectors of sleep, [keep] even the connection with the world, in reality, from which sleep, on the contrary turns away.... To sleep is neither immediate presence to the world nor pure absence. It is *being in the divergence*.[1]

Merleau-Ponty often makes clear in his lecture notes that sleep is not the same as dreams. There are of course some dreams without sleep, like daydreams, and to start dreaming is not the same as to fall asleep. The latter contradicts the psychological claim that there is in fact no sleep without dreams. But it does so by introducing an ontological claim that is less juxtapositional than medial: sleep is "being in the divergence." This statement should inform everything else in the passage before it. Even if sleep is protective and turns away from the world, and dreams in fact protect this turn away, it does not follow that the conduct of sleep is superseded and maintained by the conduct of dreams. Yet they are also not distinct conducts. If dreams are the work of imagination and sleep refuses to appear, Merleau-Ponty does not want to invite the notion that dreams and sleep are utterly distinct. Notice that it is not the world per se but only the identification of the world with the real that dreams protect against. This allows Merleau-Ponty to actually equate sleep with a non-objective world and space, and even with eventfulness. Sleep is thus being in the divergence because it is nothing in itself: it is neither pure passivity nor pure activity but rather a primordial passivity; and it would be only through dreams that I recognize a kind of world that contains my sleep. I notice this, for example, in falling into and waking from sleep. To get to the sleep that differs from dream and sense perception I nonetheless have to pass through dreams. I cannot get to straight sleep without some dreamy ephemera. Nor can I wake from sleep without them.

It is not the case, then, that sleep is to dreams as the real is to the fictive.[2] Yet Merleau-Ponty does mention in his passivity lectures that he is looking for the "exact relation" between the real and the fictive. The play of protection between dreams and sleep, in which the conduct of sleep is protected by the conduct of dreams, reveals in fact that the conduct of sleep produces and limits itself between the world and dreams. This sleep is thus also connected to a kind of symbolism for Merleau-Ponty. Such symbolism has been approached in the nature course notes where Merleau-Ponty navigates the dilemma between the being of nature and the non-being of consciousness. There, he argues that being and non-being require a primordial symbol that conducts itself in such a way as to produce both. Both our exterior and interior lives are therefore premised on this basic symbolic form. Yet, in producing these lives, the symbolic form at the same time effaces itself at the moment these differences appear. To the extent that sleep is in this way connected to the symbolic form, it is likewise non-personal and anonymous. Any phenomenology of sleep would therefore be concerned with both the life of the individual and the limits of thought itself. The question is whether there is a method appropriate to this most concrete ontological limit.

Dreams and Passivity

If it is now clear from the previous analyses of the nature and passivity lectures that Merleau-Ponty is searching for an ontology at once both concrete and symbolic, then it should also be clear that he is searching for an ontology that undermines the dialectic of being and non-being. He spends quite a lot of time in his sleep lecture on Sartre's work on the imaginary and sleep. Though at the end of that lecture Merleau-Ponty mentions that, while sleep is "the absence of a ground of being" and "considers nothingness valuable," it is just this absence and nothingness that leads into his next lecture on the difference between perceptual and imagining consciousness. Whereas for Sartre sleep is equal to the nothingness of imagination, for Merleau-Ponty sleep ultimately creates the difference between perception and imagination. This means that, in his ontology, the distinction between full and empty intentions cannot be entirely upheld. Merleau-Ponty writes that in the separation between them,

> [i]t is a matter not of hyletic distinction, empty consciousness and full consciousness, the same consciousness—but of structural distinction (Moreover, from the moment that there is *analogon*, and this *analogon* is apprehended as "evoking" the real being of the absent object, imagining consciousness is not empty.) "Full" consciousness [means] not "observation," but "focusing," i.e., spectacle presenting itself as going toward an optimum, and summoning a certain positioning of the sensory apparatus toward it, i.e, the body-spectacle relation [is] unknown. . . . "Empty" consciousness maintains this reference of the world, but distances it; I become my body not as openness to an effective space, "I can," power of a certain *bearing*, but as closedness to all that (which is a modality of the fields all the same).[3]

Here we should differentiate between a hyletic or material distinction and a structural distinction. If empty and full consciousness are structural rather than hyletic distinctions, this is because in both we in fact focus on the hyletic manifold in a different way. The imagination, for example, does not call up a real thing merely in its absence. If it did, it would merely be the full presentation of an absent object freely auto-posited by consciousness (e.g., a fullness of dreamed-objects). Husserl has already pointed out the unilateralism of phantasy objects, and this leads him to investigate further the role of phantasy in perception, and then its necessity to disclose an object out of the horizons of that perception. In that case, Husserl at least intimates the exteriority and spatialization of phantasy. Merleau-Ponty is likewise saying here that imagining consciousness, if not empty, is not free from the body's insertion in space. This insertion is one and the same depth from which we look in sense perception. It is less the kinaesthetic horizon of possible movement than an insensible and immobile hiatus within this horizon. Because no consciousness is free of this hiatus, waking consciousness is merely structurally distinct from dreaming consciousness in that it has a power to draw out from its hiatus a certain space to which it claims to be neutral and disinvested.

If sleep is "being in the divergence," the difference between dream and sense perceptions is a structural one that in fact requires at least some kind of indifference to this structure from the standpoint of the world. This invites the predicament that, inasmuch as they are structurally distinct, dream and sense perceptions are private and public, whereas, inasmuch as they are materially indistinct, dream and sense perceptions are in fact both public. The sleeping body, Merleau-Ponty says,

> is not truly nothingness of the world: 1) the world continues to exist—in the divergence; 2) the body becomes heavy, I lie there, I am its place, it marks my place; 3) though immobile, the body is not nothing; predominance of my respiration, I am its breathing; 4) finally my situation in the world remains, and I give the body satisfaction through dreams which allow me to avoid *truly* taking a position. It is relative and provisional nothingness—by de-differentiation of the discriminating systems: a-praxis, a-phasia—loss of *contours*, levels. But, ultimately, there are other beings, another science, on this side of space, not because the oneiric content is nothing and the something is forgotten, but because it is a *private object*. So the oneiric something becomes most of all projection of the individual drama where it is from, with all its roots.
>
> The symbolism, says Sartre, is primary an incapacity of *Deckung*, i.e., of "direct" or conventional consciousness [The] symbolisms reduces to negations; it is inadequate for thought. For Freud, on the contrary, the inadequation is voluntary, deliberate. For me, the interrupted dream frees a mode of thought, not hollow, as Sartre believes, not lying, as Freud believes, but impressional.[4]

Here, as above, the sleeping body is inserted into the very things from which it turns away, and, with their content, dreams preserve both this insertion and turn away. The question arises as to what the nature of this turn is if it is not a decisive disconnection from things. How can Merleau-Ponty also make sense of the privacy of dream content? He again seems to nod to Husserlian phantasy-consciousness when he says that the oneiric content of dreams is without position but not because this content covers over and elides the world. If dreams are private, it seems this privacy is for Merleau-Ponty on the other side of the things consciousness encounters when it is awake, and even on the other side of the horizon of those things. This would mean that, in the space where the body is asleep and inserted into the world, it is dreams that *permit* the sleeping body to be inserted into the world instead of becoming it.

Instead of the self-driven Freudian unconsciousness or the Sartrean negating imagination, Merleau-Ponty understands dreaming consciousness as impressional. This means, rather than experiences we live through and which are accessible to reflection, dreams impress themselves on consciousness and in fact present themselves as inaccessible to reflection. According to this view, dreams arise from some place other to me. Where for Sartre dreams are the negative act of an imagination and absolutely personal, for Merleau-Ponty they allow for a circumscription of this negation. This circumscription is nothing less than sleep and its own conduct. But this conduct is not now a positive volition: I do not will myself to wake from sleep and I do not will myself to fall into it. To sleep is, in other words, to enter into a non-objective space. This space constricts the non-being of consciousness, places it in the being of nature, and likewise constricts this nature from being positive. It is an unthinkable and concrete limit where my most interior life is susceptible to everyone and everything around me in a way that is more than objective. Perhaps because there is nothing personal about sleep but something profoundly public, even where my very existence is defined as fragile, I need to retreat from the world before I actually do fall into it. In any case, the public space in which I sleep constricts both the imagination of my dreams and the real space where I in fact lie down. This is the very event of symbolization.[5]

The Positive Symbol

The point of this reference to symbolism is to think passivity not as perfect inaction or action but wild in the sense that it only happens through what is different from it—only through sense and dream perceptions, or conscious and latent meanings. On the one side, this symbolism limits the extent to which negation negates; on the other side, it limits the extent to which the positive is real. It limits, for example, the extent to which dream perceptions and latent meanings negate and are false sense perception or conscious meanings; and it limits the extent which sense perceptions and conscious meanings are true or correct perceptions or meanings. The passivity with which symbolism is therefore associated thus takes place in a certain kind of space that constricts the negative and the positive. This constriction is itself positive to the extent that it generates itself in terms of these conceptualizations of the negative and the positive. This is why Merleau-Ponty also wants to speak of a "positive symbol" in Freud:

> Freud discovered this positive symbolism: this meaning beyond the meaning has a double sense. One usually retains only the two separate meanings from it: manifest meaning and latent meaning. The latter [would be] reinstitution of an original meaning which was then repressed, buried in memory, by censorship.... However, that is not his discovery. If the latent content were truly buried, dreams would not provide any relief from the desire. It is necessary that the latent content be accessible to him in some manner; that the one who dreams and the one who sees to the bottom of the dream are the same, and that there are not truly two persons (the unconscious and the censor, the id and the ego) but communication between them.[6]

The phrase Merleau-Ponty uses to describe Freud's positive symbolism, "meaning beyond the meaning," seems to implicate something beyond and other to the impressional consciousness that is crucial to symbolism. This would however imply a distinction between symbolism and its content. Yet "meaning beyond meaning" equally implies that there is in fact nothing other to meaning—that is, if meaning were in fact beyond meaning, it would no longer be meaning.[7] To derive a positive symbol, in other words, we need to first recognize our inability to think about the latent and inexplicit content of dreams without severing it from dream content. The positive symbol is in effect first a diagnosis: the thought that relegates the symbolic to either latent or explicit meaning is inapt to the symbolic itself.

Freud's positive symbolism is on the other hand an "unconventional thought."[8] It aims to explain both the latent and explicit meaning of symbolism. If latent meaning operates by indirect signification and explicit meaning by direct signification, a positive symbolism explains both meanings and both indirect and direct signification. It is positive, in other words, since it simultaneously explains both the ambiguous repressed meaning as well as the clear and non-repressed meaning. Were these two meanings not supported by this more basic symbolism, we would have to suppose a parallel within consciousness, an unconscious and a conscious life, each manifesting itself in exact measure and neither in fact covering over the other. In that case, we could not in fact ascribe duplicity within conscious life. A positive symbolism is not however the effect of an overarching identity of consciousness wherein consciousness is immediately available to itself. If it were, it would not be symbolic and would not defer what it means.

In effect, there is nothing like a symbol in-itself but only a "symbol of symbolism."[9] A *symbol* has to "mean something," but what it means here is *symbolism* itself. In that case, what the symbol means has no fixity, is never foreclosed, but this symbol is never evacuated of meaning. This symbol instead refers to itself as symbolic, and in doing so proliferates the very symbolism to which it refers. To say this another way: the symbol may very well refer to a meaning, but the meaning that it has is not clear, nor can ever itself be clarified, because this meaning is always altered in relation to it. Thus, it is really impossible here to spot an initial symbol that would have any definitive meaning. It always effaces itself in the meanings it produces. It is in this way a limit-situation in the same sense of the instituting aspect of institution. In fact, to make sense of institution as a symbolic matrix, like Merleau-Ponty says it is, we have to understand institution in terms of this positive symbolism.

In "Cézanne's Doubt," Merleau-Ponty does use the phrase "first word" to describe the sudden upsurge and organization of the sensible world before the painter, and it is sometimes wondered whether there is a "first word" in Merleau-Ponty's theory of the institution of expression.[10] In that case, institution would presume some dogmatic moment when latent and explicit meaning do not differ.[11] But the positive symbol is not such an instant and less an origin of the symbol. It is significant in this context that Merleau-Ponty also insists we should simply reject the "[r]ealist theory of interpretation" of the unconscious:

> The "true" meaning [would be] not only different, but still known by a second self, clearly, in a non-symbolic language, [thus] absolute knowledge; the unconscious [would be] "first," primary form of the "psychical"—What to think of this formulation of Freud's? It is inadequate for Freud himself; he speaks out against the spatialization of the agencies, and rightly so. The unconscious is not someone in me who clearly thinks a life of which I have only the appearance. By definition it is not an other. It is what I resist, of which I know that it is me, in relation to whom I organize my imperceptions. Consciousness and unconsciousness make but one divided being. Dialectic of Freudianism: by insistent on the symbolic power of consciousness, he discovers content which is latent, unconscious, but he is also prohibited from realizing it in conventional consciousness, in symbolism which would be symbolic of oneself.[12]

If we cannot presume the symbol is the "symbolic of oneself," it is because there is no origin to which the symbol refers. Merleau-Ponty may go so far as to argue that if indeed there was a "symbolic of oneself," and an unconscious that is merely referred to by a symbol, then the project of psychoanalysis, to read back from a symbol and decipher its psychopathology, would be impossible. There is no content of subjective life so deeply buried, so concealed or so distorted that it remains outside of and fundamentally distinct from its symbolization. The positive symbol points this very tension at the core of psychoanalysis and its possibility: even if explicit and latent content are not the same thing, there is always a subject on whom this latent content impresses itself and who at the same time "sees to the bottom" of this content.[13] The subject who reflects and gets to the bottom of the latent content is in other words capable of telling the difference not only between explicit and latent content but also between true and false latent content. For the subject to distinguish between the latter, however, she must surpass the distinction of explicit and latent content as well as false and true latent content. Even if she is not personally situated in relation to it—that is, even if it is not her own—the capacity for such distinctions circumambulate around a symbol that is instead anonymous. This anonymous symbolism defines the split between both meanings, and thus also between the conscious and unconscious.[14]

Now we are confronted with the peculiar kind of productivity inherent to symbolism. This productivity is understood merely as the introduction of a constriction: it constricts us from the premise of a radical negation; and it constricts us from the premise of a positive that supplants the negative altogether. Though it may at first be counterintuitive, this is also why, when describing symbolism, Merleau-Ponty equates it with resistance and with the censor. This censor would in fact be the positive articulation of the symbol that for its part resists getting closed off into either the unconscious or conscious, latent or explicit, dreaming or waking:

> The description of the oneiric structure (impossibility of expressing, dictatorship of figuration, condensation as sole means of expression) would attribute the disguise of latent thoughts as much to the condition of the dream as to [the] censor-repressed struggle—Consequently, latent content not to be represented as thought in the depth of ourselves in the mode of conventional thought, as an absolute observer would represent it. The unconsciousness of the unconscious [is the] unknown; but not known by someone in the depth of ourselves. The unconscious [is the] abandonment of the norms of wakeful expression, i.e., of the symbolic

as symbolic of self, direct language, which presupposes distance and participation in the category. But this unconscious is not distant; it is quite near, as ambivalence. The "affective content" is not even unconscious or repressed, i.e., the unconscious as pulsation of desire is not behind our back.... [The] unconscious [is the] implex, [the] animal, not only of words, but of events, of symbolic emblems. [The] unconscious [is] unknown acting and organising dream and life, principle of crystallization (*rameau de Salzbourg*), not behind us, fully within our field, but pre-objective, like the principle of segregation of "things."[15]

Freud himself affirms this reading of resistance in his "Revision of the Theory of Dreams":

You have long been aware that this censorship is not an institution peculiar to dream-life. You know that the conflict between the two psychical agencies, which we—inaccurately—describe as the "unconscious repressed" and the "conscious," dominates our whole mental life and that the resistance... is nothing other than the resistance due to [a] repression by which the two agencies are separated.[16]

Here, Merleau-Ponty uses a language familiar especially to Freudians who would come after him (e.g., Lacan, Kristeva, Lyotard) to describe the productive character of the censor, as a "latent content," that operates by a "principle of crystallization." He also uses the Freudian theme of "dictatorship." As a censor, in other words, the primordial symbol refuses to be constricted to unconscious or conscious life, latent or explicit meaning, or dreaming and waking. This formulation of symbolization avoids any simple denotational theory in which the symbolic has a real denotatum. It remains somewhat of an open question here as to whether Lacan's formulation of "the real" would come under criticism. "The real" is for Lacan what puts the symbolic and the imaginary in their places and cannot itself be symbolized. But, because this is so, "the real" relates to the death drive and the repetition compulsion. As such, it remains something unavoidable by the subject in virtue of its structure as "that which always returns to the same place."[17]

In addition to being concrete and associated with passivity, the productivity of symbolization for Merleau-Ponty is also proliferative. This goes beyond the etiology of the subject and has to do with another kind of productive constriction: if the positive symbol has no original denotata, it also has no original designatum; and when it acts like a censor, it is also "like the principle of segregation of 'things.'"

This claim is I think quite unique to Merleau-Ponty. As soon as Freud opens the unconventional thought of the positive symbol, one must recognize that symbol is located in no one special divergence but is equally between latent and explicit meaning, ourselves and the world, and between the things of the world. In this sense, the positive symbol runs a circuit through differences. Merleau-Ponty pursues an "ontological psychoanalysis."[18] This means that, in his readings of the Oedipal complex and the case of Dora, for example, promiscuity is a central theme.[19]

Freud's Dora case is initially about a young girl thought to have hysteria who turns out to have been seduced by an older, married man, and used as a pawn in a sordid interfamily drama by her adulterous father. Here "hysteria" is ultimately not a collection of symptoms but a peculiar logic that governs the way in which someone organizes relationships with people and things. With Dora, Freud also famously realized that it was no longer the diagnosis or interpretation that matters but the dynamics of transference between himself and his patient. Of this promiscuity, Merleau-Ponty writes in his lectures on Dora:

> The Freudian *decision* is the movement in the constellation where Dora is set up, is perceptual decision, i.e., not imposed by the givens of the situation, but effective only if she takes them and reorders them not as a system of objects, but as a system of tensions attached to certain beings-things.[20]

And:

> Thus, 1) no absolutely deep and superficial—No absolutely conscious and absolutely unconscious—Because unique object with facts—the back of the object is not a zero of consciousness.[21]

And finally:

> Symbolism, signifying and signified—Impossible to distribute the roles absolute, to say that one of the relationships only signifies the other. It is a relationship to Eros which has many pairs of arms and clusters of faces. In particular, [it is] impossible to establish an exclusive relationship to the past (father) and, beyond, somatic sexuality.[22]

If the relation between a signifier and a signified is not initial, neither is the relation between our conscious and unconscious. These relations merely make sense of a symbolization that has already transpired. Since Merleau-Ponty thinks symbolization is instead promiscuous and already integral within both the signifier and signified, itself unaccounted for by these terms, he must admit that symbolic formation presumes a given context and nexus of relations. But this nexus is not fundamental in any sense: it is not a universal form and it is not simply the object-world. The form of symbolization is not universal because it is not disassociated from, and in fact impossible without, the site where it arises. It is also not reducible to an object-world because it does not assume a series of punctuated referents discrete from one another but rather their being taken together. That is, after all, the very possibility of substitution and transference between people and objects or even between analyst and analysand. This symbolization, Merleau-Ponty says, occurs at the "back of the object" and in a "system of tensions attached to certain beings-things." With this non-frontal symbolization, Merleau-Ponty evidently wants to articulate an ontological symbolism and the event of symbolic formation that is not on the visible plane yet not disassociated from it. It is unclear, however, how such a symbolism could be the object of any philosophy or even how philosophy might employ language to articulate it. The relations between the signifier and the signified and the conscious and the unconscious, for example, are already outside perspectives on a symbolic formation that rigidify and thus distort it.

The Positive Symbol and Psyche

An ontological symbolism would thus question whether phenomenology in fact reaches back to the limit of the phenomenon, and also whether it is in the end an immanental science. Yet Merleau-Ponty actually appears to answer these questions in the affirmative in this startlingly radical description of the project of philosophy from "*La philosophie aujourd'hui*":

> There is only one complete psychology: it is philosophy, that is to say Psyche confined to the auto-revelation of Being (hence, reference to the Psyche of Heraclitus). If philosophy is true psychology, psychology is an incipient philosophy: But this is not only true of Psyche; the body as bearer of Psyche returns to being where all things are together.[23]

It is a matter, as Keith Whitmoyer notes, whether phenomenology "endeavors to be present at the event where sense comes into being." Such an event, accordingly, is the happening, the taking place, the manifestation of ψυχή, which we now understand to be staged in bodies as well—as inscribed within the very flesh of being. To make this return, to be present at the event of ψυχή, is to be present at the point of exhalation where all is one, to be present at the event of expression itself. Whether such presence is possible—the capacity for transcendental thought to bear witness to this event—is the essential question.[24]

There is certainly textual support to read Merleau-Ponty's phenomenology as an attempt to be present at the initial event of expression. Take this well-known passage from *The Visible and the Invisible*:

> And, in a sense, to understand a phrase is nothing else than to fully welcome it in its sonorous being, or, as we put it so well, to hear what it says (*l'entendre*). The meaning is not on the phrase like the butter on the break, like a second layer of "psychic reality" spread over the sound: it is the totality of what is said, the integral of all the differentiations of the verbal chain; it is given with the words for those who have ears to hear. And conversely the whole landscape is overrun with words as with an invasion, it is henceforth but a variant of speech before our eyes, and to speak of its "style" is in our view to form a metaphor. In a sense the whole of philosophy, as Husserl, says, consists in restoring a power to signify, a birth of meaning, of a wild meaning, an expression of experience by experience, which in particular clarifies the special domain of language. And in a sense, as Valéry said, language is everything, since it is the voice of no one, since it is the very voice of the things, the waves, and the forests. And what we have to understand is that there is no dialectical reversal from one of these views to the other; we do not have to reassemble them into a synthesis: they are two aspects of the reversibility which is the ultimate truth.[25]

Passages such as this one, of which there are plenty, counter many of Merleau-Ponty's comments about symbolism from the passivity lectures. It is in this context that readers like M.C. Dillon, for example, object to Merleau-Ponty's references to the elemental on the grounds that it supports an irreducible non-given. What Whitmoyer calls "the essential question" is whether a non-given can be brought to givenness by the method of phenomenology. I opt to read phrases like "the voice of no one" and the "voice of the things" to implicate a limit between interlocutors and things—the limit of what is phenomenal in voice and speech—that remains spatial but never subject to the phenomenal or objective plane. The limit of expression may be a non-given, then, but in a totally different sense of something merely lying in wait of expression.

When Husserl refers to the limit of the phenomenon in *The Crisis of the European Sciences* section 49, he, like Merleau-Ponty above, refers to the psyche of philosophy and Heraclitus's Fragment B45. But what does the fragment say? It reads: "ψυχς πείρατα ἰὼν οὐκ ἂν ἐξεύροιο πᾶσαν ἐπιπορευόμενος ὁδόν· οὕτω βαθὺν λόγον ἔχει." Noting the key terms of this fragment and their translations into German and French, λδος (*Grund, fondement*), ψυχῇ (*de Seele, l'âme*), βαθὺν (*Tiefe, profond*), and πείρατα (*Grenzen, forme*), Whitmoyer gives this translation of the fragment: "[T]he *logos* of the soul has such depth that we may never reach its limit—no matter what path we take or how far we travel."[26] The last term, πείρατα, also concerns a reading of the phrases "the voice of no one" and the "voice of things." The German translation has the additional sense of "limit," while the French has the sense of "sides" or "bounds" and particularly concerns the limits of shapes and bodies.[27] For Merleau-Ponty the limit is indeed what delimits the shape of things and what makes those things discrete from one another. This limit is also equated with depth, but the depth between shapes or bodies is not so deep as to be unbounded, itself lacking boundaries, or impossible to reach a bottom as a matter of principle. Though Merleau-Ponty's philosophy returns to the depths of the psyche, in other words, this psyche limits and gives shape to those things (forming them) while remaining always in the hazards of those things and intervallic.

This way of understanding the ψυχῇ has also been evidenced: whatever is in present position of strength (for example, waking), its opposite (sleeping) for Heraclitus is not symmetrically so, or else this opposite would never turn around and come to the fore; rather, the opposite is weaker and unable to sustain itself on its own. What is not presently expressing itself is also not self-sufficient enough to be properly otherwise to the present expression, and therefore every present expression will always invariably bear a lateral and latent opposition. Merleau-Ponty writes: "From the superficial to the deep—The 'conscious' is conscious precisely in order to hide the unconscious. The prevalent idea gets its strength from that which it disguises."[28] Even if philosophy draws towards the psyche, then, there is no original disguised event that can be undisguised, undone, or rendered explicit.

Inasmuch as the psyche is understood in terms of an impressional consciousness, as Emmanuel de Saint Aubert says, it implies level, size, or modulation.[29] Just like the depths of sculptural shapes and bodies in which any positional alteration in relation to it only generates other depths, so too when we draw the psyche into explicit awareness it has yet other resources. The psyche finds itself in mutation with respect to certain visible contours, modulated according to its topology, in just the same way as is depth. I would even suggest here that Merleau-Ponty anticipates a similar reading of Freud's posthumous note "*Psyche is ausgedehnt, weiss nichts davon*" that Nancy gives in the first reading of *Corpus*.[30] He also anticipates that the body contains a limit, which is impossible to sense—an interdiction to touch it. Merleau-Ponty nonetheless differs, as we have already seen, on the nature of this ignorance and interdiction.[31]

The Positive Symbol, Psyche, and λέγειν

The psyche describes the shape or contour—a limit both indistinct from the very identity it limits and confrontational with another identity. The psyche, in other words, delimits and is between or in the midst of the very identities it produces. If this psyche is also associated with the first material principle of fire, it describes the immanental limit between what shows up in the light and our ability to see within that same light. Though the psyche is never itself illuminated or illuminable, it does not oppose or synthesize the illuminated aspects of the phenomena. The psyche is in language in the same way. It takes λόγος away from an association with νόμος and reintroduces it to the more felicitous sense of λέγειν. Here λέγειν is not just verbal expression, the utterances of sounds, or signifying meaning. It also concerns their existential circumstances and involvement in a sensible world that is itself rife with tensions and paradoxes. The limit or psyche of discourse is, then, caught up in these tensions and paradoxes. What makes separate things distinct from one another is in other words also the limit of language and what makes it appear distinct from the sensible world. In a passage of *The Visible and the Invisible* that deliberately echoes Lacan, Merleau-Ponty says "language is not a mask over Being" but is instead the "most valuable witness to Being" to the extent that being is "structured as a language."[32] This is taken to extreme, beyond the regional problem Merleau-Ponty says it is in Lacan's formulation,[33] as soon as being is itself conceived in a diacritical sense and as what separates and delimits identities.

Derrida notes the sensible limit in Nancy in the chapter titled "'To self-touch you': Touching—Language and the Heart" from *On Touching—Jean-Luc Nancy*. There, he writes about the heart:

The heart is one of those interior surfaces of the body that, in principle (unless one performs the unimaginable, at least for now, operation of open-heart surgery on oneself), no "self-touching" can ever reach—what might be termed the heart's hide. A thinking of touch must at least go through a theory of skin. Now, what is skin, the pellicular, *peau*, peel, pelt, fell, or hide? In *Corpus*, Nancy has invented *expeausition*, a great and necessary word. . . . The heart: absolute intimacy of the limitless secret, no external border, absolute inside, crypt for oneself of an untouchable self-interiority.³⁴

Derrida says quite explicitly that the absolute intimacy Nancy has in mind differs from Merleau-Ponty and the overlapping of the flesh. This intimacy, Derrida notes, "is a limit that also becomes its own limit."³⁵ A limit that limits itself means that it is self-intimate and does not overlap or coincide with other things but is a proper separation and other. Even if this limit is the heart inside of me, in other words, it is nonetheless alien to me. It may at first feel like a passivity but can at any time turn out to be entirely active. That is of course what Nancy notes about his own heart attack in "The Intruder." In each limit there is an "effraction of the other," a "syncope," a "gap or dilation without return," which "does not let itself be gathered up or contracted in the relation to self."³⁶ If language contains a sensible limit, this means for Nancy that it contains a radical separation. Merleau-Ponty, too, indicates a syncope in language. His notion of the *écart* does not however alternate pure passivity and pure activity but rather pertains to the primordial passivity. Merleau-Ponty would call this passivity "the limit of language."

There are two terms adopted from Paul Valéry that are significant here: "chiasma" and "implex." The former refers to the intercrossing of the optic nerve as well as to the rhetorical structure in which two clauses are balanced against one another and then again appear in reverse order. If the sensible world and language are chiasmatic, this mean not only that they intercross but also that they balance against and reject one another. The sensible world and language are chiasmatic, in other words, because they are as much pushed apart as they are drawn together. The second term, "implex," elaborates the push and pull between language and the sensible world and refers to an inability of language to directly refer to the space of this. It thus has to do, for Valéry, with a theory of language in which the poetic is above the prosaic.³⁷ When Merleau-Ponty uses this term in the reference above, what is especially clear is that it refers to an "animal of words" that is impossible to indicate directly because of the kind of space it involves. This space is not only behind my back, but above, below, and in front. When I refer to something as "behind me," for example, I transform the intimacy of that space into something foreign. I have, in other words, made what is behind me frontal. What was previously displaced is reduced to a place, and the symbolism of displacement itself dissipates. A similar thing happens when I refer to my heart as inside me instead of also foreign to me. I reduce a non-personal aspect of my person to the inside of my person, and thus a displacement—the fact that at the most concrete level I am never present to myself—dissipates.

Such dissipation nonetheless also has a productivity. As soon as I speak, for example, my tongue and larynx suddenly appear divergent to my interior. As soon as I write, my hands suddenly appear for just a practical purpose and opposed to a free ability to call forth a whole language system. When I speak to someone else, we can agree that our discussion is "about something," but the very basis on which this agreement is may never itself be in question.[38] The implex highlights that language in fact requires a lack of intention or intentional agreement, and only on the basis of this does intention or intentional agreement appear in language. This is a raw or promiscuous symbolic emblem that makes, for example, the relation between the signifier and the signified possible.

In a slightly different context, Merleau-Ponty calls this symbolic emblem an "unspeaking speech."[39] The unspeaking speech generally refers to interior monologue. It refers, more specifically, to Freud's observation that when we dream we are talking; there are in fact no words and neither signifier nor signified is needed. This leads one to think that the unspeaking speech is possible because consciousness is directed to itself and does not need specific and discrete signs or even signification. But, for Merleau-Ponty, the connection between dreams and the primordial passivity, and the fact that passivity intervenes in dreams, already undermines such intentions and replaces them instead with a being in divergence that is capable of intervention. The unsaid is similarly neither a signifier nor a signified but intervenes within discrete signs and even signification. It is less an inner monologue, then, and more a passivity functioning as the symbolic emblem and intercepting intentional relations in language. This moment always remains mute not per se because it is where language and world coincide but rather the opposite. It is unsaid, that is, because there is no summative point between language and the sensible world. If passivity remains unsaid, it is because it is a displacement that runs through both language and the world.

This is to say that passivity is diacritical and structured like a language, and because of this both dissipates and produces—at once both repressed and expressed. When I speak and refer to a thing, for example, and thus express a relation between language and it, in the same moment my mouth and tongue become irrelevant and non-obvious to this referral. When I write, suddenly my hand and arm become less important and secondary to what the inscribed words say, and thus they are repressed. When I discuss a matter with someone, the tacit situation on the basis of which we can talk is likewise non-obvious and repressed. If, for Merleau-Ponty, the passive situation in all these examples is the delimitation of both language and world, then this situation is what, in the implex passage above, he calls a "censor-repression struggle." It is the very struggle between expression and repression. As the censor or as what limits this struggle, it is neither the direct nor indirect meaning, neither the explicit sensible meaning nor the implicit virtual meaning, but the very symbolic form according to which the various meanings are possible.

When Merleau-Ponty attributes the discovery of "oneiric structure of thinking" to Freud, he means that the limit of thought is productive of thought but itself always unthought. This symbolic form, he says, is thus "a pre-notion" and "not a notion."[40] If the limit of both expressive language and the repressed sensible world is for Merleau-Ponty the symbolic form of signification, it is not itself a notion of signification but what is effaced in all notions of signification. For example, the changes to the Homeric diphthong I discuss in the first chapter may ultimately be both practical and conceptual: a mutation occurs at both the conceptual levels of language, the syntactical and lexical, as well as at its concrete and practical elements, syncopation and meter. But, as a pre-notion, this mutation is precisely what is deleted in the thought of a difference between practical and conceptual language. This becomes more than a claim about symbolism and language. If the symbolic form limits and generates the structure of signification, it itself resists signification and delimits thought in general. The question is what kind of critique such a limit deserves or even whether it can be critiqued at all. It would be, after all, the limit of thought and even the limit of ordinary critique.

The Positive Symbol in Philosophy: Analysis and the Analyzed

In the lecture note titled "Symbolism," and with reference to Freud's work on dream interpretation and Jensen's "Gradiva," Merleau-Ponty addresses "[t]he science of the world and the science of dreams."[41] He thinks that these sciences cannot be the same, and that a science of dreams should not be reduced to the causal structure of the former science. Yet these sciences are also not completely distinct since this would imply the already theoretical claim that, in the science of dreams, the object of analysis is not in the world but a negation of it. The implication would thus be that there is a science of the negation of the world. This science would be dedicated to the various operations involved in such negation as if they can be disclosed by themselves.

Yet, as Merleau-Ponty remarks about Sartre, symbolism "consists in embodiment and the relation with others," and thus, for example, "projection and introjection are not operations of a 'consciousness.'"[42] The science of projection and introjection would thus involve at the same time a science of the world. Only now, Merleau-Ponty says, this new science no longer begins from the "rigorous distinction between the 'sensory' and the 'non-sensory'"[43] but rather from "Being and oneirism."[44] The science of symbolism implies, that is, an ontology that should allow us to "pose the problem of the imaginary and the real" in which it is no longer a question, "1) Of distinguishing them absolutely... 2) Nor, of course, of confusing them."[45] Merleau-Ponty writes the following with this ontology in mind:

> [W]hat prevents the latent meaning from being stated openly is that the very idea of *openly* or of *exactitude* makes no sense here, not simply because we are in the imaginary (formal reason), but because the unity is undivided. This sex is not sex because it is everything—ignored as sex because it is everything.[46]

In the ontological question of the imaginary and the real it is a matter of latent and explicit meaning intervening into one another. It is a matter of their unity, and of this unity being everything and everywhere. But this expanse and unity between the imaginary and the real is irreducible to formalism. The science of dreams and the science of the world are never going to be unified through a systematic appeal to their unity. Even when Freudian metapsychology seems to be guided by the notion that sexual desire structures the psyche, according to Merleau-Ponty this sex is not nowhere but everywhere. In this passage, as in other ones, the "everywhere" implies that it excludes no region so that this sexual desire is always particularized and in a context. The "everywhere" also implies here, then, that such sexual desire is not deterministic.

In fact, neither is Freud's reading of the unconscious *as* sexual desire a predetermined. In his preface to Hesnard's *L'Oeuvre de Freud*, published in 1960, Merleau-Ponty wonders whether psychoanalysis and phenomenology should instead mark a "converging" since they both provide an "archeology" of latent content.[47] This convergence, he notes, would guard against the "idealist deviation of Freudian research."[48] Here, Merleau-Ponty echoes remarks he made in the passivity lectures and his comment on "complete psychology" in "*La philosophie aujourd'hui.*" Now we see that a complete psychology demands the reorientation of both psychoanalysis and phenomenology. It allows phenomenology to give way to the psychoanalytic claim of a symbolic component that limits the deliberation of the individual. While it allows psychoanalysis to become ontological even to the degree that it may be concerned with the limits of thought itself. To the extent that an ontological symbolism is now concerned with the symbolic limit of analyses rather than the terms of these analyses themselves, it poses these analyses as in the "timber yard."[49] This is to say, that according to an ontological symbolism, analyses are understood as a work that produces its analyzed content—understood, that is, to sediment its latent content as "what it studies" and "attempts to make explicit." This avoids the duplicity between the analyzed latent content and the analysis that makes this content explicit. It avoids having two opposite sides to signification—on the one hand a repressed latent content that expresses by concealing itself, and on the other hand the expression of analysis so completely different from repression that it can unconceal latent content. Merleau-Ponty in fact wants to deny that analysis has a completely active power distinct from the latent content it analyzes, and he wants to deny that this latent content is passive and completely subjugated by analysis. He denies, for example, any "phenomenological positivism."[50] An ontological symbolism is instead an analysis of analysis in the act of sedimentation.

This is because the moment of sedimentation between analysis and the analyzed *is* the symbolic form. This is also to say that the symbolic form is not more than its specific formation. If the symbolic form is the sedimentation between analysis and analyzed, this means its ontology demands a novel analysis proper to it. Such an analysis will have to account for this reciprocity without however falling prey to the problem of ordinary analysis—without conceiving itself as an analysis that achieves the full expression of latent content. Quite remarkably, then, Merleau-Ponty calls for a,

> [m]ethod proper to the understanding of dreams: reverie over dreams, hermeneutical reverie. Because it is not something said, but an echo through totality. It is this system of echoes which also constitutes the oneirism of wakefulness (cf. Blanchot's unspeaking speech).[51]

This hermeneutical reverie will have to be executed in some way that exceeds the confines of ordinary critique. From the beginning, ordinary critique assumes distinctions such as being and non-being or dream-perception and sense-perception. It remains ignorant of these distinctions as already having been limited and formed by a symbolic form. The hermeneutical reverie, on the other hand, is analysis of a symbolic form in the act of limitation and formulation and cannot begin with what ordinary critique takes for granted. Neither will it attempt to clarify what is taken for granted in ordinary critique. It will not clarify, for example, the non-being of dreams apart from the being of the world. In fact, it will clarify neither non-being nor being and is properly speaking not clarificatory at all. This is why Merleau-Ponty calls for reverie to be a method. But this reverie is still hermeneutical and will therefore not be uncritical. It is critical in a different sense than the critique of a speculative philosophy of reflection, which deduces from experience its necessary conditions. One could say instead that a hermeneutical reverie amounts to a sort of psychoanalysis of the philosophy of reflection and indeed of philosophy in general. Like Merleau-Ponty suggested in the earlier institution lecture titled, "Artistic Creation as Institution," here he is again claiming that a truly critical thought, concerned with the very limits of ordinary critique, must recognize itself as formed by a symbolism that is always overdetermined; and it must also offer a method of analysis adequate to this recognition.

Some Remaining Questions

A hermeneutical reverie would be crucial to a symbolic form applicable to both latent analyzed content and explicit analysis of it. It would be crucial to the symbolic form that intervenes on both imaginary and real. But the hermeneutical reverie would also seem to require a singular mode of expression capable of grasping the limit of thought. That is, it would seem to emphasize the poetic. In her introduction to Merleau-Ponty's recently published lectures, *Recherches sur l'usage littéraire du langage*, Benedetta Zaccarello notes that, for Merleau-Ponty, literary language "falls under the sign of doubt, questioning, and the difficulty of forging a language, rather than adapting it to an intention of meaning given beforehand."[52] It would seem, in other words, that for Merleau-Ponty the literary usage of language effects a phenomenological reduction on language in general, and that the former serves as an analytic of the latter. For example, Merleau-Ponty repeatedly returns to Stendhal during his lectures because he thinks that, more than anyone else's, Stendhal's writing teaches us that subjectivity is constituted in the act of writing and shaping language and in fact cannot be found otherwise.[53] Whereas, in a merely philological concern with it, language is submitted to some initial meaning that hovers above it.[54] Even more problematic is the philosophical employment of language. Here the use of conceptual language to clarify ideas assumes a subject automatically capable of going straight to the internal meaning of language. It assumes, in other words, that the subject commands meaning. But Merleau-Ponty is struck by the fact that thought has to happen in language and is possible only in the middle of it. The literary activity of forging a language tells us that any anonymity in language has less to do with a pre-existent and pre-given meaning than with a mutation of meaning available only through that language.

The question famously posed by Émile Bréhier to Merleau-Ponty seems wholly appropriate in this light: why is phenomenology not better served by art and literature? But if indeed literature operates a reduction, it would not be a matter of switching out one kind of language for another, just as phenomenology does not per se replace the natural subject with another subject. Had Merleau-Ponty followed Bréhier's suggestion, he would in fact end up eliding the philosophical worth of literature. There is a philosophical reason, in other words, that Merleau-Ponty did not write literature under his own name. He in fact rejects Sartre's claim that, because it acquires its creative and prosaic meaning from a free play of words, literature has both an aesthetic and revolutionary role. Sartre is most critical of Bataille, Blanchot, and the surrealists, for example, because he thinks they do not understand the difference between reality and imagination radically enough and consequently miss the revolutionary potential of literature. Merleau-Ponty rather thinks that literary language lives inside ordinary language and that they form a chiasm. He thinks that what is new in ordinary language can only appear and become a phenomenon through the literary transformation of language. He thus wants to explore instead the possibility of a middle way between the languages.[55]

As Zaccarello already notes, furthermore, the title of the 1953 lectures does not have to do with literature only but the literary use of language.[56] If an analysis of the literary use of language goes beyond literature, then in an important way *Recherches sur l'usage littéraire du langage* goes beyond the inclination to make poetic language a reduction on language in general. This suggests the point Merleau-Ponty makes in his 1961 lecture *"L'ontologie cartésienne et l'ontologie d'aujourd'hui,"* given during his last course at the Collège de France, that contemporary culture is described by a convergence between the art forms—the novel, painting and cinema.[57] This convergence, Merleau-Ponty says, is in fact architectonic or ontological and presents a "spontaneous philosophy."[58] The lectures on literary language not only indicate a convergence between the languages but also a generation and novelty of language. This novelty is just the constellation of linguistic forms.

It is in this context that I read the following passage of *The Visible and the Invisible*, which appears just past the middle of the book:

> Language in forming itself expresses, at least laterally, an ontogenesis of which it is a part. But from this it follows that the words most charged with philosophy are not necessarily those that contain what they say, but rather those that most energetically open upon being, because they more closely convey the life of the whole and make our habitual evidences vibrate until they disjoin. Hence it is a question whether philosophy as the re-conquest of brute or wild being can be accomplished by the resources of the eloquent language, or whether it would not be necessary for philosophy to use language in a way that takes from it its power of immediate or direct signification in order to equal it with what it wishes all the same to say.[59]

The initial claim here, that language formally expresses something more than itself, is already familiar. Merleau-Ponty is reiterating that language both refers to a meaning and is unable to elucidate this meaning in full. It does not however follow that meaning preexists language and that the examination of language is an examination of meaning: "[T]he examination of the significations in themselves," Merleau-Ponty says, "would give us the world reduced to our idealizations and our syntax."[60] The fact that language refers to the very meaning it is unable to elucidate only means that it is incapable of circumnavigating itself to say something beyond it. It is better to say, in other words, that language signifies through some retrospective and sedimenting view. In fact, the subject appears to itself in retrospective view of language as well. If it were true that the subject is free from language, there would be no reason to speak and write since thought could directly signify what it means. But if language is incapable of expressing a meaning beyond it, then the very notion that there is a subject who thinks independently of language appears only in the context of language. Merleau-Ponty makes this an ontological claim: language, he says, is "ontogenesis."

What Merleau-Ponty wants to show, in other words, is that language generates meaning and its referent, that this meaning and referent appear in light of language, and thus that this meaning and referent are never the condition of language. In effect, he wants to show a matrix:

that, in the very generation and determination of its meaning, language possesses an indeterminate, unsignified, and unsignifiable meaning. That there is an ontogenesis of language, but this ontogenesis is not what language is about. This is what lies at the heart of both "the paradox of being"[61] and "the paradox of expression"[62] and what reveals them as one and the same paradox. The reconciliation between being and non-being is impossible in language since it is language that generates the paradox and where the paradox is recognized. There is likewise no language that can undo itself and analyze its own emergence and retrieve what makes us speak and write. This is because language is in fact at every ontological tier: there is no being that antedates it but rather their relation is the reverse. That is, language is the limit of ontology. If there is an ontogenesis of language, then, this undermines the very notion that language is "about something" and even that it has a denotational structure.

This is to say, language is organized around a disorder, which, in determining the meaning of this disorder, it deforms and makes coherent. Merleau-Ponty very often borrows from André Malraux the phrase "coherent deformation."[63] The phrase implies that coherence at once deforms, that form is a deformation of the deformed. If phenomenology must show language as a deformation of the deformed, it will have to take this matrix of language to its most extreme limit. In doing so, it poses a fundamental issue, of which Merleau-Ponty indeed seems aware: "But then I will have to disclose a non-explicated horizon: that of the language I am using to describe all that—And what co-determines its final meaning."[64] What language, Merleau-Ponty asks here, would disclose all this? What language could possibly reveal the ontogenesis of language that no language could ever be about?

The answer is: none. Or, rather, none in particular. Merleau-Ponty suggests that the eloquent and the philosophical have to be written into one another. He denies any essential difference between these languages. But he seems to think that this denial is in fact the disclosure of the impossible limit of language. This should inform his claim that, when it comes to language, the impossibility of the reduction *is* the reduction and that this impossibility reveals a savage ontology.[65] The eloquent language does not reveal an essential poetic truth of language. While conceptual language does not clarify otherwise eloquent language and make its poetic meaning static. The "non-explicated horizon" refers not only to the fact that there is a horizon of language that cannot be explicated or that is inexplicable. It also situates Merleau-Ponty's phenomenology of language as an indirect phenomenology that concerns the entirety of language. If ontology is indirect, and as such a transversal slice of both non-conceptual and conceptual usages of language, it shows that there never is an original meaning to which language is directed or from which it is originated. It shows that language has no start or finish, is dispersed throughout the signified and the signifier or the conscious and the unconscious, and belongs instead to an ontology "as on the first day."

It is important to consider in this context that some of Merleau-Ponty's most central philosophical notions are taken right from literature: in addition to "chiasma" from Valéry,[66] "coherent deformation" from André Malraux,[67] even "flesh of the world" comes from Claude Simon.[68] We know too from Claude Lefort's introductory and editorial remarks for *The Prose of the World* that Merleau-Ponty intended for the book to contain a second section with studies of Stendhal, Proust, Valéry, Breton, and Artaud, and a third section that considered the redefined notions of poetry and prose in terms of the world in general.[69] He also writes the following in a note titled "Philosophy and Literature":

> Philosophy, precisely as "Being speaking within us," expression of the mute experience by itself, is creation. A creation that is at the same time a reintegration of Being: for it is not a creation in the sense of the commonplace *Gebilde* that history fabricates: it knows itself to be *Gebilde* and wishes to surpass itself as *pure Gebilde*, to find again its origin. it is hence a creation in a radical sense: a creation that is at the same time an adequation, the only way to obtain an adequation.
>
> This considerably deepens Souriau's views on philosophy as supreme art: for art and philosophy together are precisely not arbitrary fabrications in the universe of the "spiritual" (of "culture"), but contact with Being precisely as creations. Being is what requires creation of us for us to experience it. Make an analysis of literature in this sense: as inscription of Being.[70]

Merleau-Ponty cannot make any of these claims in a direct way. He does not in the end "make" an analysis of literature in this context. As a result, at the end of *The Visible and the Invisible*, he seems to use Proust as an analogy for his own phenomenological insights. But this contradicts the claim that Proust offers a hermeneutical reverie and thus also a method phenomenology should follow. Merleau-Ponty also does not say his philosophy effects a "supreme art"—a philosophy that creates the very being which runs through us and which, through this very creation, is *then to be* experienced. But, I suggest, the literary phrases that characterize Merleau-Ponty's late ontology do in fact open lines of previously impossible conceptual analyses. For example, they introduce an ontology of embodiment beyond the lived-body discovered through rigorous description. If so, this should also give us grounds to reconsider the role of Proust in ontology.

The issue is, in other words, not whether Merleau-Ponty takes us back to the original event of expression, or to an ontology before language, but whether in writing the non-conceptual and conceptual languages into one another he effects an event of expression and therefore also shows its ontological limit. As "Baudelaire already said," Merleau-Ponty notes, "there are finished works which we cannot say have ever been completed, and unfinished works which say what they meant. What is proper to expression is to never be more than approximate."[71] Does Merleau-Ponty follow what is proper to expression? That is, does he not event it and at this very moment retrace it? This is again a matter of the symbolic form of critique.

Chapter 5

Philosophical Language—Literary Language

One of the dominant themes in Sartre's *What Is Literature?* is recognition.[1] The author writes, Sartre says, for recognition in Hegel's sense: for the sake of mutual recognition between one consciousness and another. The reader also reads in the hopes of satisfying a desire for recognition between consciousnesses. The literary work, on this view, requires in its very creation the freely given collaboration of author and reader. For this reason, Sartre thinks literature gives a picture of a socialist politics that involves the future participation and mutual recognition of free equals. Behind this politics, though, is a theory of what Sartre calls "disclosure" of consciousnesses in general[2]: literature expresses what would otherwise be repressed, whereas ordinary language represses what would otherwise be expressed. Merleau-Ponty, on the other hand, thinks that literary and ordinary language cannot be without each other and are always mutually imbricated. This entails a double bind: when literary language phenomenalizes what is novel in ordinary language, it also represses other possible forms of ordinary language. This of course means that ordinary language also suppresses literary language and even other possible forms of itself. This does not mean, however, that Merleau-Ponty undermines the connection between language and politics, only the connection between language and Sartre's idealist politics. Ultimately, for Merleau-Ponty, the connection between language and politics requires a practical politics, a politics that requires continual effort. Since it continually represses other political forms such as idealism or fascism and could always be otherwise, it needs to always work to uphold itself.

Sartre also makes a series of distinctions between art forms in his essays on writing and literature. Most importantly, he distinguishes poetry, which falls on the side of painting, sculpture, and music, from prose. The latter, he writes, is "committed writing." It "uses" language to an end. For his part, Merleau-Ponty points out in his *"L'ontologie cartésienne et l'ontologie d'aujourd'hui"* lecture that contemporary culture marks a convergence of the arts. To take this broader view is to deny a special role to prose writing. The very fact of this convergence, according to Merleau-Ponty, amounts to an ontology that would seem to abide a double bind similar to that between languages: this ontology is "spontaneous"—it is in some sense emergent and new—as well as evidence of an ontology before ontology. That is, it is "primitive" as Merleau-Ponty might say. I argue that such an ontology results from the pursuit of philosophy "from behind philosophy" or a philosophy "as on the first day." To the extent that this spontaneity is a-philosophical, Merleau-Ponty cannot make sense of it as purely poetic or metaphorical. These, I think, fail to explain both the double bind of languages and ontology. They result instead in some notion of self-identity—in the case of language a unified power of signification and in the case of ontology a unified being—before difference. On the other hand, what Merleau-Ponty calls the "hermeneutic reverie" in Freud and Proust does not prize the poetic and metaphor above all. The hermeneutical reverie is critical philosophy insofar as it is concerned with the limits of thought, though it understands the spontaneity of these limits not ideologically but as in a reverie: as the continuous delimitation between one thing and another, these limits are themselves alterable. This non-ideological ontology is in effect a primordial or positive symbolic form; and it will evidence equally in both indirect and direct language but resist the position of some further truth beyond them.

Ontology, Not Metaphorical Ontology

Renaud Barbaras's argues in "Métaphore et Ontologie" that being is equivalent to metaphor, and in particular, that *écart* is an "originary metaphoricity."[3] He argues that the *écart* itself allows us to understand how a thing may be "another thing while also not being that other thing," and this "permits us to remove the paradox [of being] in such a way that a being would never be itself except in not fully being itself."[4] This only at first glance makes ontology antithetical to self-identity since, in its initial situation, being is always other to itself and therefore dispersed amongst visible things.

To say that ontology operates at the level of metaphor and vice versa is to deny the difference between being and non-being and between ontology and the language that expresses it. Barbaras wants to deny the division between linguistic and sensible plenitudes that opens up when metaphor is understood according to its classical conception in rhetoric. Aristotle writes in *Poetics*, for example, that "to be happy in the use of metaphors," involves the, "discernment of resemblances," and consists in bringing previously "remote" terms together so that they suddenly appear "close." This definition of metaphor involves showing a new kinship between heterogeneous ideas so that they "make sense."[5] In particular, it involves the transfer of sense from the everyday use of a word or words to another use; and in this transfer the sensible world is substituted with a linguistic one. As Ricoeur points out, furthermore, there is nothing to prevent us from extending this definition of metaphor to the level of sentence and to refer to metaphorical statements. Here, the transfer of sense bears on language itself to destroy the consistent or lexical meanings of the terms it employs.[6] This in turn implicates in metaphor a "semantic innovation" and a new use of the imagination that is non-logical and opposite to the coherent use of the imagination in everyday language.[7] Whereas for Barbaras the "paradox" is at the level of the phenomenon, I would argue its ontological removal works in the same way as metaphorical statements and implies a non-logical innovation and elision of the difference between being and non-being. This elision is, however, nowise in the visible or in expression. For example, I do not directly witness precisely where or when the real and the imaginary converge. I note, following Derrida, that metaphysical language requires its negative concepts to be raised to the level of reality while metaphor is demoted to pure fiction and to negatives that are unreal.[8] While Barbaras's notion of an originary metaphor works in exact measure in the reverse: it implies that being and non-being are brought together and that this is an ontological creation independent of the visible and its expression. But, problematically, this is ontological difference *as such*.

It is crucial that Barbaras calls the convergence between ontology and metaphor "originary." Although he claims to transgress the limit of metaphor according to Ricoeur, for whom it differs from ontology, in the end he does so by saying this ontology bears the rules of metaphor and marks a convergence with poetry as opposed to the scientific discourse that essentially veils being.[9] Yet Merleau-Ponty is quite clear on the issue: "There is no *metaphor* between the visible and the invisible."[10] Consider, furthermore, this passage from his "Indirect Language and the Voices of Silence":

> A language which only sought to reproduce things themselves would exhaust its power to teach in factual statements. On the contrary, a language which gives our perspectives on things and cuts out relief in

them opens up a discussion which does not end with the language and itself invites further investigation. What is irreplaceable in the work of art? What makes it far more a voice of spirit, whose analogue is found in all productive philosophic or political thought, than a means to pleasure? The fact that it contains, better than ideas, matrices of ideas—the fact that it provides us with symbols whose meaning we never stop developing.[11]

Merleau-Ponty's thesis here is that the sense of language is always overdetermined by a meaning that is inexhaustible and ever different. But he does not say that this meaning is itself innovative or that it is veiled by scientific discourse. The reference to art and creativity here is akin to Merleau-Ponty's reference to art, noted last chapter, in the context of sleep and primordial passivity. Because it is nothing less than symbolism or oneirism itself, and therefore manifest through difference, this primordial passivity is neither externally caused nor internally self-causing. To draw a connection between language and this primordial passivity therefore implies that language does not simply come from the world but neither does it cover that world. In other words, Merleau-Ponty accepts that language and ontology operate at the same level, but he denies the outright distinction between kinds of discourses, where the scientific veils ontology and the poetic is ontology. He suggests that *within* the sense of conceptual and scientific language there is already some non-conceptual meaning allowing it to extend beyond the world of facts and to be altered. If a non-conceptual meaning alters conceptual language, then, it is not through the collapse of logical space and the sudden novel announcement of non-logical space. In general, I think, for Merleau-Ponty language transgresses both scientific and poetic discourse and is a matrix between them. In fact, his formulation of language seems broader than originary metaphor since he defines it precisely in terms of its chiasm between its conceptual and non-conceptual usages. One should not take Merleau-Ponty's references to the figured, figurative, or figuration to refer only to metaphor.

The difference between figurative and metaphorical language is however difficult to decipher. Ricoeur points out, for example, that the word "figure" as it is used to describe language (linguistic figure, figure of speech, figure of language, etc.) is already a metaphor.[12] The metaphor of the figure indicates that, because language makes sense of disparate and juxtaposed terms that do not go together in common reference, it has its own space and shape. In other words: the word "figure" is itself a spatial metaphor we use to indicate that metaphor requires a totally new use of the imagination in language. It is therefore said that the spatial metaphor is itself already the result of a transfer of sense from sensible to linguistic space. It is already a use of the imagination to indicate this very use of the imagination in language, and already the destruction of the concepts that are consistent or lexical to indicate very ability of language to exceed itself in this way. In this case, the metaphor of a figure expresses a notion otherwise impossible to express and forms the circumference of a purely linguistic space and its own imagination.

Merleau-Ponty has to deny this kind of suspense if he thinks meaning configures sense from within it. As an internal delimitation instead, the spontaneity of meaning is not outside or apart from the everyday sense. The claim that language contains matrices works precisely because Merleau-Ponty does not pose non-conceptual language against conceptual language. He assumes instead a matrix that figures equally between both languages. There is a matrix in the languages to the extent that a non-concept continually intervenes in conceptual language and can never be made conceptual. In this sense, language announces a detour; we move through language without however knowing, or needing to know, every possible permutation of that language. This feature may be the basis for understanding language as a self-contained system of signs. But, following Merleau-Ponty, we can also question whether this chiasm would at the same time be the limit, mentioned last chapter, between articulation and the world that remains inarticulate or unspeakable. When we note that there is a symbolic matrix between speaking and the world, we note a symbolism at the very site where, as Merleau-Ponty says, "by a certain dehiscence the body opens up in two,"[13] exterior to my interior and inarticulate in my ability to articulate.

I mention earlier that Merleau-Ponty can follow Heidegger's claim that λόγος is originally associated with λέγειν, and even that λέγειν is in some sense a locus of otherwise disparate significations. But even if language brings disparate significations together, this does not mean for Merleau-Ponty that it itself is always already gathered. He does not abide the distinction between symbolic and concrete spaces. The apparently distinct matrices between a constellation of signs and a site of speech are for Merleau-Ponty anything but distinct. The ability for language independent of distinct significations does not cover over the fact that one exists in and between those significations, which are themselves deviated against one another. In effect, Merleau-Ponty refuses to use the spatial metaphor of a figure to describe the virtual character of language. This has repercussions for the chiasmatic structure between the languages to which he wants to return. To the extent that Merleau-Ponty finds this chiasm and matrix between the languages, he also finds a method of hermeneutical reverie adequate to a symbolism that is also ontological. It is this ontological symbolism that would be the limit of thought.

Finding a Hermeneutical Reverie with Proust

I want to mention here one of Miguel de Beistegui's arguments in *Proust as Philosopher* where he refers, through Proust, to a different definition of metaphor from the Aristotelian one that emphasizes innovation:

> For Aristotle, metaphor's a form of comparison, and this means that it's always geared towards extracting an identity from two distinct terms, a similarity from something dissimilar. It's another story altogether with Proust, who doesn't compare anything since what allows him to bring two terms or two series of terms together isn't of the same *kind* or *nature* of those terms or series in their respective, individuated and ordinary state, which alone can be compared with another. If we can still speak of something "similar" it's only in the sense of another level of reality that *emerges* from metaphor and emerges from it as its pre-individual horizon, thereby making it essentially different from a genus or a species. To my mind, metaphor will turn out to be the transposition of the poetic level of an otherwise philosophical issue, namely that of difference. The distinctiveness of metaphor lies in its ability to present or schematize difference: metaphor is the sensible figure of difference, its poetic schema.[14]

Proust, de Beistegui argues, effects a notion of metaphor in which differences do not have to conform to a novel sense that flaunts the rules of ordinary language. Rather than a sense produced from their convergence, for de Beistegui the Proustian metaphor expresses a level of existence in which differences are figured rather than reconciled. This metaphor articulates, in other words, an existential texture in which things are asymmetrical or irreconcilable, which then becomes the very basis for a poetic schema. If one concedes to this, one can also note that Proustian metaphor may also conform to the structure of chiasmus. In a chiasmatic poetics, for example, there is not a simple logic of crossing or exchange between two terms but rather a production of "continual movement" and "reverberation" that is "triggered by their arrangement in [a] mirror image format" as in "the fair is foul and the foul is fair."[15] The chiasmus has thus also been described as a "face-threatening act"[16] or even possessing an "asocial tendency" because it works through counter-position.[17] This counter-positioning prohibits complete identification and prevents a simple overlap between two opposing things or points of view. It therefore does not let us identify differences, identify with what is other to us, or allow for a final and shared experience, but only "offers stability only to oscillate and then to spin off something beyond the binary, something asymmetrical."[18] The chiasmus is for this reason also considered a "thoroughly multi-vocal trope."[19]

There is plenty of secondary literature on Merleau-Ponty and Proust. For the former, after all, Proust is in many ways a tutelary figure. Most of this literature, my own included, focusses on the usefulness of classic Proustian issues such as nostalgia and the effect of the past in the present or whether the present genuinely retrieves the past. In the same passage that Merleau-Ponty writes of an "architectonic time" and "indestructible past" in Proust, he also speaks of a "myth time." Here, he also notes, the past works according to institution.[20] In the narrative structure of myths, in other words, the past is both architectonic and indestructible because it configures itself in the present without explicitly announcing itself as such. The present, then, unbeknownst to it, comes face-to-face with its past and for this reason is neither self-sufficient nor lasting. This means, too, that there is a displacement between the two times. It is also useful, then, to highlight the reverse aspect of the chiasm between present and past in Proust, the effect the present has over the past. To the extent that the present is reconfigurable in terms of the past, this past means nothing in itself and is instead a plurality that works itself through times other than itself. One could say that, in Proust, the past and present are like the fair and foul in *Macbeth*. The search for lost time, as Joshua Landy writes,

> is not involuntary memory, not metaphor.... There is a further stage to be reached beyond it, namely the process of giving style to one's character in everyday life, reinterpreting, concealing, foregrounding, even inventing elements *de toutes pièces* if necessary, but optimally preserving as much of the given arrangement as possible and aiming for a maximal multiplicity beneath the single controlling principle.[21]

Indeed, Proust affirms this multiplicity in his letters when he writes: "As there is a geometry in space, so there is a psychology in time, in which the calculations of a plane psychology would no longer be accurate."[22] A psychology in time is in other words a depth psychology. This depth psychology evidences a chiasmatic texture of existence in which temporal moments, and indeed opposing arrangements in general, each supplant one another rather than flow directly through one another without any complication whatsoever. Merleau-Ponty:

> It is necessary to conceive all of what Freud has described (domination of the past and childhood, domination of oneself over the other) and Proust (if one is open to oneself then one is closed to oneself) not as the dogmatic explication of the human (there are forces of sublimation) but as hermeneutical reverie, introducing [some] unknown but not exclusive factors.[23]

In fact, where Freud comes to the margins of the ontological symbolism as an "unconventional thought," I want to suggest that Proust at least intimates the method of a hermeneutical reverie most proper to elaborating this symbolism. To this end, there are three issues that typically surround Proust and his work on which I would like to focus: whether Proust evidences a chiasm between conceptual and literary language; whether Proust evidences a chiasm between the real and the fictive; and, in this connection, whether Proust evidences a chiasm between localized space and non-localized time.

The Chiasm between Conceptual and Literary Language

Readers of *In Search of Lost Time* often note the difficulties in separating the book's descriptive sentences from those that are expressive. Proust was himself critical of description:

> [T]he sort of literature which is content to "describe things," to provide nothing more of them than a miserable list of lines and surfaces, despite calling itself realist, is the furthest away from reality, the most impoverished and depressing, because it ceremoniously cuts all communication between our present self and the past, the essence of which is retained in things, and the future, where things prompt us to enjoy it afresh. It is this that any art worthy of the name must express.[24]

He describes here what de Beistegui calls the "realist's lie."[25] The notion that descriptive language has a fealty to the real ignores the way in which language and the real do not in fact coincide. The realist's lie and descriptive language thus fall victim to Plato's prohibition of mimesis. Whereas, de Beistegui argues, Proust wants an "expressionist truth," and an expressive language that does not bear fidelity to the real as such but to its depths.[26] In committing itself to these depths, expressive language circumnavigates the logic of mimesis and Plato's prohibition. Though such language does not seem to give us the traditional sense of a philosophical truth, it is also not a literary lie. For it to avoid being a literary lie, however, literature for Proust also cannot be complete fabulation and abandon description altogether. One notices in *In Search of Lost Time* historical and biographical facts, the work of other writers and poets, descriptions of famous artworks, etc.

I note the similarity between the ambiguity of kinds of language in Proust and Merleau-Ponty's claim that phenomenology requires eloquent language. This phenomenology is no longer descriptive in Husserl's sense but becomes instead "an expression of experience by experience, which in particular clarifies the special domain of language." This is an issue of whether phenomenology can show that, when language expresses the world of experience, it sediments that world, and that this sedimentation is a limit of language produced by language—an internal delimitation of language itself rather than something preceding or other to it.

The Chiasm between the Real and the Fictive

The inability to fully distinguish the languages in Proust's work creates yet another ambiguity—namely, between the fiction of a novel and the realism of autobiography. It is often said that the fictional character of Marcel is an allegory for Proust himself, and that at the end of the novel, when Marcel is at last able to write the novel we have just read, the distinction between him and Proust is undermined. But at the end of the novel Marcel is also about to write the novel we have just read. It is this context, as Joshua Landy points out, that Marcel's fictional autobiography resides in the future perfect. It comes as no surprise, Landy remarks, that a novel such as Proust's, in which sentences delay their completion, the hero begins writing a novel without finishing it, and in which the world is a series of misconceptions, appropriately concludes with the adoption of a fictional future perfect perspective: "[W]e should not be asking what we are—for we will always only be a tangle of unfulfilled possibilities—but wondering, instead what *we will have been*," and it could be that, "Proust considers authentic selfhood to involve not just illusion but *lucid* illusion."[27]

Marcel is Proust's lucid illusion. He is also the person who, at the end of this illusion, is about to write what we have just read—setting out to accomplish what has just been accomplished. Whereas Proust is no one other than the person who writes *In Search of Lost Time*. Even if Marcel is on the way to becoming Proust, in other words, we should not think that Proust is Marcel. Their relation does not turn on some realist identification that would clear the ambiguity between the realism of autobiography and the fiction of a novel. In the above, the question was whether Merleau-Ponty's phenomenology, like Proust's own work, proceeds into the depth underneath both real things and the purely descriptive language we use to refer to them. This same question is now posed in terms of the real and the fictive. We know that Merleau-Ponty wants to expose their "exact relation" and that doing so involves an exposition of the positive symbol. In his institution lectures, he claims to want to avoid the philosophy of symbolic forms in favor of revealing the symbolic form of philosophical criticism.

Whereas for Proust the notion of identity revolves around a lucid illusion, for Valéry the idea of authorial intent in literature is, as Merleau-Ponty notes, the result of its "false illusions (*impostures*)."[28] Both the lucid and false illusion, it seems to me, asks us to resist a passive relation to the text, and to instead see both oneself and the author of the text as equally indebted to language.[29] One could say here that for Proust and for Valéry on Merleau-Ponty's reading, the literary work effects a double eclipse of both reader and author, to show instead a language neither inside nor outside us, neither absolutely proximate nor irremediably distant. The ambiguity between realist autobiography and fictive novel is never truly rectified in an objective or theoretical way. It is neither the author nor the reader that creates the meaning of a literary text but rather *language* that constitutes the meaning of both what is written and what is read. This meaning of this language belongs, in a certain sense, always to someone and someplace else: it is with her, over there, and only because of this alterity can words have sense.[30]

In his introduction to *The Visible and the Invisible*, and referring specifically to that text, Claude Lefort notes a similar medial aspect between author and reader:

> It is therefore not saying much to say that the work survives the writer, that, when its incompletion will be forgotten, we will know only the plenitude of its meaning. This plenitude is de jure. The work alone seems to have a positive existence, for, even though its fate be suspended on the decision of future readers to let it speak, at least each time they will turn to it, it will come to interpose itself, as on the first day, between him who reads and the world to which he is present, compelling him to question that world in it and to relate his own thoughts to what it is. Such is the fascination the finished work exercises on its reader that for a moment

it renders vain all recrimination of the death of the writer. The writer disappears just when he was preparing for new beginnings, and the creation is interrupted, forever beneath the expression it announced, from which it was to draw its final justification.[31]

Lefort's claim here is, I think, quite remarkable considering it is about a classic work of ontology. He says that, in this work, language intervenes between writer and reader and that this tentative position is in fact central to *The Visible and the Invisible* and the continuity of its meaning for us. This continuity rests on a language which, for the author, always fails to express and, for the reader, can always be reinvigorated. But this behavior of collapse and emergence turns out to also be the behavior of an ontological institution. That is, the work produces an ontology that is "as on the first day." Yet this ontology is not sui generis so much as it always demands an excursus each time new.

The Chiasm between Localized Space and Nonlocalized Time

Merleau-Ponty wants to consider philosophical critique as an alteration of symbolic form. But this still implies he wants to provide a philosophical critique. That is, he wants to show the limit of philosophy, and he thinks only a philosophy that recuperates itself in terms of its symbolic form will do this. It is this recuperation that I think Lefort recognizes in his description of a medial language between Merleau-Ponty's text and its readers. If this alteration transpires "as on the first day," this is because its very occurrence undermines the idea of a concealed being behind or other to the symbolic form of such a language. A symbolic event that happens as on the first day is, in other words, an event that is not parasitic on the difference between being and beings. This event is naïve, and it is rather the case that any ontological difference would depend on it. In that way, the symbolic is less some self-identity underneath beings than it is a matrix. It is less a singularity than a plurality. There is, in other words, no contradiction between the first day of a symbolic matrix and its adventure. One could also say that there is no ontological oblivion.

One should also stress here that for Merleau-Ponty the symbolic form is a matrix to the extent that it has the characteristic of anonymity. There is one passage in his passivity lectures, in a reference to Proust, which I believe elaborates the anonymity of a symbolic matrix in a special way. The passage appears, unsurprisingly, in "The Problem of Memory" lecture and reads:

> [The] past thus enclosed in the I can of my body, modalized in power without contact. Why do I speak of the body and not of consciousness? Because we cannot speak of consciousness, nothing to say about it, if it is truly nothing. One can only describe the phenomena of which it is the mainspring, the invisible lining, and which, moreover, it animates only by closely wedding them: my body, language. Sartre turns this nothingness into another being, a productivity.
>
> Cf. Proust's text on the reference of the surroundings to the body which inhabits them and of the past body to the present: they are variations of one another and the surroundings are an explication of them. But of course, the body is substituted here for consciousness only as the place of our eruption into the world. As empirical body, it is no less determined than determining (it "turns" in the course of the search)— We consider it as a vinculum of the temporal and spatial distance, and transformer of space into time: *Erinnerung*.[32]

Here, the matrix between space and time and that which produces temporality against the grain of spatiality is named *Erinnerung*. It is crucial to note the more literal translation of *Erinnerung*, which is "interiorization." That is, rather than memory, the matrix between space and time and the production of temporality against spatiality is a moment of interiorization by which some external horizon becomes an internal horizon. Whereas Husserl was unable to explain this vinculum, conceiving instead of an interior and neutral horizon of phantasy juxtaposed against a spatial horizon, here Merleau-Ponty pits Proust against such a view but does not simply reverse the terms. Indeed, interiorization depends on the fact that there is a body deposited into space and with a spatial horizon. But, where for Husserl phantasy is neutral, for Merleau-Ponty reading Proust this space and spatial horizon are not at all neutral. That is, they are not passively awaiting reception or merely to be recuperated. The body takes the place of consciousness, Merleau-Ponty writes, because it is where in fact the world erupts precisely as the world. This implies that there is the event of some installation whereby which space and time become distinct from one another as two separate horizons. It also implies that the place of this installment is not self-integral and merely non-visible but non-objective in a totally different sense. That is, interiorization is not from the outside per se but from a non-objective space by which the outside becomes what it is and counter-posed against the inside. In this way, I think, interiorization describes a primordial passivity and the same divergence that is sleep. In fact, I would even suggest, it is exactly where sleep delimits what appears and to whom it appears. In the "Proust-Memory" lecture, and after quoting at length some opening passages from *Swann's Way* that describe the middle state between sleeping and waking, Merleau-Ponty wonders how one regains one's orientation in the world from the previous disorientation of sleep and the immobility of things: "Someone will say, but he remembers. No, what is at issue is not a portion of recollections—or the recollections are themselves conditioned by something else, by a global view, by a system in which they are set up."[33]

The phenomenology of sleep is in effect concerned with site of convergence between the personal and the ontological. This explains Merleau-Ponty's enigmatic description of his ontology as "a sort of time of sleep."[34] To say that being is equal to time is to say it has an interior horizon that flows uninterruptedly and is an interior into which the space of particular things does not penetrate. It is also to say, then, that the space of particular things is equally undisruptive and has an interiority of its own and of a different sort than the interior of time. To say that being is the time *of sleep*, however, is to say that both this time and space, and their mutual exclusion from one another, involve at a more basic level an ontological disruption or divergence—for this is what sleep is—by which space and time can be seen as essentially distinct from one another. If Merleau-Ponty wants to perform a phenomenology of the "time of sleep," it is because he wants to examine ontology from inside ontology, where there is no ontological oblivion but rather a production—a dark sleep that lets time and space diverge.

Carbone writes about this "time of sleep" in "The Time of Half-Sleep: Merleau-Ponty between Husserl and Proust":

> Merleau-Ponty emphasizes that subjectivity is a *"fissure,"* not in the Sartrean sense of pure nothingness, of an emptiness or "hole" immediately filled with the plenitude of being, but in the sense of a "hollow," hollowed out precisely by the woof of sensible being's differentiations. In fact, this woof culminates by folding itself back into a sensible, which, on the other side—the side of absence of its presence to that being, the "spiritual side spoken" of by Husserl—is also sensing. By virtue of this, therefore, the sensible-sensing sketches a hollow inside the sensible by which the reflexivity of this very sensible exerts itself. [35]

If, as Carbone writes a little later, "Proust's work in its entirety, in fact, describe[s] a life without reflective consciousness, an experience emerging precisely as in sleep or in one of those states of half-sleep,"[36] it is because the work takes as its starting point neither the continuous flow of time nor an equally non-disruptive and objective exterior space.

To say that Proust's work is one of interiorization is not only to say that it exposes the "time of sleep." To the extent that the time of sleep is a hollow in the sensible world, it disrupts the simple separation between phantasy time and real space, between latent and explicit meaning, or even between indirect and direct signification. It thus also marks a rupture in the sensible world that at the same time intercepts language. One will notice from the previous chapter the confluence between the phenomenology of sleep and the phenomenology of language in that they ultimately expose resistance and censorship, a production that creates the difference between sensible and linguistic plenums and effaces itself in this production.

I am at last prompted to ask to what extent has Merleau-Ponty's phenomenology, as a philosophy that shows the symbolic form of philosophical critique, interiorized literary language and Proust's work specifically. What really is the relation between literary and philosophical language in his thought? This is a distinct question from whether poetic language performs a reduction on language in general. Whereas Merleau-Ponty gives the final say to Saint Exupéry in last section on freedom in *Phenomenology of Perception*, for example, literary phrases such as "chiasma," "coherent deformation," and "flesh of the world" appear in *The Visible and the Invisible* now as phenomenological insights. With these phrases, it seems, Merleau-Ponty's phenomenology is as wide open to the beginnings of philosophy as at beginnings of philosophy. This is as much a claim about a secret rupture of symbolism than it is about going back to this symbolism. On its own, the attempt to retrace and recuperate this symbolism as the limit of thought would be a failed project according to the very character of this symbolism. When Lefort suggests *The Visible and the Invisible* is in virtue of the symbolic form, this suggestion is in the spirit of the symbolic form itself. It implicates a symbolism, Lefort rightly points out, irreducible to its author and its reader and medial instead—neither proximate nor distant, neither interior nor exterior. Here we again come back to the issue of the symbolic form as a "negation of negation," or a positive constriction, which keeps it from being absolutely individuated or absolutely other. This is also a positive constriction that thus keeps language from being a free expression of what would otherwise be alien and completely repressed. Merleau-Ponty is more concerned instead to use language in a productive way so as to show itself as at once both expressing and repressing. Such a language will not be distinct from ontology but instead its inner-possibility and, in fact, the only way phenomenology might offer a new adventure in philosophy.

Some Remaining Questions

Where Sartre juxtaposes the role of literary and ordinary language, Merleau-Ponty claims that each is in fact inextricable from the other. If for Sartre literature alone has the capacity to be revolutionary, for Merleau-Ponty all language effectuates some transformation. There is nothing like a pure literature, according to him, for the simple reason that literary language expresses something already repressed in conceptual language. This of course also means that there is nothing like a pure conceptual language. Ultimately, for Merleau-Ponty, there is no pure language at all. This is why he has to reject poetic language as the analytic truth of language, the only language that can phenomenalize what is new in language in general. At last, Merleau-Ponty thinks, phenomenology must become a phenomenology *of language*. That is, it must disclose the expressive and repressive nature of both the literary and conceptual. It is on such grounds, I think, that the project of Proust's *In Search of Lost Time* is proximate to the project of Merleau-Ponty's later phenomenology. It is likewise on these grounds that Merleau-Ponty might think to write eloquent language into conceptual language and consequently to provide a language capable of transforming itself from out of itself.

To do this would not be to lose sight of a philosophical critique. Such philosophical critique would however indicate the profoundest correspondence between phenomenology and crisis. Where for Sartre the relation between literary and ordinary language turns on a notion of disclosure between consciousnesses, I think the chiasm between literary and conceptual languages in Merleau-Ponty's turns on a symbolic form that *cannot* be disclosed. This involves a claim about the central role of the symbolic form in Merleau-Ponty's ontology. If one language cannot be the analytic truth of the other, it is because of a symbolic form that is the ontological limit of both. While this limit produces both literary and conceptual language, it effaces itself in their separation. If it is the very condition of the thought of their difference, it lacks a precise destination or end. In the final analysis, that is, phenomenology recognizes itself as beginning and ending in crisis, at every step of the way constellated and animated by an impossible limit. It is on this basis that phenomenology also recognizes itself as in an adverse position.

The notion of crisis and adversity brings us to one more issue: if literature is for Sartre committed to a political project of mutual recognition between free equals, is there a political project for Merleau-Ponty's medial phenomenology of language? We know that this phenomenology aims to show the symbolic form of critique in general. But if there is such a similarity between Merleau-Ponty and Proust why insist so strongly that the former is still after philosophical critique? And to what is this critique committed? His project seems eminently dangerous and vulnerable to become some philosophy of un- or post-truth.

Conclusion

If the world has a coherent sense, it also has a non-sense. We are deposited equally into sense and non-sense, and, in fact, it is because of the latter that the world does have sense and appears senseful. This is what Merleau-Ponty calls the silence or mute meaning of the world. Such meaning cannot be clarified or apprehended according to the terms of sense. It cannot be suddenly given the form of sense, and to think that it could is precisely to misapprehend it. While the phenomenology of institution may be an elaboration of the mute meaning, it cannot *exhibit* it. This is to say that, for Merleau-Ponty, the meaning that lapses and slips out from sense also configures sense, recoils in it, but always remains mute. It is this most confounding relation between sense and meaning that makes the former alterable rather than essential.

Husserl conceives the relation between sense and meaning in terms of an inner-horizon of time consciousness. But, for Merleau-Ponty, this is not the most primordial association between between sense and meaning because it ignores the disruptive nature of a silent meaning within sense. This disruption implies an institution conceived in terms of an event that exceeds but also seizes the inner-horizon of time consciousness, and this problematizes the very notion that consciousness is continuous with itself and self-relational. It implies that the meaning with which we are ultimately concerned is also spatial, and not an objective space that would be unable to invade the interior life of any consciousness. This space is barbarous and wild rather than measurable. It surges up in our interior lives but refuses to be thematized. Where Husserl understands the continuity and self-relationality of consciousness in terms of phantasy, placing phantasy against space, Merleau-Ponty mentions Proust in the passivity lectures to problematize this consciousness, phantasy, and space. With Proust, Merleau-Ponty finds a space that, configurationally, makes both the inner-horizon of phantasy and the objective world of real objects. This space means but is not merely on the other side sense. It is properly generative, a space that does not abide sense at all but forms a matrix with it.

Sedimentation, Elementality

The term Merleau-Ponty uses to describe Proust's work, *Erinnerung*, is usually translated as "memory" but is more literally "interiorization." This term refers neither to the continuous flow of interior time nor to the undifferentiated exterior of real space, but rather to the very means by which the two are torn apart and confrontational with one another. It is less a mechanism than the event of some non-objective space that, while swelling and surging, articulates itself reflexively in terms of the fictive and the real. One could say that interiorization is akin to sleep, since sleep it is the divergence between latent and explicit meaning, and dreaming and waking, etc.

One finds these same insights in Merleau-Ponty's discussions of Schelling in the nature lectures, and specifically in his remarks on *Urwissen* in Schelling as the "symbol of primordial knowing." When Schelling associates the symbol of primordial knowing with light, for example, it is because this light is not itself luminescent so much as it is seen through and according to. Like the association symbolism has in the passivity lectures with a sleep that is between waking and dreaming, the symbol's association with light in the nature lectures implies some event impossible to apprehend except merely through what is evident or non-evident of it—through what is explicit or latent, shown or hidden. It makes the reflective stance on consciousness against objective space possible, then, but for its part penetrates everywhere and explores everything. The symbolic form is for this reason also morphogenetic or procreational. It is nowhere but in the production of the very terms of thought that prove impossible to apprehend it. In an important sense, then, the symbolic configures an impossible matrix even if it is not external to the terms of that matrix. This same impossibility is noted between consciousness and nature. Nature cannot be idealized: it is impossible for consciousness to become the nature of nature. Nor can consciousness be naturalized and for nature to be its interior: it is impossible for nature to be the consciousness of consciousness. This is to some extent already discerned in psychoanalysis: it is impossible for the son to be the father of the father, or for the infant to be the mother of the mother, but these impossibilities inform the relationships between generations. Imagine, though, if the relationship between generations was a matter of manifesting such impossibilities *as such*, if freedom for the son really was to become the father. The result would be repetition and stagnation.

The primordial symbol is not this for Merleau-Ponty. It is impossible, according to him, because it resists opposite terms and manifests them as what they are. It is for this reason interiorized and is interiorization itself. The symbol is not objective or else it could not invade the scene of subjective lives. It is not subjective or else what is eternal to the subject could not mean according to it. Interiorized into the intentional structures between such relations, the primordial symbol is, for its part, not an externally directing limit and is in fact not directedness in any sense. It is impossible, then, only because it invades, animates, and configures from within the lives of children and parents or consciousness and nature. The symbol intervenes like Merleau-Ponty says Freud himself intervenes in the life of Dora: "qua object for a transference in the imago of the father, [the symbol] intervenes in this constellation, but intervenes not in the context of the 'real' life ... but as a present-absent, revealer of this barrier."[1] That is, the symbol phenomenalizes the conflict between child and parent, or even between consciousness and nature, but is equally between these terms and is, as such, itself impossible to phenomenalize.

If the primordial symbol is the interiorization and sedimentation of intentional structures and itself non-intentional, this puts a phenomenology concerned with the genesis of these structures in a difficult position. Such a phenomenology risks misapprehending the very impossibility of the symbolic form if it is conceived according to the terms of the structures to which it gives rise. A phenomenology proper to the symbolic form would in fact have to take a stance against this risk and grasp it indistinctly from the visible and as the matrix between what appears and what does not. In this sense, the symbol has to be grasped in its ontological behavior even before it accords by the terms of ontological difference. It is therefore better, I suggest, to think of this ontological symbolism in Merleau-Ponty in terms of the elemental, which neither has nor is an exterior dialectical term. The elemental, and in particular the element of fire-light, does not oppose the illuminated phenomena but is within them even as it is not itself illuminable. This hiddenness is in fact the basis on which the phenomena are apparent. This is why I have argued Merleau-Ponty's references to the "incitement" and "spark" of fire in "Eye and Mind" are significant; these are the non-visible moments that show up both the sensing and the sensed. The elemental is in this way matrixed into the sensible. It delimits sensible things against each other as well as my sensations of those things. It is therefore promiscuous, runs a circuit, and resists origins and destinations. It is, in short, on an adventure and anonymous.

The Different Politics of Metaphor and Symbolism

In his 1949 "Note on Machiavelli," although now in terms of the power of authority and power, Merleau-Ponty seems to indicate a dynamic very much akin to the interiorization of a symbolic form. He writes in the *Note*, for example:

> There is no power which has an absolute basis. There is only a crystallization of opinion, which tolerates power, accepting it as acquired. The problem is to avoid the dissolution of this consensus, which can occur in no time at all, no matter what the means of coercion, once a certain point of crisis has been passed. Power is of the order of the tacit.[2]

If no power has an absolute basis or ground, this means no power gives itself absolutely. It follows, too, that no subject of power is absolutely receptive, and that power is never itself through recognition alone. With this, Merleau-Ponty avoids both the idea that power is completely self-authorizing and that it is a total chimera. It is in fact legitimated and made the dominating force it is though the subjects of that power, who thereby institute it by recognizing it. The institution of power and the recognition of power therefore ground each other. But this co-grounding only works when the subjects of power also fail to recognize that their recognition of it also institutes it—when they fail to see themselves within power. Thus Merleau-Ponty writes that, "power does not coerce or persuade; it thwarts—and we are better able to thwart by appealing to freedom than by terrorizing;"[3] and, "[t]he power which is called legitimate is that which succeeds in avoiding *contempt* and *hatred*."[4]

If the subject of power is to remain ignorant of its own role in power's institution, and if this power is to avoid being absolute and instead work through its subjects, power must play a deception of its own. In fact, Merleau-Ponty thinks this specific insight takes Machiavelli beyond the claim that power is either undergoing or exercising coercion and into the basic play of deception itself:

[W]hat is original about Machiavelli is that, having laid down the source of struggle, he goes beyond it without ever forgetting it. He finds something other than antagonism in struggle itself. "While men are trying not to be afraid, they begin to make themselves feared by others; and they transfer to others the aggression that they push back from themselves, as if it were absolutely necessary to offend or to be offended." It is the same moment that I am about to be afraid that I make others afraid; it is the same terror which threatens me that I spread abroad—I live my fear in the fear I inspire.⁵

Here Merleau-Ponty suggests Machiavelli gives us a politics that hints at its psychoanalytic and ontological origins. Even more radically, I think, what is original about Machiavelli for Merleau-Ponty is that he gives us a politics requiring and working *from within* its psychoanalytical and ontological origins. Merleau-Ponty does not however see the play of deception in power as an essential problem because he thinks there is no way out of it that does not lapse into total ideology, and there is no total ideology that is not fundamentally dogmatic. Rather, if the insight from Machiavelli is the ontological play of power itself, it is this same play by which our politics can or even ought to work. This involves a reorientation of the distinctions between our thought and its practice; it requires us "to rethink our political concepts in an ontological light and our ontological concepts in a political one."⁶ Politics and ontology, and practice and thought, can indeed be conceived in view of one another for Merleau-Ponty because in fact their scenarios are one and the same. In the political and practice, our experience of the authorial is the very means by which it becomes so; our experience of the authorial makes it so. In the ontological and thought, being and non-being or the concepts of the real and the fictive, are realized though a symbol that effaces itself in the recognition of these terms. Merleau-Ponty attributes this to the primordial or positive symbol. Thus, power, like being itself, cannot be absolute: it is impossible for absolute power to have a subject. Nor can the subject of power be the absolute of power: it is impossible for the subject to absolutely recognize a power that does not dominate it.

It is this ontological symbolism, I also argue, of which metaphor remains ignorant. Therefore, I think, metaphor operates a different politics of power than the one just outlined. Where metaphor destroys the consistent or lexical structures of language and indicates a novel use of the imagination against its coherent uses, ontological metaphor requires us to say that being is likewise novel and spontaneous and opposite to the coherent order things. This means that being possess an original meaning distinct from ordinary meaning. This original meaning implies that being is not instituted through its recognition but in fact opposes its recognition and consequently also self-authorizes. If the politics of power marks a refusal of absolute power and an acceptance of the positive role of its subjects, ontological metaphor involves a politics of absolute power and a purely passive role of its subjects. It is for this reason "dangerous," as Hölderlin, Nietzsche, and Benjamin all admit of language in general. I submit that the ontology of metaphor is implied in the so-called post-truth politics of today in which facts are spontaneous and simplistically alternate to one another.

One of the things we ultimately learn from Merleau-Ponty, I think, is that the real and the fictive are close to one another in that they both depend on a symbolism. This is not to say that the symbolic is a more general structure that makes the real and the fictive indecipherable. Because it is irreducible to both terms, the symbolic is not the truth of the real and the fictive. Where at least part of the tradition of philosophy would seem to depend on the essential distinction between the real and the fictive and between truth and untruth, Merleau-Ponty allows us to see that this essential distinction presumes a symbolism that works in discordance with this very tradition. It is the ultimate task of philosophical critique, then, to recognize itself as having transpired according to a limit that is nowise philosophical—that is, to recognize itself for having altered the very same symbolic form that conditions it. Every coherent sense configures an impossible meaning. But for this same reason, according to Merleau-Ponty, there is no absolutely novel an innovative meaning that escapes all coherent senses. The impossible is internal to all senses, configuring them from within. This matrix, between sense and the meaning that cannot possibly make sense, implies that no sense ever exhausts its non-sense. Thus, conflicting senses are not simplistically alternate to one another but alternate to one another on account their abiding inability to be fully coherent. Any ideological position will therefore abide a series of other positions held in a less ideal way. One can refuse or deny this position, but even the refusal or denial is at the same time a recognition, and therefore institution, of this series of non-ideal meanings. I believe that, for this reason, Merleau-Ponty's account of language in general, and its matrix between conceptual and non-conceptual, cannot be disentangled from his politics. In fact, I think, he does not have a poetics or an ontology that is not political. For the play between held ideals and held non-ideals is exactly how the subject of power fails to recognize its own recognition of power, and how power can therefore "thwart" us from seeing its play.

Merleau-Ponty may note, however, that in Proust this very eclipse is no longer thwarted but recognized precisely as the play of deception that it is. Indeed, *In Search of Lost Time* refuses the very passive relation to language that prohibits its reader from thinking either that she creates the work's meaning or that the work contains an intentional meaning of its author. It is, in other words, recognized in terms of a double eclipse of both reader and author effected by a symbolic form irreducible to either. Surely, Merleau-Ponty sees in Proust's work usages of language that situate language in terms of its medial symbolic form—a language proximate and internal to the subject having been formed by a symbolism distant and external to it. This same eclipse is what Claude Lefort claims in his introduction that *The Visible and the Invisible* accomplishes. But there is an important difference between Merleau-Ponty and Proust in that the former, though concerned with the figures of language, is after a unique *philosophical* critique. This critique shows the symbolic form of philosophical critique.

In this sense, I think, the stakes of phenomenology are raised to indicate a "supreme art." It has to reveal itself as having interiorized the ability to recognize rather than thwart the play of deception. That is, it has to recognize itself as having interiorized a work such as *In Search of Lost Time*. In this sense phenomenology cannot avoid making evident the double eclipse between reader and author and thus also the medial symbolic form. This does not mean that philosophy and philosophical language has to now suddenly illuminate the symbolism on which everything depends. It is critical to the extent that it understands itself as having taken place within a symbolism. This symbolism in which critique operates is however primordial: it acts towards both the sensible world and the language we all borrow and use. There is a sense in which Merleau-Ponty agrees with Hegel that philosophy is what is needed when opposites lose their life and we enter into simple dichotomy, forgetting what limits these opposites. But the point of philosophy for Merleau-Ponty is only to rehabilitate the life of these opposites. If he does not have a philosophy of symbolic form per se, it is ultimately because he departs from the wholly philosophical point that these forms are general and universal ones. They are in this sense neither essential being nor essential non-being. At the heart of Merleau-Ponty's thought seems to lie an impossible matrix event: his is a philosophy ultimately concerned with the symbolic form that operates as a limit-situation within such difference and indeed all categories of difference that arise from it; but also, if this is the symbolic form with which it is concerned, Merleau-Ponty's phenomenology breaks from direct philosophy. There is no form at which to aim and phenomenalize. The only way to phenomenalize the symbolic form, then, is to transform the old language of philosophy by altering it according to what is non-conceptual within it—that is, to produce a new adventure of thought from out of the old thought.

Politics, History, and Elements

This phenomenology, recognizing it begins and end with crisis, is thus always in an adverse position because it is nonetheless also critical. We must ask now what it means for phenomenology to interrogate to such an extent that it comes to an un-thought as its start and finish. This is more than reminiscent of the procreational dialectic Merleau-Ponty, through Schelling, points out: phenomenology and non-phenomenology are both older and younger to one another. If each comes both before and after the other, this means they do not reach towards a higher or synthetic order. Instead, they set into relief a "quasi-concept" in common to both that never itself comes to light except in fragments. In the philosophy of reflexion, these fragments are a consciousness that reflects and the object reflected upon or even what is unreflected and on the opposite side of this object. In the philosophy of history, it would be contingent human acts and the whole of their trajectory through which they take a detour and which has a logic of its own. If these fragmented thoughts are by virtue of the "primordial symbolism" that could never itself comes to light, one could say that they are of philosophies in the dark.

To the extent that a phenomenology of symbolism is, on the other hand, concerned with the elemental nature of these fragments, it is concerned with a basis for the relation between *analysis* and *what it analyzes*. For instance, there is a relation between the signifier and the signified or the relation between the conscious and the unconscious. But, according to the phenomenology of symbolism, such relations are specific symbolizations of what is for its part non-directional and deformed. In this sense, the phenomenology of symbolism involves an interrogation of how certain directions arise from what is always constellated, matrixed, or mutated through what is other than it. Were the phenomenology of symbolic form to somehow conceive this investment something to which it could directly attend, as something like an ideal form, it would likewise lose the basis of investment. That is why, at most, such a phenomenology calls this non-direction, constellation, and matrix "events" that require not singular but plural times and spaces—nothing analyzable *in itself*. The reason no thought absolutely illuminates things is because it is always invested in this symbolic form of events—that is, at once in different times and spaces, and yet does not think about such investment. To phenomenalize this investment would however entail another kind of study than the one that it is: a study of itself as a symbolization or a study in its own symbolic formation. This in turn means that it becomes a study of itself as occurring on the basis of what it cannot think. From the point of view of such analyses, furthermore, we can also see why Sartre's absolute imagination is equally invested in an unthought. The very commitment to the future participation and mutual recognition of free equals is committed to something more than this future. That does not mean it is wrong. It only means it cannot be a non-exclusionary ideal.[7]

This is precisely why all thought is committed and why Merleau-Ponty writes in *Humanism and Terror* that "even *laissez faire* involves a commitment."[8] It is possible to grasp how Merleau-Ponty's ontological symbolism might in the end undergird this claim about the impossibility of non-commitment. It is possible to see that, in this ontology, Merleau-Ponty is ultimately attuned to the elements and at the same time what he calls the "maleficence in history" or the "history of the event."[9] In the "Origin of Truth" working note to *The Visible and the Invisible*, for example, he says he wants to show "the divergence between physics and the being of *Physis*." He says he wants to show the lived-history of the incarnate subject and a non-abstracted nature of the blind spot. And, quite remarkably, he says this: "[I]t would be necessary in principle to disclose the 'organic history' under the historicity (*Urhistorie, erst Geschichtlichkeit*) of truth [. . .] as the infinite horizon of science—This historicity of truth is also what animates Marxism."[10] Compare this to another comment from *Humanism and Terror*: "Marxism is not a philosophy of history; it is *the* philosophy of history and to renounce it is to dig the grave of Reason in history. After that there remain only dreams or adventures."[11] In the *Visible and the Invisible* reference, the elemental is what would animate the acts of history and even the philosophy of history that is Marxism. There, "adventures" are not thought of as aleatory, as they apparently are in *Humanism and Terror*. They are rather thought in terms of events, and ontological events in particular—that is, events that are instituting insofar as they alter the meaning-field by virtue of their hidden configuration in the present. The phenomenology of such events would in effect operate a cross section of both history and its philosophy. But, if so, it can never be more than an interrogation of how, at a given time, history and the philosophy of history are according to the terms of something they cannot grasp or think: their symbolic form.

Notes

Introduction

1. Alain Badiou, *Being and Event*, trans. Oliver Feltham (United Kingdom: Continuum, 2006). See, for example, pages 6, 67, 68, 86–90, 131, 186–89, 421, 432, 500, 525.
2. See ibid., page 30, where Badiou defines the "axial theme of the doctrine of being" as "pure inconsistent multiplicity."
3. Ibid., 90.
4. Gilles Deleuze, *The Logic of Sense*, trans. Mark Lester and Charles Stivale (United Kingdom: Athlone Press, 1990), 98.
5. *IP*, 44/13, 52–54/18–20, 57/22, 85/47, 163/121, 167/125, 213/160, 221–23/168–69, 244/187, 264/203.
6. Ibid., 53/18.
7. Ibid., 44/13.
8. *NC*, 84.
9. *S*, 259/159.
10. *VI*, 224–25/173.
11. It is admittedly more complicated than this. For Husserl, the mode of being of the noema is "*intentionalen Beschlossenseins.*" This "intentionally enacted being" does not oppose the mundane transcendence of things. It cuts across ontological regions of essences and individual things, the nonexistent and the existent, for the sole reason that it is not an ontological concept but a genuinely phenomenological one. True, Husserl does say that this noema is "meaning." But for him meaning is ambiguous enough to permit equivocation. The intentional object is "meaning in the sense of reference," whereas the noema is "meaning in the sense of sense." That is why Husserl also speaks of the "noematic nucleus" to describe what appears and the "noematic horizons" to describe the transcendence to which what

appears refers. Only in the former is there "meaning in the sense of sense"—that is, only in the former is sense distinguishable from reference. Husserl thus proposes *Bedeutung* and *Sinn* differently: in the former, meaning at the conceptual, logical level; in the latter, sense for meaning in the broadest sense. The former applies to acts of expressing exclusively, and the latter to all acts. The "noematic nucleus" is the *Sinn* of the noetic act but not the conceptual or logical meaning. I think Merleau-Ponty strongly emphasizes, however, that the intentional correspondence between the noetic act and the noematic nucleus is always *an act of signification of some kind*, whereas the noematic horizon refers to a transcendence of this sense and even to a transcendence of the intentional object as the "meaning in the sense of reference." He thinks that this transcendence conveys a meaning that is unreferenced and unsignified, silent or mute, but always at the crossroads of "meaning in the sense of reference." That is, while intentionality is an act of signification it arises on the basis of a meaning that is not itself an act of signification. One could say that, for Merleau-Ponty, meaning does not merely signify: in every sense, and for this sense to be, there is non-sense. This matrix is the formation of the intentional relation between sense and meaning. From here on, I will mention the intentional relation between sense and meaning and the fact that Merleau-Ponty complicates the unilateralism of this meaning and thus intentionality itself. This particular matter is complicated further by the multiple meanings of the French word *sens*: it means direction and signification, as well as sensation and feeling, and more.

12. In the 1959 Working Note to *The Visible and the Invisible* titled "*Einströmen*—Reflection," Merleau-Ponty continues: "Because there is *Einströmen*, reflection is not adequation, coincidence: it would not pass into the *Strom* if it placed us back at the source of the *Strom*" (*VI*, 224/173).
13. *IP*, 159/118.
14. Ibid., 53/18–19.
15. Discussing the connection between the institution and passivity lectures, Robert Vallier writes the following:
    Merleau-Ponty is thus attempting to think the temporal meaning-structure of the always-already, which forms our horizon before we are born, forms our shared tradition and common history, our "world," and thus also to rethink the form of a philosophy of history in terms of institution. While the temporal accent in the course on institution is placed on the future, all institution depends on the operation of this fecund ontological anteriority. And this in turn gives us a hint as to why the two courses on institution and passivity are complementary: as we learn in the second course, passivity is

not a state of consciousness, not the antonym of activity, but rather refers to the ontological anteriority that would deposit a meaning in me, and would dispose me towards a future.

See Robert Vallier, "Institution: The Significance of Merleau-Ponty's 1954 Lectures at the Collège de France," *Chiasmi International* 7 (2006): 293.

16. VI, 266/216.
17. IP, 82/44. Merleau-Ponty also criticizes Cassirer's distinction between a "community of being" and a "community of sense" in *Phenomenology of Perception*, a distinction that in advance prevents us from grasping the ontological place of sense that is consciousness. Merleau-Ponty:

> The "symbolic function" or 'representation function' certainly underlies our movement, but it is not an ultimate term for the analysis, it in turn rests upon a certain ground. Intellectualism's error is to make it depend upon itself, to separate it from the materials in which it is realized, and to recognize in us, as originally, a direct presence in the world. For beginning from the transparent consciousness, and from this intentionality that does not admit of degrees, everything that separates us from the true world—error, illness, madness, and, in short, embodiment—is reduced to the status of a mere appearance. Of course, intellectualism does not set up consciousness apart from its materials, and for example, it explicitly resists introducing a "symbolic consciousness" behind speech, action, and perception that would be the common and numerically single form of linguistic, perceptual, and motor materials. There is no "general symbolic faculty," says Cassirer, and reflective analysis does not look to establish a "community of being," but rather a "community of sense" among the pathological phenomena that concern perception, language, and action. Intellectualist psychology, given that it has definitely left causal thought and realism behind, would be capable of seeing the sense or the essence of the disorder and of recognizing a unity of consciousness that is not observable on the level of being and that is self-affirmed upon the level of truth. But precisely this distinction between the community of being and the community of sense, the consciousness passage from the order of existence to the order of truth, and the reversal that allows for the affirmation of sense and value as autonomous are, in practice, equal to an abstraction, since, from the point of view ultimately adopted, the variety of phenomena becomes meaning-less and incomprehensible. If consciousness is placed outside of being, then consciousness can never be penetrated by being. (*PP*, 145/124–25)

18. Ép/IPP, 61/61.
19. Ibid., 58/57–58.
20. VI, 242/192.

21. Ibid., 267/218.
22. M.C. Dillon, *Merleau-Ponty's Ontology*, 2nd Edition (Evanston, IL: Northwestern University Press, 1997), 61.
23. Rajiv Kaushik, *Art and Institution: Aesthetics in the Late Works of Merleau-Ponty* (United Kingdom: Continuum Books, 2011) and *Art, Language, and Figure in Merleau-Ponty: Excursions in Hyper-Dialectic* (United Kingdom: Bloomsbury, 2013).
24. Ferdinand de Saussure, *Course in General Linguistics*, trans. Roy Harris (Peru, IL: Open Court, 2009), 9; *VI*, 137/102–3.
25. See my chapter 3 from *Art, Language, and Figure*, titled "The Devolution of Language."
26. *VI*, 266/217, 273/224.
27. Ibid., 243/192.
28. *N*, 67–68/42–43.
29. Ibid., 66/43.
30. *OE/EM*, 21/163.
31. *IP*, 195–96/148.
32. Ibid., 201–2/152.
33. *VI*, 182/139.
34. *IP*, 202/152.
35. *VI*, 137/102–3.
36. Ibid., 217/166–65.
37. Ibid., 270/221.
38. Ibid., 137/102.
39. Ibid., 260/210.
40. Ibid., 229–30/178.
41. *IP*, 204; 205/154; 155.

Chapter 1

1. Martin West, "Homer's Meter," in *A New Companion to Homer*, ed. Ian Morris and Barry B. Powell, 227 (New York: Brill, 1997). The reference to Homer's *Odyssey* is to: Walter W. Merry, (ed.), *Homer's Odyssey* (United Kingdom: Clarendon Press, 1886), 9.151–12.7.
2. Martin West, "Homer's Meter," 227.
3. Charles Anthon, "Metrical Index," in *First Three Books of Homer's Illiad, According to Ordinary Text and with the Digamma* Restored (United Kingdom: William Tegg, 1866), 289.
4. I have used the following translation of Homer, which of course did not yet exist for Anthon: Homer, *The Iliad*, trans. A.T. Murray (Cambridge, MA: Harvard University Press, 1924), i., 358, i., 209; i., 23, i., 37. However, I have placed the breaks in the appropriate places according to Anthon's text to illustrate the metrical rule.
5. Carl Wilhelm Lucas. *Forms of the Ionic Dialect in Homer: With an*

Appendix on the Principal Dialectic Peculiarities of Heroditus (United Kingdom: Whittaker and Co., 1846), 24–26.
6. Giorgio Agamben, *The End of the Poem: Studies in Poetics*, trans. Daniel Heller-Roazen (Palo Alto, CA: Stanford University Press, 1999), 75.
7. Ibid., 76.
8. References to Plato are from Plato, *The Complete Works*, ed. John M. Cooper (Indianapolis, IN: Hackett, 1997); *Sophist*, 242c.
9. Ibid., 244b–c.
10. Ibid., 244d.
11. Søren Kierkegaard, *The Concept of Anxiety: A Simple Psychologically Orienting Deliberation on the Dogmatic Issue of Hereditary Sin*, trans. Reidar Thomte (Princeton, NJ: Princeton University Press, 1981), 84.
12. *Parmenides*, 141e.
13. Martin Heidegger, *Being and Time*, trans. John Macquarrie and Edward Robinson (New York: Harper and Row, 1962).
14. Martin Heidegger, *Plato's Sophist*, trans. Richard Rojcewicz and André Schuwer (Indianapolis: Indiana University Press, 2003), 361–94. These concern sections 253b–254b, 254b–257a, 257b–259d of *Sophist*.
15. Ibid., 7.
16. I am referring to Edmund Husserl, "Third Logical Study: the idea of an absolute grammar that would be logic," in *Logical Invesigations*, trans. J.N. Findlay (United Kingdom: Routledge and Kegan Paul, 1975), 435–89.
17. *Cratylus*, 385d.
18. Ibid., 386e, 389d.
19. Ibid., 439d–e.
20. Ibid., 440d.
21. Ibid., 439b.
22. H.D. Rankin, *Sophists, Socratics and Cynics* (New York: Routledge, 2014),170.
23. *Phaedo*, 78d; *Republic*, VI 490b, VII 532a, VI 476.
24. *Sophist*, 266b.
25. Paul Ricoeur, *Being, Essence and Substance in Plato and Aristotle*, trans. David Pellauer and John Starkey (United Kingdom: Polity, 2013), 88, 96.
26. Ibid., 89.
27. Ibid., 99.
28. VI, 273/224.
29. Ibid., 22/7.
30. Ibid., 7.
31. Ibid., 273/224.
32. Ibid., 266/217.
33. I am referring here to section 22, "The Reproach of Platonic Realism: Essence and Concept," in Edmund Husserl, *Ideas Pertaining to a Pure*

Phenomenology and to a Phenomenological Philosophy—First Book: General Introduction to a Pure Phenomenology, trans. F. Kersten (The Netherlands: Kluwer Academic, 1982), 40–43.
34. VI, 22/7–8.
35. Ibid., 193/149.
36. Ibid., 263/213–14.
37. Ibid., 266/217.
38. Ibid., 146/110.
39. Ibid., 155/117.
40. Ibid., 112/82.
41. Ibid., 266/217.
42. Ibid., 162/128.
43. Ibid., 313/265.
44. Ibid., 318/270.
45. Ibid., 191/148.
46. Ibid., 162/123.
47. Ibid., 23/8.
48. S, 270/166.
49. Glen A. Mazis, *Merleau-Ponty and the Face of the World: Silence, Ethics, Imagination, and Poetic Ontology* (Albany: State University of New York Press, 2016), 310.
50. Ibid.
51. Ibid., 35.
52. OE/EM, 78–79–185.
53. Mazis, *Merleau-Ponty and the Face of the World*, 35.
54. VI, 94/66.
55. Ibid., 212/161.
56. Ibid., 266/216.
57. Ibid., 217/166–65.
58. Ibid.
59. Ibid., 270/221.
60. Ibid., 277/228.
61. Ibid., 277/227–28.
62. Martin Heidegger, "Aletheia" in *Early Greek Thinking*, trans. David Farrell Krell and Frank A. Capuzzi (San Francisco: Harper and Row, 1984), 104.
63. Ibid.
64. Ibid., 110.
65. Ibid., 110–11.
66. I refer to the original German here: "*das niemals Untergehende.*" Martin Heidegger, *Gesamtausgabe* vol. 55, entitled *Der Anfang des abendländischen Denkens Logik. Heraklitis Lehre vom Logos*, ed. Manfred Frings (Germany: Vittorio Klostermann, 1994), 141.
67. Note Heidegger's phrase here: "*das ständig Aufgehende*"; the verb *aufgehen*, literally "to go up," has several senses, some clearly

relevant here: to self-open, rise, come up (for example, of plants). It is also used in the phrase "to go up in flames" in "Aletheia," 111.
68. This is a somewhat literal translation of Heidegger's, "*das doch ja nicht Untergehen je.*" Heidegger, *Gesamtausgabe* vol. 55, 141.
69. Ibid.
70. Ibid., 143.
71. Jean Bollack and Heinz Wismann, *Héraclite ou la separation* (France: Editions de Minuit, 1972), 197.
72. The numbering system for the pre-Socratic fragments derive from Hermann Alexander Diels and Walther Krantz, and is referred to as DK. They identified each pre-Socratic with a number. Heraclitus is 22, and his fragments are either A or B Fragments. The first fragment here is therefore DK22B1. I refer only to the last two designations throughout for simplicity.
73. I am grateful to Drew Dalton for this point, which was made during a talk at Brock University in April, 2017. It can be found in Dalton's chapter, "Ethics and the Absolute: Tyranny and Resistance" from: Drew Dalton, *The Ethics of Resistance: Tyranny of the Absolute* (United Kingdom: Bloomsbury, 2018).
74. Jean Bollack and Heinz Wismann, *Héraclite ou la separation*, 12–14.
75. Véronique Fóti, *Vision's Invisibles: Philosophical Explorations* (Albany: State University of New York Press, 2003), 14.
76. Ibid.
77. Robin Reames in "Heraclitus' Doublespeak: The Paradoxical Origins of Rhetorical Logos":

> *Logos* is not a word or principle that exists above or beneath matter as a cosmic law or universal measure, but it is concomitant with the matter itself, and as such, is marked by the same strife, tensions, and flux that mark the river, the sea, the bow, and the lyre. Moreover, to uncover the tension of opposites that inhere within Heraclitean *logos* is to enter into the riddle and play that is constructed within the paradox of the first fragment.

In *Logos Without Rhetoric: The Arts of Language Before Plato*, ed. Robin Reames, 73–74 (Columbia: University of South Carolina Press, 2017).
78. In *Introduction to Metaphysics*, Heidegger also considers that the fundamental sense of λέγειν found in the German "*lesen,*" which most commonly means "to read" but more originally means "to collect, to gather." Martin Heidegger, "The Resistriction of Being," in *Introduction to Metaphysics* 2nd edition, trans. Gregory Fried and Richard Polt (New Haven, CT: Yale University Press, 2014), 137. "To read," Heidegger thinks, is derived from the original significance and so is a sort of gathering that brings together while allowing what the things brought together to be what they are through the relations constituted by the gathering. The act of reading, for example, brings otherwise separate significations together, and in this act the significations become

what they are and take on their specific meanings. Later in his Heraclitus lectures, Heidegger refines his understanding of the Greek λόγος to indicate exactly how discourse makes manifest—namely, by providing a gathering or context where things show themselves in relation with and in contrast to other things both collectively and individually. Λόγος as gathering is no longer an attribute or *existentiale* of Dasein but rather of the bringing together and setting apart of beings performed by language (*die Sprache*). Here language is conceived more broadly than the mere totality of words that humans possess: *it is the jointure* between revealing and concealing and holds humans under *its* power. The significance of Heraclitus's use of λόγος—already in the sense of "word" and "talk"—lies in the acknowledgment of the practical equivalence of language and the event of Being, and the affinity of both of these with the notion of gathering. Heidegger, "Logos," in *Early Greek Thinking*, 76–78. On the notion that speech is eventful of being, Merleau-Ponty and Heidegger are, I think, profoundly of apiece. On whether this point assumes the primacy "jointure," they are definitely divided.

79. William K.C. Guthrie, "The Earlier Presocratics and the Pythagoreans," in *The History of Greek Philosophy, Vol. 1* (United Kingdom: Cambridge University Press, 1962), 432.
80. In fact, Guthrie may be guilty with what Agamben describes as an uninterrogated persistence of a theological foundation" in the "formalist" rendering of λόγος: "What thus comes to the foreground of formalist criticism, however, is ... a purely theological supposition: the dwelling of the word in the beginning, of *logos* in *archē*, that is, the absolutely primordial status of language. This uninterrogated persistence of a theological foundation shows itself in the fact that the original structure of the poetic work remains marked by negativity: the primordiality of *logos* thus quickly becomes a primacy of the signifier and the letter, and the origin reveals itself as trace. (*The End of the Poem*, 77)
81. VI, 313/265.
82. Ibid.
83. Ibid., 273/224.
84. Ibid., 251–52/201.
85. Heidegger asserts that Greek mathematicians used λέγειν in the same way as reading, and he also cites a passage from Homer where the best translation of "λέξαιτο" is "[if] one were to gather." Heidegger, "The Restriction of Being," in *Introduction to Metaphysics*, 137.
86. VI, 200/154.
87. Leonard Lawlor, "Eliminating Some Confusion: The Relation of Being and Writing in Merleau-Ponty and Derrida," in *Écart and Différance: Seeing and Writing in Merleau-Ponty and Derrida*, ed. M.C. Dillon, 86. (United Kingdom: Humanities Press, 1997).

Chapter 2

1. Edmund Husserl, *Crisis of The European Sciences and Transcendental Phenomenology*, trans. David Carr (Evanston, IL: Northwestern University Press, 1970), 119.
2. Ibid., 127.
3. Edmund Husserl, *Ideas I*, 157–60.
4. Delia Popa, "The Relation between Space and Imagination in Husserl's Phenomenology," *Internationales Jahrbuch für Hermeneutik* 14 (2015): 83.
5. Eugene Fink, "Vergegenwärtigung und Bild," in *Studien zur Phänomenologie* (1930–1939) (The Netherlands: Martinus Nijhoff, 1966), 21§8.
6. *Ideas I*, 106.
7. Popa, "The Relation between Space and Imagination," 86.
8. *Ideas I*, 109.
9. Edmund Husserl, "Ding und Raum," in *Vorlesungen 1907, Hua 16*, ed. Ullrich Claesges, 55–60 (Hamburg: Meiner, 1973).
10. Ibid., 58–59.
11. Ibid., 56.
12. Husserl, *Ideas I*, 156–60.
13. Husserl, *Crisis*, 149.
14. Ibid., 159.
15. Ibid., 160.
16. Ibid., 149.
17. Ibid.
18. Ibid., 25.
19. Edmund Husserl, "The Origin of Geometry," in *Husserl at the Limits of Phenomenology*, ed. Bettina Bergo and Leonard Lawlor, 113 (Evanston, IL: Northwestern University Press, 2002).
20. Husserl, *The Crisis*, 25–26.
21. Ibid., 38, 128, 127, 139.
22. Jacques Derrida, *An Introduction to Edmund Husserl's Origin of Geometry*, trans. John P. Leavey Jr. (Lincoln: University of Nebraska Press, 1989), 126. See also Edmund Husserl, *Formal and Transcendental Logic*, trans. Dorion Cairns (The Netherlands: Springer, 1969), 126.
23. Derrida, *Edmund Husserl's Origin of Geometry*, 126.
24. Ibid. Husserl affirms this in *Crisis*, 34.
25. John Sallis, *The Logic of the Imagination: The Expanse of the Elemental* (Indianapolis: Indiana University Press, 2012), 162.
26. Ibid., 162–63.
27. Ibid., 163.
28. "l'espace orienté," in *PP*, 118/101.
29. Ibid., 145/124.
30. See Maurice Merleau-Ponty, *Les Sciences de l'homme et la phénoménologie* (France: Centre de documentation universitaire, 1975). English translation: *PrP*, 43–95.

31. Ibid., 24/60.
32. *IP*, 164/121–22.
33. Emmanuel Alloa, "Could Perspective Ever Be a Symbolic Form?" *Journal of Aesthetics and Phenomenology* 2:1 (2015): 51–71. Alloa argues that Cassirer could not agree with Erwin Panofsky in "Perspective Is a Symbolic Form." To the extent that Merleau-Ponty is critical of Cassirer's placement of consciousness outside of being, he ultimately can and does agree with Panofsky. Except he is careful to say:
    > Do we have to say, with Panofsky, "symbolic form," *Weltgefühl*, and assimilate this invention to a historicized, enlarged criticism (Cassirer)? This supposes that we consider at least this kind of perspective as a point of maturity, equilibrium [according to which there is nothing but oscillation towards the ultra-objective (Italian painting) and the ultra-subjective (baroque)]. But this is the conventional image of the Renaissance academic commonplace according to the painters.... Therefore, this is an "aesthetic-social choice" and not a law of nature of even the acquisition of a pictorial, critical consciousness which would be ultimate. (*IP*, 84/46)

    This is the context in which he argues that in painting the "symbolic form" is in fact a labor rather the basis of a choice; and that this labor takes place of the "field of painting." Here, "[e]ach painting is a matrix of different symbols of what is its own" (*IP*, 85/47).
34. See, for example, OE/EM, 23–25/164–65 and 49/174.
35. Ibid., 29–30/167.
36. Ibid., 71/182, 67–69/181–82; also concern the "system of equivalencies" between line and color.
37. Henry Moore, *Writings and Conversations*, ed. Alan Wilkinson (Berkeley: University of California Press, 2002), 190.
38. Martin Heidegger, *Bemerkungen zu Kunst—Plastik—Raum* (St. Gallen: Erker-Verlag, 1996), 6.
39. Martin Heidegger, "Art and Space," trans. Charles H. Seibert as *Man and World* 6 (1973): 3–8, and reprinted with the same title in *The Heidegger Reader*, ed. Günter Figal (Bloomington: Indiana University Press, 2007), 305.
40. Heidegger, *Bemerkungen zu Kunst—Plastik—Raum*, 13–15.
41. "[t]urning subtle shapes into perfect cubes or cylinders, or all curves into sections of a circle," this "kind of abstract art cannot have great meaning or lasting interest" (Moore, *Writings and Conversations*, 190).
42. I should also refer here to this Working Note from *The Visible and the Invisible*:
    > Superficial interpretation of Freudianism: he is a sculptor because he is anal, because the feces are clay, molding, etc. But the feces are not the cause: if they were, everybody would be sculptors. The feces

give rise to a character (*Abscheu*) only if the subject lives them in such a way as to find in them a dimension of being—It is not a question of renewing empiricism (feces imprinting a certain character on the child). It is a question of understanding that the relationship with feces is in the child a concrete ontology. Make not an existential psychoanalysis but an ontological psychoanalysis. . . . The whole architecture of the notion of the psycho-logy (perception, idea—affection, pleasure, desire, love, Eros) all that, all this bric-a-brac, is suddenly clarified when one ceases to think all these terms as positive (the more or less dense "spiritual") in order to think them not as negatives or negentities (for that brings back the same difficulties), but as differentiations of one sole and massive adhesion to Being which is the flesh (eventually as "lace-works"). (*VI*, 317/269–70)

I discuss this note at length in my article, "Psyche and Civilization: The Far Reaches of Merleau-Ponty's Natural Ontology," *Internationales Jahrbuch für Hermeneutik* 14 (2015): 347–66.

43. OE/EM, 22–23/164.
44. Ibid.
45. Ibid., 23/164.
46.
Merleau-Ponty goes so far as to call this seeing farther "*voyance*," explaining that this "*voyance*" "renders present to us what is absent." Beware, though: the *voyance* consists in seeing "farther than one sees," in showing us the invisible as "the outline and the depth of the visible." Precisely for this reason, the *voyance* "renders present to us what is absent" not simply by *presentifying it*, but rather in *creating it* as a particular presence which, as such, had never been present before. . . . In fact, this happens because seeing "farther than one sees" is seeing "according to, or with" what one sees.

—Mauro Carbone, *The Flesh of Images: Merleau-Ponty between Painting and Cinema*, trans. Marta Nijhuis (Albany: State University of New York Press, 2016), 6.

47. *VI*, 54/33, 107/78, 295–96/247–48, 303/255.
48. *N*, 239/183.
49. Ibid., 68/43.
50. Ibid., 239/183.
51. Ibid., 68/43.
52. *S*, 290/178.
53. *N*, 68/43.
54. Ibid., 67–68/42–43.
55. Ibid., 67/43.
56. Ibid.
57. Ibid., 239/183.
58. Ibid., 66/42. Following the relatively recent publication of

Merleau-Ponty's *Nature* course notes, there has been some extraordinary research on the relationship between Merleau-Ponty's late ontology, what he calls the psychoanalysis of nature, and the thought of Schelling. See, for example: Patrick Burke and Jason M. Wirth, *The Barbarian Principle: Merleau-Ponty, Schelling, and the Question of Nature* (Albany: State University of New York Press, 2013); and Dylan Trigg, "The Indestructible, the Barbaric Principle: The Role of Schelling in Merleau-Ponty's Psychoanalysis," *Continental Philosophy Review* 49, no. 2 (2016): 203–21.
59. Ibid., 68/43.
60. *VI*, 229/177.

Chapter 3

1. Martin Jay. *Downcast Eyes: The Denigration of Vision in Twentieth-Century French Thought* (Berkeley: University of California Press, 1994), 29.
2. Ibid.
3. Ibid.
4. As opposed to a "light mysticism." See Hans Blumenberg, "Licht als Metapher der Wahrheit," Studium Generale 10 (1953): 434.
5. Martin Jay, *Downcast Eyes*, 30. In any case, it is mostly agreed that vision is the highest sense for the Greeks. Hans Blumenberg writes, for example: "The light in which the landscape and things that surrounded the life of the Greeks stood gave to everything a clarity and (in terms of optics alone) unquestionable presence that left room for doubt regarding the accessibility of nature to mane only late and only as a result of thought's experience with itself" (*The Legitimacy of the Modern World*, trans. Robert M. Wallace [Cambridge, MA: MIT Press,1983], 243).
6. In his Phenomenon of Life, Hans Jonas describes this assumption:
    Sight includes at any given instant an infinite manifold at once, and its own qualitative conditions open the way into what lies beyond. The unfolding of space before the eye, under the magic of light, bears in itself the germ of infinity—as a perceptual aspect. Its conceptual framing in the idea of infinity is a step beyond perception, but one that was taken from this base. The fact that we can look into the unbounded depth of the universe has surely been of immense importance in the formation of our ideas. (*The Phenomenon of Life: Toward a Philosophical Biology* [Evanston, IL: Northwestern University Press, 2001], 151)
7. Rodolphe Gasché argues, for example, that the reflection of the speculum was potentially an absolute one. *The Tain of the Mirror: Derrida and the Philosophy of Reflection* (Cambridge, MA: Harvard University Press, 1986), 43.

8. In fact, I think both Merleau-Ponty and Nancy share a project with Lyotard, even if Lyotard would perhaps disagree:

    Merleau-Ponty spoke of the chiasmus of the eye and the horizon, a fluid in which mind floats. The solar explosion, the mere thought of that explosion, should awaken you from this euphoria. Look here: you try to think of the event in its quod, in the advent of "it so happens that" before any quiddity, don't you? Well, you'll grant the explosion of the sun is the quod itself, no subsequent assignment being possible.... Solar death implies an irreparably exclusive disjunction between death and thought: if there's death, then there's no thought. Negation without remainder. No self to make sense of it. Pure event. Disaster. All the events and disasters we're familiar with and try to think of will end up as no more than pale simulacra. (Jean-François Lyotard, *The Inhuman: Reflections on Time*, trans. Geoffrey Bennington and Rachel Bowlby [Palo Alto, CA: Stanford University Press, 1991], 11)

9. *MPR*, 435. The word *"filigrane"* appears in *The Visible and the Invisible* as "filigree" *VI*, 265/215. It appears in the text in a Working Note, "Avril 1960. Chair," from the section "New Working Notes from the Period of The Visible and the Invisible" in *The Merleau-Ponty Reader*, and it is a matter of some interpretational debate. It can be translated in a figurative sense as a "showing just beneath the surface" or to refer to a watermark on a piece of paper that allows light to pass through so that something is made visible without the mark itself being visible. I use it here in the latter sense and believe to have grounds to do so, since it appears alongside such phrases to describe *"écart"*: *"le même à distance," "plein du vide (définition du sensible, qui fait qu'il est aussi imperception),"* and *"Les perspectives, ni l'Erfüllung* ("perspective possible") *ne sont du positif"* (*MPR*, 435).

10. *VI*, 267/218.

11. In his *Resistance of the Sensible World*, Emmanuel Alloa gives insightful and succinct commentary on this note on the elements. They are obviously not perceptible in the same way as an object. It requires a specific operation to visualize the spacing between things; one can thematize as an object what is simply a transitive element, but only at the cost of losing the transitivity that made it operative That is the reason one never paints a color but always only something colored, just as one cannot depict the content of a sensation, a sound in itself, and so on. (Emmanuel Alloa, *Resistance of the Sensible World* [New York: Fordham University Press, 2017], 94]

12. I am in dialogue here with Alloa's following claim that Merleau-Ponty is pulled in two different directions at once:

    [T]oward a phenomenological cosmology, like the one that Czech phenomenologist Jan Patočka proposed, for example, and toward a phenomenology of fields, which, however, does not manage to rid itself of the eidetic model. It is as if the field were only the background of an object, as if one had only to turn one's attention away from the objects and toward the space between them is to understand what produces their appearance. But experimental psychology has demonstrated that, when one shifts one's gaze from the focal area to the margins, the paradigm of objectification is not thereby undone. (Ibid., 94–95)

But, then, I also agree to the basic premise of what Alloa calls a "dia-phenomenology":

What appears does not appear purely and simply to the eye; it appears through a milieu, which Aristotle calls diaphanous (from dia-phanēs, "visible through"). That operative medium is both the perceptual milieu of vision and the structure of visibility. This notion accounts for the remarkable structure of visual perception itself, in that it cannot occur without combining distance and continuity, cannot forgo a paradoxical form of relationship operating between beings. If there were total continuity between beings, no experience would be possible; only where there is spacing between them can experience occur. (Ibid., 97)

13. Jean-Luc Nancy, *Multiple Arts: Muses II*, trans. Simon Sparks (Palo Alto, CA: Stanford University Press, 2006), 171.
14. Jean-Luc Nancy, *The Muses*, trans. Peggy Kamuf (Palo Alto, CA: Stanford University Press, 1996), 33.
15. William Watkin, "Poetry's Promiscuous Plurality: On a Part of Jean-Luc Nancy's The Muses" in *Jean-Luc Nancy and Plural Thinking: Expositions of World, Ontology, Politics, and Sense*, ed. Peter Gratton and Marie-Eve Morin, 199 (Albany: State University of New York Press, 2012).
16. Nancy, *The Muses*, 34.
17. Jean-Luc Nancy, "Euryopa: Blick in die Weite/Euryopa: le regard au loin," Ulrich J. Schneider, Beiträge/contributions, 2 issues: *La philosophie européenne de la culture et le projet "Logos" de 1910*, International Symposium, University of Leipzig, May 1994. (cf. collectifs 67), 5–15. English translations are my own.
18. Ibid., 5.
19. Ibid., 6.
20. Ibid., 10.
21. Ibid.
22. Nancy, *The Muses*, 9.
23. Jean-Luc Nancy, *The Sense of the World*, trans. Jeffrey S. Librett (Minneapolis: University of Minnesota Press, 1998), 62.

24. Jean-Luc Nancy, *The Ground of the Image*, trans. Jeff Fort (Palo Alto, CA: Stanford University Press, 2006), 4.
25. *PP*, 360–61/312.
26. Ibid., 376–77/326.
27. *NC*, 305; PNP, 40.
28. *PrP*, 92/36.
29. Ibid., 92/36–37.
30. Ibid., 90–91/36.
31. *NC*, 305; *PNP*, 40. "The Vieldeutigkeit is not a shadow to be eliminated from true light."
32. OE/EM, 21/163.
33. Ibid., 86/188.
34. Ibid., 65/180.
35. Aristotle, *Metaphysics, Books I–IX*, trans. Hugh Tredennick (Cambridge, MA: Harvard University Press, 1996), 983b6.
36. Eugen Fink and Martin Heidegger, *Heraclitus Seminar*, trans. Charles H. Seibert (Evanston, IL: Northwestern University Press, 1997), 139.
37. Ibid., 137.
38. Ibid., 138.
39. Ibid., 130. In sleep, Veronique Fóti writes, "[O]ne's life continues unbroken in the embrace of night, one touches then—with one's eyes cut—upon what it may mean to be dead" (*Vision's Invisibles*, 21).
40. Fink and Heidegger, *Heraclitus Seminar*, 130.
41. A comparison with John Sallis's analysis of smoke and fire in Heraclitus is helpful:
    At the limit of the fragment which I have attempted to read, at the point from which it speaks, its beginning—here one comes up against the issue from which perhaps all the fragments of Heraclitean thinking ultimately rebound—the issue, to say it phenomenally: How do fire and smoke belong together? One can also ask it mythically: Where likes the joint which joins the domain of the sun to that of Hades, Zeus' lightning to Hades' withdrawal into darkness, revealment to concealment? Where is that joint by which, as Heraclitus himself says (Fr. 15), Hades and Dionysus are held together in the unity of sameness? This would also be the joint of the soul, the joint which as λόγος sunk into the depths of the soul gathers the soul into its limits. (*Delimitations: Phenomenology and the End of Metaphysics* [Indianapolis: Indiana University Press, 1995], 193)
42. Fink and Heidegger, *Heraclitus Seminar*, 139–40.
43. Ibid., 145.
44. Ibid., 140–41.
45. Ibid., 145.
46. Heidegger, "Aletheia," 104.
47. *IP*, 196/148.

48. Ibid., 185/139. Also, in a June 1961 Working Note to *The Visible and the Invisible* titled "Dream, Imaginary," Merleau-Ponty critiques "the philosophy that adds the imaginary to the real" and suggests instead that "[t]he dream is the inside in the sense that the internal double of the external sensible inside, it is on the side of the sensible wherever the world is not—this is that 'stage,' that 'the-atre' of which Freud speaks, that place of our oneiric beliefs" (*VI*, 310/262).
49. *VI*, 275-76/226-27 and 279/229.
50. *PP*, 245/211-12.
51. *IP*, 185/139.
52. Ibid., 189/142.
53. Ibid., 185/139.
54. Ibid., 189/142.
55. Ibid., 275/213.
56. Ibid., 275/212.
57. Ibid., 189/142.
58.
> But into the night, as into sleep, we do not go with our eyes closed. When our eyes are closed, sleep has already won the sleeper. But the instant just before, when eyelids have slipped over our eyes and they for one more moment have remained seers behind their curtain and through the darkness spread everywhere in what we call the bedroom, that is the vault, the curving dome that seals space from sleep by separating it from the celestial vaults themselves—eyelids, bedroom, "canopy [ciel de lit]," sublunary world, world of beneath, crypt hidden to itself —at that instant the gaze has seen the night into which it was entering. What it saw was nothing but the absence of all vision and all visibility. Even that, it saw. He had to bear this sight all the time it took to fall asleep, and it is possible that this horror, worse than a blinding, penetrated the marrow of his sleep to pursue him there and to prevent him finally from truly, profoundly falling asleep.
>
> Not seeing connects with some possibility of help or hope for sight. We do not see in the darkness, which in a way can be dissipated. But seeing that we see nothing and that there is nothing to see, seeing signs clinging to itself as to its sole object, that is like seeing the invisible, surely, but is only like its other side or its negative. To sojourn in just that other side, not to try to discern the invisible, that is the blind task of sleep. (Nancy, *The Fall of Sleep*, trans. Charlotte Mandell [New York: Fordham University Press, 2009], 48)

59. *IP*, 197-98/149.
60. I respond here to Nicolas de Warren's essay on sleep, which is a response to Jean-Luc Nancy's claim that there is no phenomenology

of sleep. One can see in Merleau-Ponty a third option between Nancy and Husserl:
> By the same token, the "self-abstention" of consciousness from itself, its suspension of the patent distinction between pour soi and en soi is itself constituted in absolute time-consciousness much as, within waking life, we have the transformation within retention consciousness, and thus, within time-consciousness, of near retentions into far retentions. When Husserl speaks of *"unwache Zeitigung"* he means the expression *"unwache"* as equivalent to "life-less" and "unconscious," but not in the sense of lacking consciousness, or, indeed, of lacking an intrinsic self-consciousness, but rather in the sense of without force. Sleep is an affection of consciousness in which affections lack force, but also, self-affection of consciousness itself—its self-temporalization—must also lack force, and thus, in this sense, be seen as temporarily neutralized from within, as if consciousness absented itself from itself, that is, rendered itself immune to the affective force of its own self-affection. (Nicolas de Warren, "The Inner Night: Towards a Phenomenology of (Dreamless) Sleep" in "The Inner Night: Towards a Phenomenology of (Dreamless) Sleep" in *On Time: New Contributions to the Husserlian Phenomenology of Time*, ed. Dieter Lohmar and Ichiro Yamaguchi, 290-91 [The Netherlands: Springer, 2010])

De Warren's analysis is complemented by Dan Zahavi's analysis in *Self-Awareness and Alterity* of the dreamless sleep in Husserl. Zahavi makes clear that, for Husserl, the dreamless sleep is present and undifferentiated consciousness (208-10).

61. *IP*, 200/151.
62. Ibid., 197/149.
63. F.W.J. Schelling, *The Ages of the World: Third Draft*, trans. Jason M. Wirth (Albany: State University of New York Press, 2000), 24.
64. Sigmund Freud, *The Uncanny*, trans. David McLintock (United Kingdom: Penguin Books, 2003), 132.
65. *IP*, 203/154.
66. Freud, *The Uncanny*, 212.
67. Jean-Paul Sartre, *The Imaginary: A Phenomenological Psychology of the Imagination*, trans. Jonathan Webber (United Kingdom: Routledge, 2004), 49.
68. Ibid., 48.
69. Ibid.
70. *IP*, 186/140-41.
71. Ibid. This claim is in reference to long passages from Sartre's work on the imaginary.
72. Ibid., 191, 192 /143, 144.
73. Ibid., 193/146.

Chapter 4

1. *IP*, 196/148.
2. This question occupies much of the secondary literature on Merleau-Ponty, but perhaps no one has examined the matter as closely and consistently as Annabelle Dufourcq. See for example: Annabelle Dufourcq, *Merleau-Ponty: une ontologie de l'imaginaire* (The Netherlands: Springer, 2012).
3. *IP*, 196/148.
4. Ibid., 196–97/148–49.
5. Ibid., 197/149.
6. Ibid., 201–2/152.
7. I am very grateful to Duane Davis for pointing out this phrasing to me at a conference at The University at Buffalo in April 2017.
8. *IP*, 203–4/154.
9. Luca Vanzago, "Passivity and Time: On Merleau-Ponty's Lectures on Passivity," *Epekeina: Hermeneutical and Phenomenological Ontology* 1, no. 1–2 (2012): 127–41.
10. *SNS*, "*première parole*," 25/19.
11. Ricoeur in fact makes just this point when talking about *Cartesian Meditations* in his collection of essays *From Text to Action*:
    [T]hanks to this *Rückfrage*, reflection glimpses, in the thickness of experience and through the successive layers of constitution, what Husserl calls a "primal institution"—an *Urstiftung*—to which these layers refer. The primordial is thus the intentional limit of such a reference. So there is no need to search, under the title of "sphere of belonging," for some sort of brute experience that would be preserved at the heart of my experience of culture, but rather for an antecedent that is never given in itself. Hence, in spite of its intuitive kernel, this experience remains an interpretation. "My own too is discovered by explication and gets its original meaning by virtue thereof" (51). Husserl quotations found in: Edmund Husserl, *Cartesian Meditations: An Introduction to Phenomenology*, trans. Dorion Cairns (The Netherlands: Matinus Nijhoff Publishers, 1960), 111 and 102.
12. *IP*, 211–12/159.
13. Ibid., 212/152.
14. I am very much borrowing here from Rudolf Bernet's extremely insightful analysis of "the Freudian subject" in his most recent book *Force—Pulsion—Désir*. In discussing the truth and falsity of desire, and our ability to distinguish them, Bernet also notes that, in addition to the desire providing the difference between fidelity and infidelity, the ability to distinguish is inevitably "the subject of speech," and that it is speaking that allows the subject to retrace its steps and restore fidelity to the symbol of desire (386–87). My translation.

15. *IP*, 210–11/158–59.
16. Sigmund Freud, "Revision of the Theory of Dreams," in *Essential Papers on Dreams*, ed. Melvin R. Lansky, 39 (New York: New York University Press, 1992).
17. Jacques Lacan, "Book 11" in *The Four Fundamental Concepts of Psycho-Analysis*, trans. Alan Sheridan (New York: W.W. Norton, 1978), 49. This is in the context of reading Freud's *Beyond the Pleasure Principle*. The notion of "the real" was first introduced by Lacan in a 1953 lecture called "Le symbolique, l'imaginaire et le reel" in *Bulletin de l'Association Freudienne* 1:4–13.
18. *VI*, 317/270.
19. See also Emmanuel de Saint Aubert, "La 'promiscuité' Merleau-Ponty à la recherche d'une psychoanalyse ontologique," *Archives de Philosophie* 1 (2006): 11–35.
20. *IP*, 238/182.
21. Ibid., 241/184.
22. Ibid., 242/185.
23. *NC*, 83. Quote can be found in English in Whitmoyer, "The Sense of the Transcendental," 205. The translation here is Whitmoyer's. Keith Whitmoyer, "The Sense of the Transcendental: ΨYXH in Heraclitus, Husserl, and Merleau-Ponty," *Chiasmi International: Trilingual Sudies Concerning Merleau-Ponty's Thought* 18 (2016): 199–214.
24. Whitmoyer, "The Sense of the Transcendental," 205.
25. *VI*, 201/155.
26. Whitmoyer, "The Sense of the Transcendental," 203.
27. Ibid., 205.
28. *IP*, 239/183.
29. Saint Aubert, "La 'promiscuité' Merleau-Ponty à la recherche d'une psychanalyse ontologique," 16. See also Saint Aubert, "'Conscience et expression,' avant-propos à Merleau-Ponty," in *Le monde sensible et le monde de l'expression. Cours au Collège de France, Notes, 1953* (Switzerland: Métispresses, 2011), 7–38.
30. Jean-Luc Nancy, *Corpus*, trans. Richard A. Rand (New York: Fordham University Press, 2008), 21–24.
31. "noli me tangere," *IP*, 254/195.
32. *VI*, 165/126.
33. Ibid.
34. Jacques Derrida, *On Touching—Jean-Luc Nancy*, trans. Christine Irizarry (Palo Alto, CA: Stanford University Press, 2005), 267.
35. Ibid., 267–77.
36. Ibid., 281–82.
37. In many ways, Merleau-Ponty's reading of Valéry's implex tracks the one Derrida gives his study of Valéry's sources. Valéry develops the "implex," a pure condition of "potentiality to act," to break off communication with the exterior and give up the "affirmation of

mastery by means of the exercise of style." Derrida notes, however, that because the implex is a "self presence whose dynamic virtuality" in *resistance* against the "contingent, conditional," it is ultimately an inviolability of the self against the impact of an "irreducible difference" in Jacques Derrida, *Margins of Philosophy*, trans. Alan Bass (Chicago, IL: University of Chicago Press, 1982), 295, 303.

38. This is why Ricoeur argues, for example, discourse is work and this work

> appears a practical mediation between the irrationality of the event and the rationality of meaning. The event is stylization itself, but this stylization is in dialectical relation with a complex, concrete situation presenting conflictual tendencies. Stylization occurs at the heart of an experience that is already structured but that is nevertheless characterized by openings, possibilities, indeterminacies. (*From Text to Action*, 81)

> Note that Ricoeur, following the phenomenological school, gives "the word *meaning* a very broad connotation that covers all aspects and levels of the *intentional exteriorization* that, in turn, renders possible the exteriorization of discourse in writing and speaking" (Ibid., 80).

39. IP, 201/152. Merleau-Ponty refers to Maurice Blanchot in "Death of the Last Writer," and Blanchot's reference there to unspeaking speech:

> There is also chatter and what has been called interior monologue, which does not in the least, as we well know, reproduce what a man says to himself, for man does not speak to himself, and the deepest part of man is not silent but most often mute, reduced to a few scattered signs. Interior monologue is a coarse imitation, and one that imitates only the apparent traits of the uninterrupted and incessant flow of unspeaking speech. Let us recall that the strength of this speech is in its weakness; it is not heard, which is why we don't stop hearing it; it is as close as possible to silence, which is why it destroys silence completely. Finally, interior monologue has a center, the "I" that brings everything back to itself, while that other speech has no center; it is essentially wandering and always outside. (*IP*, 200–1/151–52)

40. Ibid., 202/152.
41. Ibid., 204/154.
42. Ibid., 205/155.
43. Ibid.
44. Ibid., 204/154.
45. Ibid., 204/154–55.
46. Ibid., 204/154.
47. Hes, 8-9/71.
48. Ibid., 8/70–1.

49. Ibid., 8-10/70-71. Galen Johnson writes about this metaphor as well:
    Merleau-Ponty's metaphor is more active [than Heidegger's], more physical, more visceral and perspiring. A timber yard is a logging site, the place where work is being done and trees are being felled, limbed, and prepared for the mill, a place of uprootedness and fallenness, where there is disarray and disorder of life. The timber yard is filled with exquisite, stunning beauty and magnificence, alongside dismemberment and horror. (254-55)

    Galen Johnson, "The Problem of Origins: In the Timber Yard, Under the Sea," *Chiasmi International:Trilingual Studies Concerning Merleau-Ponty's Thought* 2 (2000): 249-56.
50. *Hes*, 8/70.
51. *IP* p. 204/154.
52. Benedetta Zaccarello, "Pour une littérature(-)pensée," avant-propos à Merleau-Ponty, *RLL*, 22.
53. Rudolf Bernet presented an exceptional paper to the 41st Annual International Merleau-Ponty Circle in 2016 on Merleau-Ponty's lectures on literature and mentions the importance of Stendhal:
    What language and imagination did for Stendhal's own personality, when he invented the fictional lives of literary figures, they can also do for us, when we re-invent our own personal identity. To come to understand our own personal identity in analogy with the creation of a fictional literary figure, belongs to the most important things literature can teach us. Writing and reading literature can inspire us to relate to our own personality and character, to our acts and feelings in a way that is similar to how we relate to a literary fictional figure: neither entirely from the inside nor entirely from the outside; neither in absolute proximity nor from an unbridgeable distance. The capacity to adopt such a medial or literary distance in the relation to our own person, acts and feelings may be a necessary condition for the possibility of leading a free and fruitful life. While experiencing our actual life in a first-person perspective, we would then relate to our possible personal identity in an imaginative mode of a second person's perspective. While truly living our life, we would live it in the familiar, yet uncertain and surprising *company* of ourselves.

    This paper has now been published as: Rudolf Bernet, "Philosophy and Literature—Literature and Philosophy," *Chiasmi International: Trilingual Studies Concerning Merleau-Ponty's Thought* 19 (2018): 268.
54. *RLL*, 33.
55. Ibid., 149sq.
56. *RLL*, 3.
57. *NC*, 391.
58. Ibid.

59. VI, 137/102-3. Here again, Merleau-Ponty's references to Schelling (and his distinctions from Fichte) in the nature lectures prove highly valuable. Consider this passage:

> Hegel and Schelling: There is a terrain where the two philosophies meet: the terrain of poetry, in opposition to Logic and Gnosticism. "There is an element of poetry in philosophy," Schelling sometimes says, more or less taking poetry in its etymological sense. This is the best clue. Thus the letter, stupidly feminine, from Caroline Schlegel to Schelling: "You have poetry and Fichte does not. It leads you directly to the level of production, and he, by the acuity of his perception, was led to consciousness. He had light, in its clearest clarity, but you, you had the heat in addition; the former can only clarify, and the latter produces." Schelling is trying for a nonprosaic conception of consciousness, wherein consciousness is entirely clear to itself and knows the object at which it aims, an object that is nothing other than its aiming. A poetic consciousness recognizes that it does not possess its object totally, that it can understand it only by a true creation, and that it creates clarity by an operation that is not deductive but creative. Poetic consciousness, overcoming by its object, must get hold of itself again, but without ever being able to separate itself from its history. There is an act of faith in the meeting of passivity and spontaneity, of which the effort of art is the best "document." He is seeking a Reason that is not prosaic, a poetry that is not irrational. (N, 74/50)

60. VI, 136/102.
61. Ibid., 178/136.
62. Ibid., 187/144.
63. Perhaps the best-known instance of Merleau-Ponty's references to Malraux's "coherent deformation" comes in "Indirect Language and the Voices of Silence," first when speaking about the origination of the painter's style from out of the sensible world: "There is signification when we submit the data of the world to a 'coherent deformation.' . . . For each painter, style is the system of equivalences that he makes for himself for the world which manifests the world he sees. It is the universal index of the 'coherent deformation' by which he concentrates the still scattered meaning of his perception and makes it exist expressly" (S, 88/54–55). Later in the same essay, Merleau-Ponty denies that literary language is different from style and the expression of the sensible world:

> [L]anguage is literary (that is, productive) only on the condition that we stop asking justifications of it at each instant and follow it where it goes, letting the words and all the means of expression of the book be enveloped by that halo of signification that we owe to their singular arrangement, and the whole writing veer toward a second-order value where it almost rejoins the mute radiance of

painting. The meaning of a novel too is perceptible at first only as a *coherent deformation* imposed on the visible. And it will never be otherwise. Criticism may well compare one novelist's mode of expression with another's and incorporate one type of narrative in a family of other possible ones. This work is legitimate only if it is preceded by a perception of the novel in which the particularities of "technique" merge with those of the over-all project and meaning, and only if it is intended to explain what we have already perceived. (Ibid., 125–26/78)

64. *VI*, 230/178.
65. Ibid.
66. *RLL*, 103.
67. *Par*, 339.
68. *NC*, 209.
69. *PW*, xvi/xxiii–xxiv.
70. *VI*, 247–48/197.
71. *S*, 380/233.

Chapter 5

1. Jean-Paul Sartre, *What Is Literature? and Other Essays* (Cambridge, MA: Harvard University Press, 1988).
2. In the essay "What is Writing?" Ibid., 37.
3. Renaud Barbaras, *Le tournant de l'experience* (France: Librarie Philosophique J. Vrin, 2009), 281.
4. Ibid., 274, 275. Commenting on this very claim by Barbaras, Mazis writes in Merleau-Ponty and the *Face of the World: Silence, Ethics, Imagination and Poetic Ontology*:

    The idea of metaphor that Merleau-Ponty employs is resonant with a world in which each being is a dimension, like the red of the dress in the "Chiasm" chapter that we discussed, which is implicitly and pre-reflectively enmeshed with the robes of bishops, the Russian revolution, the flames of hell, and so on. Each sensible being is inseparable from a matrix of relations that are internal to each being's identity. The individual is a dimension stretching out in space-time in such a way as to gather together a multiplicity of beings that are internally related to each other through the sense of their perceptible qualities that become what they are only through this nexus of interrelation at the heart of embodied perception. This is far different from the traditional idea of metaphor that assumes one meaning of an object is substituted or transferred onto another to create a comparison between the two, but this is merely a "subjective" consideration brought to bear upon two discrete entities. Merleau-Ponty's idea of metaphor is as the expression of the

dimensionality of all beings that is a manifestation of their interconnectedness. Poetic metaphor is central to the ontology of the flesh for it expresses the promiscuity of being that comprises the flesh. (290)
5. Aristotle. *Poetics*, trans. George Whalley (Canada: McGill-Queens Press, 1997), 1459a 4–8.
6. Ricoeur, *From Text to Action*, 8.
7. Ibid., 9.
8. Derrida asks in *White Mythologies*: "Is there metaphor in the text of philosophy, and if so, how?" In the text of philosophy, it is assumed that language is the proper elucidation of real events. But this is an untenable assumption. If words truly pointed to such events, they would not themselves be elucidatory. The text is instead, according to Derrida, surreptitiously metaphorical and non-conceptual and holds within it what he calls a "surplus value." This surplus value is most evident in the metaphysical language that is driven to "concepts in the negative" such as *"ab-solute, in-finite, non-Being"* (121). These are also supposed to be real events in the absence of specificity, and metaphysical language is supposed to properly elucidate them. But if such language truly pointed to negative events, one could argue that, properly speaking, it would not be elucidatory.
9. Barbaras, *Le tournant de l'experience*, 267–68.
10. VI, 271/221. Merleau-Ponty extends this argument: VI, 271/221–22. Notably, "There is no metaphor: 1) because thought involves a quasi-locality that has to be described."
11. S, 124–25/77.
12. I refer the reader to Derrida's long and sustained defense of *White Mythologies* against Ricoeur's criticisms of the text in *The Rule of Metaphor*. This defense is found in a chapter called "The *Retrait* of Metaphor" in Jacques Derrida, *Psyche: Inventions of the Other Vol. 1* (Palo Alto, CA: Stanford University Press, 2007), 48–91. Derrida professes to be in a difficult position, since he is often the object of Ricoeur's criticisms even though in *White Mythologies*, he thinks, he makes many the same claims about metaphor as does Ricoeur.
13. VI, 162/123.
14. Miguel de Beistegui, *Proust as Philosopher: The Art of Metaphor*, trans. Dorothée Bonnigal Katz with Simon Sparks and Miguel de Beistegui (Abingdon, VA: Routledge, 2013), 77.
15. Robert Hariman, "What Is a Chiasmus? Or, Why the Abyss Stares Back," in *Chiasmus + Culture*, ed. Boris Wiseman and Anthony Paul, 51 (New York: Berghahn Books, 2014).
16. Penelope Brown and Stephen Levinson, "Universals in Language Usage: Politeness Phenomena," in *Questions and Politeness: Strategies in Social Interaction*, ed. Esther N. Goody, 65, 72 (United Kingdom: Cambridge University Press, 1978).

17. Robert Hariman, "What Is a Chiasmus? Or, Why the Abyss Stares Back," 62.
18. Ibid.
19. Ivo Strecker, "Chiasmus and Metaphor," in *Chiasmus + Culture*, ed. Boris Wiseman and Anthony Paul, 75 (New York: Berghahn Books, 2014).
20. *VI*, 291–92/243.
21. Joshua Landy, *Philosophy as Fiction: Self, Deception, and Knowledge in Proust* (United Kingdom: Oxford University Press, 2004), 124.
22. Marcel Proust, *Letters of Marcel Proust*, ed. and trans. Mina Curtiss (New York: Random House, 1949), 226.
23. *IP*, 205/155.
24. Marcel Proust, "Finding Time Again," in *In Search of Lost Time* vol. VI, trans. James Grieve (United Kingdom: The Penguin Press, 2002), 193.
25. Beistegui, *Proust as Philosopher*, 69.
26. Ibid.
27. Landy, *Philosophy as Fiction*, 125.
28. *RLL*, 111sq., 115sq.
29. Ibid., 80.
30. Ibid., 233.
31. *VI*, 337/xiv–xv.
32. *IP*, 254/195.
33. Ibid., 275/212.
34. *VI*, 315/267.
35. Mauro Carbone, *The Thinking of the Sensible: Merleau-Ponty's A-Philosophy* (Evanston, IL: Northwestern University Press, 2004), 11.
36. Ibid., 13.

Conclusion

1. *IP*, 246/189.
2. *S*, 345/212.
3. Ibid., 346/212.
4. Ibid., 345–46/212–13.
5. Ibid., 344/211–12.
6. Frank Chouraqui, "The Paradox of Power," *Chiasmi International: Trilingual Studies Concerning Merleau-Ponty's Thought* 19 (2018): 82–83.
7. In fact, Merleau-Ponty makes a comment about political ideals that could easily be placed in today's context:
   > In 1939 we were still living under the liberal order. We had not yet come to understand that the "legitimate diversity of opinion" always presupposes a fundamental agreement and is only possible on the basis of what is uncontested. Albert Sarrault really marked the limits of liberalism when he exclaimed in the chamber, "Communism is not a viewpoint, it is a crime!" That was the moment for us to have seen the dogmatic basis of liberalism and the way it

only grants certain liberties by taking away the freedom to choose against it. (*HT*, 37–38/35)
8. "*le laisser-fair est un faire,*" *HT*, 43/39.
9.
> There is a sort of maleficence in history: it solicits men, tempts them so that they believe they are moving in its direction, and then suddenly it unmasks and events change and prove that there was another possibility. The men whom history abandons in this way and who see themselves simply as accomplices suddenly find themselves the instigators of a crime to which history has inspired them. And *they are unable to look for excuses or to excuse themselves from even a part of the responsibility.* For at the very moment when they were following the apparent curve of history, others were deciding to back off and to commit their lives along another road to the future. Thus it was not completely beyond human powers. (Ibid., 43/40)

10. *VI*, 228/167.
11. *HT*, 165/153.

Bibliography

Agamben, Giorgio. *The End of the Poem: Studies in Poetics*. Translated by Daniel Heller-Roazen. Palo Alto, CA: Stanford University Press, 1999.
Alloa, Emmanuel. "Could Perspective Ever Be a Symbolic Form?" *Journal of Aesthetics and Phenomenology* 2, no. 1 (2015): 51–71.
———. *Resistance of the Sensible World*. New York: Fordham University Press, 2017.
Anthon, Charles. "Metrical Index." *First Three Books of Homer's Illiad, According to Ordinary Text and with the Digamma Restored*. United Kingdom: William Tegg, 1866.
Aristotle. *Metaphysics, Books I-IX*. Translated by Hugh Tredennick. Cambridge, MA: Harvard University Press, 1996.
———. *Poetics*. Translated by George Whalley. Canada: McGill-Queens Press, 1997.
Badiou, Alain. *Being and Event*. Translated by Oliver Feltham. United Kingdom: Continuum, 2006.
Barbaras, Renaud. "Life, Movement, and Desire." *Research in Phenomenology* 38 (2008): 3–17.
———. *Le tournant de l'experience*. France: Librarie Philosophique J. Vrin, 2009.
Beistegui, Miguel de. *Proust as Philosopher: The Art of Metaphor*. Translated by Dorothée Bonnigal Katz with Simon Sparks and Miguel de Beistegui. Abingdon, VA: Routledge, 2013.
Bernet, Rudolf. *Force–Pulsion–Désir: Un autre philosophie de la psychoanalysis*. France: Librarie Philosophique J. Vrin, 2013.
———. "Philosophy and Literature—Literature and Philosophy." *Chiasmi International: Trilingual Studies Concerning Merleau-Ponty's Thought* 19 (2018): 255–71.
Blumenberg, Hans. *The Legitimacy of the Modern World*. Translated by Robert M. Wallace. Cambridge, MA: MIT Press, 1983.

———. "Licht als Metapher der Wahrheit." *Studium Generale* 10 (1953): 432–47.
Bollack, Jean, and Heinz Wismann. *Héraclite ou la separation*. France: Editions de Minuit, 1972.
Brown, Penelope, and Stephen Levinson. "Universals in Language Usage: Politeness Phenomena." In *Questions and Politeness: Strategies in Social Interaction*, edited by Esther N. Goody, 56–24. United Kingdom: Cambridge University Press, 1978.
Burke, Patrick, and Jason M. Wirth. *The Barbarian Principle: Merleau-Ponty, Schelling, and the Question of Nature*. Albany: State University of New York Press, 2013.
Carbone, Mauro. *The Flesh of Images: Merleau-Ponty between Painting and Cinema*. Translated by Marta Nijhuis. Albany: State University of New York Press, 2016.
———. *The Thinking of the Sensible: Merleau-Ponty's A-Philosophy*. Evanston, IL: Northwestern University Press, 2004.
Chouraqui, Frank. "The Paradox of Power." *Chiasmi International: Trilingual Studies Concerning Merleau-Ponty's Thought* 19 (2018): 69–85.
Dalton, Drew. *The Ethics of Resistance: Tyranny of the Absolute*. United Kindgom: Bloomsbury, 2018.
Deleuze, Gilles. *The Logic of Sense*. Translated by Mark Lester and Charles Stivale. United Kingdom: Athlone, 1990.
Derrida, Jacques. *An Introduction to Edmund Husserl's Origin of Geometry*. Translated by John P. Leavey Jr. Lincoln: University of Nebraska Press, 1989.
———. *Margins of Philosophy*. Translated by Alan Bass. Chicago, IL: University of Chicago Press, 1982.
———. *On Touching—Jean-Luc Nancy*. Translated by Christine Irizarry. Palo Alto, CA: Stanford University Press, 2005.
———. *Psyche: Inventions of the Other, Vol. 1*. Palo Alto, CA: Stanford University Press, 2007.
———. *White Mythologies: Writing History and the West*. Translated by Robert J.C. Young. United Kindgom: Routledge, 1990.
de Warren, Nicolas. "The Inner Night: Towards a Phenomenology of (Dreamless) Sleep." In *On Time: New Contributions to the Husserlian Phenomenology of Time*, edited by Dieter Lohmar and Ichiro Yamaguchi, 273–95. The Netherlands: Springer, 2010.
Dillon, M.C. *Merleau-Ponty's Ontology*. 2nd ed. Evanston, IL: Northwestern University Press, 1997.
Dufourcq, Annabelle. *Merleau-Ponty: une ontologie de l'imaginaire*. The Netherlands: Springer, 2012.
Fink, Eugen, and Martin Heidegger. *Heraclitus Seminar*. Translated by Charles H. Seibert. Evanston, IL: Northwestern University Press, 1997.
Fink, Eugen. "Vergegenwärtigung und Bild." In *Studien zur Phänomenologie*, 178. The Netherlands: Martinus Nijhoff, 1966.

Fóti, Véronique. *Vision's Invisibles: Philosophical Explorations*. Albany: State University of New York Press, 2003.
Freud, Sigmund. "Revision of the Theory of Dreams." In *Essential Papers on Dreams*, edited by Melvin R. Lansky, 32–52. New York: New York University Press, 1992.
———. *The Uncanny*. Translated by David McLintock. United Kingdom: Penguin Books, 2003.
Gasché, Rodolphe. *The Tain of the Mirror: Derrida and the Philosophy of Reflection*. Cambridge, MA: Harvard University Press, 1986.
Guthrie, William K.C. *The History of Greek Philosophy, Vol. 1*. United Kingdom: Cambridge University Press, 1962.
Hariman, Robert. "What Is a Chiasmus? Or, Why the Abyss Stares Back." In *Chiasmus + Culture*, edited by Boris Wiseman and Anthony Paul, 45–69. New York: Berghahn Books, 2014.
Heidegger, Martin. "Art and Space." *Man and World* 6 (1973): 3–8.
———. *Being and Time*. Translated by John Macquarrie and Edward Robinson. New York: Harper and Row, 1962.
———. *Bemerkungen zu Kunst—Plastik—Raum*. St. Gallen: Erker-Verlag, 1996.
———. *Early Greek Thinking*. Translated by David Farrell Krell and Frank A. Capuzzi. San Francisco, CA: Harper and Row, 1984.
———. *Gesamtausgabe*, Vol. 55, *Der Anfang des abendländischen Denkens Logik. Heraklitis Lehre vom Logos*, edited by Manfred Frings. Frankfurt am Main: Vittorio Klostermann, 1994.
———. *The Heidegger Reader*, edited by Günter Figal. Bloomington: Indiana University Press, 2007.
———. *Introduction to Metaphysics*. 2nd ed. Translated by Gregory Fried and Richard Polt. New Haven, CT: Yale University Press, 2014.
———. *Plato's Sophists*. Translated by Richard Rojcewicz and André Schuwer. Indianapolis: Indiana University Press, 2003.
Homer. *The Iliad*. Translated by A.T. Murray. Cambridge, MA: Harvard University Press, 1924.
Husserl, Edmund. *Cartesian Meditations: An Introduction to Phenomenology*. Translated by Dorion Cairns. The Netherlands: Matinus Nijhoff Publishers, 1960.
———. *Crisis of The European Sciences and Transcendental Phenomenology*. Translated by David Carr. Evanston, IL: Northwestern University Press, 1970.
———. "Ding und Raum." In *Vorlesungen 1907, Vol. 16*, edited by Ullrich Claesges. Hamburg: Meiner, 1973.
———. *Formal and Transcendental Logic*. Translated by Dorion Cairns. The Netherlands: Springer, 1969.
———. *Ideas Pertaining to a Pure Phenomenology and to a Phenomenological Philosophy—First Book: General Introduction to a Pure Phenomenology*. Translated by F. Kersten. The Netherlands: Kluwer Academic, 1982.

---. *Logical Investigations*. Translated by J.N. Findlay. United Kindgom: Routledge and Kegan Paul, 1975.

---. "The Origin of Geometry." In *Husserl at the Limits of Phenomenology*, edited by Bettina Bergo and Leonard Lawlor, 93–117. Evanston, IL: Northwestern University Press, 2002.

Jay, Martin. *Downcast Eyes: The Denigration of Vision in Twentieth-Century French Thought*. Berkeley: University of California Press, 1994.

Johnson, Galen. "The Problem of Origins: In the Timber Yard, Under the Sea." *Chiasmi International: Trilingual Studies Concerning Merleau-Ponty's Thought* 2 (2000): 249–56.

Jonas, Hans. *The Phenomenon of Life: Toward a Philosophical Biology*. Evanston, IL: Northwestern University Press, 2001.

Kaushik, Rajiv. *Art and Institution: Aesthetics in the Late Works of Merleau-Ponty*. United Kingdom: Continuum Books, 2011.

---. *Art, Language, and Figure in Merleau-Ponty: Excursions in Hyper-Dialectic*. United Kingdom: Bloomsbury, 2013.

---. "Psyche and Civilization: The Far Reaches of Merleau-Ponty's Natural Ontology." *Internationales Jahrbuch für Hermeneutik* 14 (2015): 347–66.

Kierkegaard, Søren. *The Concept of Anxiety: A Simple Psychologically Orienting Deliberation on the Dogmatic Issue of Hereditary Sin*. Translated by Reidar Thomte. Princeton, NJ: Princeton University Press, 1981.

Lacan, Jacques. *The Four Fundamental Concepts of Psycho-Analysis*. Translated by Alan Sheridan. New York: W.W. Norton, 1978.

---. "Le symbolique, l'imaginaire et le reel."*Bulletin de l'Association Freudienne* 1 (1982): 4–13.

Landy, Joshua. *Philosophy as Fiction: Self, Deception, and Knowledge in Proust*. United Kingdom: Oxford University Press, 2004.

Lawlor, Leonard. "Eliminating Some Confusion: The Relation of Being and Writing in Merleau-Ponty and Derrida." In *Écart and Différance: Seeing and Writing in Merleau-Ponty and Derrida*, edited by M.C. Dillon, 71–93. United Kingdom: Humanities Press, 1997.

Lucas, Carl Wilhelm. *Forms of the Ionic Dialect in Homer: With an Appendix on the Principal Dialectic Peculiarities of Heroditus*. United Kingdom: Whittaker and Co., 1846.

Lyotard, Jean-François. *The Inhuman: Reflections on Time*. Translated by Geoffrey Bennington and Rachel Bowlby. Palo Alto, CA: Stanford University Press, 1991.

Mazis, Glen A. *Merleau-Ponty and the Face of the World: Silence, Ethics, Imagination, and Poetic Ontology*. Albany: State University of New York Press, 2016.

Merleau-Ponty, Maurice. *Éloge de la Philosophie et autres essais*. France: Gallimard, 1960.

———. *Humanism and Terror: An Essay on the Communist Problem.* Translated by John O'Neill. Boston, MA: Beacon, 1969.

———. *Humanisme et terreur, essai sur le problème communiste.* France: Gallimard, 1947.

———. *In Praise of Philosophy and Other Essays.* Translated by John O'Neill. Evanston, IL: Northwestern University Press, 1970.

———. *Institution and Passivity: Course Notes from the Collège de France (1954–1955).* Translated by Leonard Lawlor and Heath Massey. Evanston, IL: Northwestern University Press, 2010.

———. *L'Institution, Passivité: Notes de Cours au Collège de France (1954–1955).* Paris: Éditions Belin, 2003.

———. *The Merleau-Ponty Reader,* edited by Ted Toadvine and Leonard Lawlor. Evanston, IL: Northwestern University Press, 2007.

———. *Nature: Course Notes from the Collège de France.* Translated by Robert Vallier. Evanston, IL: Northwestern University Press, 2003.

———. *La Nature, Notes, Cours du Collège de France.* France: Seuil, 1995.

———. *Notes de cours: 1958–1959 et 1960–1961.* France: Gallimard, 1996.

———. *Parcours deux, 1951–1961.* France: Verdier, 2000.

———. *Phénoménologie de la perception.* France: Gallimard, 1945.

———. *Phenomenology of Perception.* Translated by Colin Smith. United Kingdom: Routledge, 1992.

———. *Philosophy and Non-Philosophy Since Merleau-Ponty,* edited by Hugh J. Silverman. United Kingdom: Routledge, 1988.

———. "Préface" dans A. Hesnard, *L'Œuvre de Freud.* France: Payot, 1960.

———. *Primacy of Perception and Other Essays,* edited by James E. Edie. Evanston, IL: Northwestern University Press, 1964.

———. *Le Primat de la perception et ses conséquences philosophiques.* France: Verdier, 1996.

———. *La Prose du monde.* France: Gallimard, 1969.

———. *The Prose of the World.* Translated by John O'Neill. Evanston, IL: Northwestern University Press, 1973.

———. *Recherches sur l'usage littéraire du langage: Cours au Collège de France Notes, 1953.* Switzerland: MētisPresses, 2013.

———. *Sense and Non-sense.* Translated by Hubert L. Dreyfus and Patricia Allen Dreyfus. Evanston, IL: Northwestern University Press, 1964.

———. *Signs.* Translated by Richard C. Mcleary. Evanston, IL: Northwestern University Press, 1964.

———. *Signes.* France: Gallimard, 1960.

———. *The Visible and the Invisible.* Translated by Alphonso Lingis. Evanston, IL: Northwestern University Press, 1968.

———. *Le Visible et l'invisible, suivi de notes de travail.* France: Gallimard, 1964.

Merry, Walter W., ed. *Homer's Odyssey.* United Kingdom: Clarendon Press, 1886.

Moore, Henry. *Writings and Conversations*, edited by Alan Wilkinson. Berkeley: University of California Press, 2002.

Nancy, Jean-Luc. *Corpus*. Translated by Richard A. Rand. New York: Fordham University Press, 2008.

———. "Euryopa: Blick in die Weite/Euryopa: le regard au loin." Ulrich J. Schneider, Beiträge/contributions, 2 issues: *La philosophie européenne de la culture et le projet "Logos" de 1910*. International Symposium, University of Leipzig, May 1994.

———. *The Fall of Sleep*. Translated by Charlotte Mandell. New York: Fordham University Press, 2009.

———. *The Ground of the Image*. Translated by Jeff Fort. Palo Alto, CA: Stanford University Press, 2006.

———. *Multiple Arts: Muses II*. Translated by Simon Sparks. Palo Alto, CA: Stanford University Press, 2006.

———. *The Muses*. Translated by Peggy Kamuf. Palo Alto, CA: Stanford University Press, 1996.

———. *The Sense of the World*. Translated by Jeffrey S. Librett. Minneapolis: University of Minnesota Press, 1998.

Plato, *The Complete Works*, edited by John M. Cooper. Indianapolis, IN: Hackett, 1997.

Popa, Delia. "The Relation between Space and Imagination in Husserl's Phenomenology." *Internationales Jahrbuch für Hermeneutik* 14 (2015): 80–91.

Proust, Marcel. *In Search of Lost Time*. Translated by James Grieve. United Kingdom: Penguin, 2002.

———. *Letters of Marcel Proust*, edited and translated by Mina Curtiss. New York: Random House, 1949.

Rankin, H.D., *Sophists, Socratics, and Cynics*. New York: Routledge, 2014.

Reames, Robin. "Heraclitus' Doublespeak: The Paradoxical Origins of Rhetorical Logos." In *Logos Without Rhetoric: The Arts of Language Before Plato*, edited by Robin Reames, 63–78. Columbia: University of South Carolina Press, 2017.

Ricoeur, Paul. *Being, Essence, and Substance in Plato and Aristotle*. Translated by David Pellauer and John Starkey. United Kingdom: Polity, 2013.

———. *From Text to Action: Essays in Hermeneutics II*. Evanston, IL: Northwestern University Press, 1991.

Saint Aubert, Emmanuel de. "'Conscience et expression' avant-propos à Merleau-Ponty." *Le monde sensible et le monde de l'expression. Cours au Collège de France, Notes, 1953*. Switzerland: Métispresses, 2011.

———. "La 'promiscuité' Merleau-Ponty à la recherche d'une psychanalyse ontologique." *Archives de Philosophie* 1 (2006): 11–-35.

Sallis, John. *Delimitations: Phenomenology and the End of Metaphysics*. Indianapolis: Indiana University Press, 1995.

———. *The Logic of the Imagination: The Expanse of the Elemental*. Indianapolis: Indiana University Press, 2012.
Sartre, Jean-Paul. *The Imaginary: A Phenomenological Psychology of the Imagination*. Translated by Jonathan Webber. United Kingdom: Routledge, 2004.
———. *What Is Literature? and Other Essays*. Cambridge, MA: Harvard University Press, 1988.
Saussure, Ferdinand de. *Course in General Linguistics*. Translated by Roy Harris. Peru, IL: Open Court, 2009.
Schelling, F.W.J. *The Ages of the World: Third Draft*. Translated by Jason M. Wirth. Albany: State University of New York Press, 2000.
Strecker, Ivo. "Chiasmus and Metaphor." In *Chiasmus + Culture*, edited by Boris Wiseman and Anthony Paul, 69–90. New York: Berghahn Books, 2014.
Trigg, Dylan. "The Indestructible, the Barbaric Principle: The Role of Schelling in Merleau-Ponty's Psychoanalysis." *Continental Philosophy Review* 49, no. 2 (2016): 203–21.
Vallier, Robert. "Institution: The Significance of Merleau-Ponty's 1954 Lectures at the Collège de France." *Chiasmi International* 7 (2006): 281–302.
Vanzago, Luca. "Passivity and Time: On Merleau-Ponty's Lectures on Passivity." *Epekeina: Hermeneutical and Phenomenological Ontology* 1, no. 1–2 (2012): 127–41.
Watkin, William. "Poetry's Promiscuous Plurality: On a Part of Jean-Luc Nancy's The Muses." In *Jean-Luc Nancy and Plural Thinking: Expositions of World, Ontology, Politics, and Sense*, edited by Peter Gratton and Marie-Eve Morin, 191–212. Albany: State University of New York Press, 2012.
West, Martin. "Homer's Meter." In *A New Companion to Homer*, edited by Ian Morris and Barry B. Powell, 218–38. New York: Brill, 1997.
Whitmoyer, Keith. "The Sense of the Transcendental: ΨΥΧΗ in Heraclitus, Husserl, and Merleau-Ponty." *Chiasmi International: Trilingual Sudies Concerning Merleau-Ponty's Thought* 18 (2016): 199–214.
Zahavi, Dan. *Self-Awareness and Alterity: A Phenomenological Investigation*. Evanston, IL: Northwestern University Press, 1999.

Index

adventure, xiii, xx, 50, 117, 120, 126, 130, 131
affect, affection, affective, affectivity, 1, 19, 89, 143, 149
Agamben, Giorgio, 4, 140n80
animal, xvi, 89
animal of words, 95–96
  and human, xii, xviii
  see also implex
anonymity, anonymous, anonymous-intentions, xvii, xxvii, 50, 51, 54, 58, 62, 126
  and symbolism, xix, xx, 88, 117
  in language, 101
  in sleep, 82
Artaud, Antonin, 104

Badiou, Alain, xi, 133n1
Barbaras, Renaud, 108, 155–56n4
Baudelaire, Charles, 105
Blanchot, Maurice. 99, 101, 152n39
blind spot, 51, 53–54, 56, 62, 74, 75, 123, 131
  according to Jean-Luc Nancy, 58, 60–62, 148n58
Blumenberg, Hans, 55, 144n4
Breton, André, 104

Cassirer, Ernst, xviii, xxi, 135n17, 142n33

Cézanne, Paul, 45, 87
censor, xxvii, 86–89, 97, 120
  see also implex; promiscuity; psychoanalysis
chiasm, chiasmatic, chiasmus, 95, 104, 112–14, 115, 120, 145n8
  between forms of language, 101, 110, 111–12, 114, 121
  between speaking and hearing, 28, 111
coherent deformation, 103, 104, 120, 154–55n63
cosmology of the visible, 27, 58

Deleuze, Gilles, xi, xii, 17
depth, 16–17, 31, 45–46, 49–51, 56, 83, 93–94
  and the symbolic form, 88–89
depth psychology in Proust, 113–114
  versus plane in Husserl, 31–32
Derrida, Jacques, xxiii, 39, 49, 94–95, 109, 151–52n37, 156n8
diacritics, diacritical, xxii, xxiii, 4, 5, 10, 28–29, 44, 94, 96
  relation to *écart*, xxiii, 1–2, 11, 15–16, 18, 20
  relation to Heraclitus's opposites, 21
Dillon, M. C., xxii, 91

écart, xx, xxiii, xxiv, 25, 45
   in Jean-Luc Nancy, 61 (*see also* blind spot)
   problem of passivity and activity, 95
   problem of separation and continuity, 19, 28, 62
   relation to diacritics, 1–2, 11–13, 16, 18, 28
   relation to metaphor, 108
   elements, elemental, elementality, xxii, xxv–xxvi, 54, 58, 65, 92, 131, 145n11
   and intentionality, xxi–xxii, xxvi, 57, 76, 130
   have "no name in the history of philosophy," xxvii
   in relation to psychoanalysis, xxi–xxii, xxvii, 125–26, 130
Euclid, 31
expression, 21, 75, 88, 92–93, 94, 97, 99, 104–5, 112, 115, 117, 120, 154–55n63, 155–56n4
   paradox of expression, xxvii, 87, 102–3, 109
   in Proust, 114, 120

figure, figured, figuration, figurative, xxii, 38, 39, 45, 46–47, 110–12
   and space, 48–50
Fink, Eugen, 34, 54, 58, 67–69, 74, 81
fire, xxvi, 26–27, 54, 65–68, 71, 94, 125–26, 147n41
   see also Heraclitus: elements, kindling; Heidegger, Martin: setting sun in Heraclitus's Fragments
flesh, xx, xxiii, 13, 28, 53, 95, 142–43n42
flesh of the world, 104
Freud, Sigmund, xii, 54, 58, 76–77, 87, 89, 94, 96, 97, 108, 148n48
   Oedipal Complex, 90
   the Dora Case, 90, 125
   the unconventional thought, 77, 86–87, 113

Galileo, 31

Hegel, Georg Wilhelm, 18, 57, 129
   critique of art in, 61
Heidegger, Martin, xxiii, 20, 21, 31, 54, 56, 58, 67–71, 74, 81, 138n62, 139–40n78
   on Plato's *Sophist*, 6
   on sculpture and space, 47–48
   on sleep in Heraclitus's fragments, xxv–xxvi, 66, 81
   setting sun in Heraclitus's fragments, 21–22
Heraclitus, xxiii, 2, 20, 21–22, 58, 67–71, 93
   division in the first fragment, 25
   first fragment, xxiv
   kindling, 27, 54, 66, 67
   Merleau-Ponty's approximation of, 24–25
   opposites and their separation, 23, 147n41
   waking, dreaming, and sleeping, xxv
hermeneutical reverie, 99–100, 105, 108, 113
Homer, xxiii
   diacritics in Homeric poetry, 4
   digamma in Homeric poetry, 3
   hiding in the *Odyssey* according to Heidegger, 21
   separation of diphthong, 3–4
homogeneous space versus oriented space, 41
Husserl, Edmund, xiii–xvi, xxiii–xxv, 7, 12, 13–15, 17, 19, 58, 115, 123
   absolute sense-bestowing consciousness, xii, 45, 50

body and the *hylē*, 37
critique of Kant, xv
freedom of geometry, 38
geometry cannot proceed descriptively but deductively, 39
mathematization of the universe, 31
meaning and sense, 133–34n11
not a Platonic Realist, 12
phantasy consciousness, xxiv, 34, 118, 123
phenomenological reduction and its sedimentation, xvi
sensible world and morphological essences, 38
space versus time, 34–36
see also depth: verses plane in Husserl; institution: difference between institution in Husserl and Merleau-Ponty

image, xxvi, 13, 17, 33, 46, 53, 142n33
and non-being, 19, 42, 51
hypnogogic image, 77–78
see also Husserl, Edmund: phantasy consciousness
implex, 95–96, 151–52n37
institution, xii–xvi, 43, 86, 87, 100, 113, 123, 134–35n15, 150n11
as a symbolic matrix, xvii–xix, xxiii, 87
difference between institution in Husserl and Merleau-Ponty, xvi
in language, 116–17
in relation to passivity, xvii
institution of power, 126–27, 128

Jonas, Hans, 144n6

Kant, Immanuel, xv

Kierkegaard, Søren, 5
Klee, Paul, xiii, 45, 47
Kristeva, Julia, 89

Lacan, Jacques, 89
language:
as ontogenesis, xxviii–xxix, 102
as ontological limit, 95
conceptual and non-conceptual language, 110–11, 121, 128
eloquent language, xxviii, 102
literary language, 100–1, 154–55n63
speech, xii, 4–5, 7, 26, 28, 92, 96, 99, 111–12
see also implex; mute meaning; signification
Lascaux, 50–51
light, xxv–xxvi, 23, 25, 46, 54, 63–65, 71, 74, 144n5
and passivity in sleep, 73
and phenomenality, 57, 59–60
essential character of, 62
in Schelling, xxv, 52–53, 124
in the history of philosophy, 54–56
logic of, 62–63
lux versus *lumen*, 56 (*see also* Jean-Luc Nancy)
sculpture and, 49–50
see also elements; fire; Heraclitus: kindling; Martin, Heidegger: setting sun in Heraclitus's fragments
Lévi-Strauss, Claude, xiii
Lyotard, Jean-François, 89, 145n8

Machiavelli, Niccolò, 126–27
Malraux, André, 104, 154n63
Matisse, Henri, 45, 47
metaphor, 108–9, 110, 112, 127–28
defined by Aristotle, 109
"originary metaphoricity," 108, 109

Index

Moore, Henry, 47, 49–50, 142n37
motor-intentionality, 41
mute meaning, xxi, 29, 96, 104, 123, 134, 152n39
   as unsaid meaning, 96

Nancy, Jean-Luc, xxiii, 56, 57, 58, 74–75, 94, 94–95, 148–49n60
   lux versus *lumen*, 59–60
   on the blindspot, 61
   notion of *écarts*, 61–62
negation, xviii, xxv, 43, 45, 53, 57, 76, 79, 84, 85, 88, 98, 145n8
   and critique of non-being, 27
negation of negation, 18–20, 42, 53–54, 120
natural negativity or natural negation, 19–20, 25, 42
   see also Sartre: Merleau-Ponty's critique of negation in

painting, xviii, 45–47, 101, 108, 142n33, 154–55n63
   see also Lascaux
Panofsky, Edwin, 45, 142n33
Parmenides, 2
passivity, xiv–xv, xix, 14, 15, 34, 65, 72–73, 74, 82, 117, 124, 134–35n15, 154n59
   and symbolism, xxvii, 54, 85, 89–92, 96–97
   primordial passivity, xvii, 74, 76, 95–96, 110, 118
   see also sleep
Plato, xxiii, 1, 20, 31, 56, 115
   dialectical situation of being in *Sophist*, 1–2, 6
   language and math, 8
   problem of the One and the many, 5
positive symbol:
   and "unconventional thought" in Freud, 86–87, 88–89
   in relation to negation, 85–87
   the space of, 86
   see also primordial symbolism
power, 126–27
primordial symbolism, xxv, xxvi, xxvii, 76–77, 78, 91, 108, 125, 130
   and the fictive and the real, 77
   in relation to negation, 54
   in relation to the censor, 89
   in Schelling, xxxv, 53, 76
   see also positive symbol
promiscuity, xii, 14, 89–91, 126
Proust, Marcel, 104, 105, 108, 122, 129
   architectonic time, 113
   expression, 112
   sleep, 118–20
psychoanalysis, 87, 100, 123–24
   and nature, 144–43
   non-anthropological or ontological psychoanalysis, 87, 99, 142–43n42
   phenomenology and psychoanalysis, 91, 98–99

reflexion, xvii, xix, 9, 13, 33, 130
   and sedimentation, xiv–xv, xvii, xxviii
   and symbolism, xvii–xviii
   see also elements: and intentionality
Rembrandt, 46
Ricouer, Paul, xxiii, 109, 150n11, 152n38
   on Plato's *Sophist*, 9–10
Rodin, Auguste, 17

Sallis, John, 40, 147n41
Sartre, Jean-Paul:
according to Gilles Deleuze, xi–xii
   Merleau-Ponty's critique of negation in, 18–19, 42–43, 83, 85
   on the hypnogogic image, 77–78

on the imaginary life, 41
on literature, 100, 107–8, 121
Saussure, Ferdinand de (or Saussurean), xxii, 28
Schelling, Friedrich Whilhelm Joseph von, xxv, 51–52, 56, 76, 123, 130, 154n59
  on light as quasi-concept, 53–54
  see also primordial symbol: in Schelling
Simon, Claude, 104
silence, 28–29, 48–49, 123, 152n39
  in Heraclitus's first fragment, 26
  problem of silence in Plato, 10
  see also mute meaning
Slee, 58
  and passivity, 72–74, 82
  being in divergence, xxvi, 72, 74, 81, 84, 118
  dreamless, 66–67, 81–82
  in relation to primordial symbolism, xxvi, 54, 76, 82, 85
  the phenomenology of, 74–75, 82
signification, xx–xxi, xxii, xxvi, xxvii, 8–9, 11, 28–29, 86, 89–91, 94, 96–97, 102, 108, 111, 120, 139–40n78, 154n63

intentionality and, 28–29, 72, 96, 133–34n11
theory of the sign, xxi, 91
see also sleep; speech: speaking discourse; symbolic matrix
speech. xii, 4, 26, 27–28, 92, 111, 135l7n, 139–40n78, 150n14
  as the limit of ontology, 29, 92
speaking discourse, 7, 28
  unspeaking speech, 96, 99, 152n39 (*see also* mute meaning: unsaid meaning)
Stendhal, 100–1, 104, 153n53
Surrealism, 49–50, 101
symbolic matrix, xii, xvi, xviii, xx–xxvii, 29, 87, 111, 117, 125, 142n33
  see also signification; institution: as a symbolic matrix

theory of extramission (fiery vision thesis), 55, 70–71

Valéry, Paul, 95, 104, 115, 151n37

www.ingramcontent.com/pod-product-compliance
Lightning Source LLC
Chambersburg PA
CBHW070337240426
43665CB00045B/2187